Anecdotes & Scripture Notes

for All Occasions

Rev. John G. Hillier

TWENTY
THIRD *23rd*
PUBLICATIONS

Twenty-Third Publications
A Division of Bayard
One Montauk Avenue, Suite 200
New London, CT 06320
(860) 437-3012 or (800) 321-0411
www.23rdpublications.com

The Scripture passages contained herein are from the *New Revised Standard Version of the Bible*, copyright ©1989, by the Division of Christian Education of the National Council of Churches in the U.S.A. All rights reserved.

ISBN 978-1-58595-570-1
Library of Congress Catalog Card Number: 2006939022
Printed in the U.S.A.

Anecdotes & Scripture Notes for All Occasions

FOREWORD

Priests and deacons know quite well how a memorable story, an anecdote, or an amazing fact can illustrate and enliven the point of a homily. In fact, teachers, preachers, parents, and conversationalists know that adults and children alike enjoy interesting stories, anecdotes, and relevant facts. Didn't Jesus himself used parables for this very reason? Was he not a storyteller?

Anecdotes and Scripture Quotes for All Occasions does not disappoint. It will serve as a useful tool for those who give formal speeches and spiritual conferences, for those who preach, for teachers of various grade levels, and it will be equally valuable for those who wish to use the thematic reflections for personal spiritual reading and private meditation.

This unique collection of stories, anecdotes, and facts, coupled with a spiritual and theological commentary, is instructive and faithful to Scripture and church Tradition. Drawing upon a wide range of illustrative material, Father Hillier's commentaries shed light on God's word and help the reader to discover God's abiding presence and providential concern in the ordinary and sometimes mundane circumstances of life. A wide range of human experiences—achievement, tragedy, patience, adversity, bitterness, history, prejudice, humor, perseverance—all find their way into the pages of this informative and stimulating volume.

Anecdotes and Scripture Quotes for All Occasions came about in part due to the determination of one man, a priest who never stopped giving of himself even when, because of a chronic and disabling disease, days were long and nights were even longer. When his physical pain became increasingly intense and his mobility grew more and more limited, Father Hillier would use the long hours to collect and create the stories in this book and to write an accompanying reflection. Although initially intended for his own enrichment, this anthology is now offered for the spiritual instruction and formation of others.

Very Reverend Edward C. Puleo
Diocese of Metuchen, New Jersey

PREFACE

I cannot imagine any task in life more satisfying than sharing the Good News, which is Jesus Christ, and bringing the light of faith to another human being or brightening it in another. This, in part, is what motivated me to write *Anecdotes and Scripture Notes for All Occasions*. Whether you are charged with teaching faith formation classes, leading a sacramental preparation course, RCIA sessions, retreats, catechetical talks, spiritual conferences, or Bible study groups, you will find this book a handy resource for teaching and sharing the fine treasures of our Catholic Christian faith. Others involved in pastoral ministry will also find this book a welcomed addition to their personal libraries. Following the welcome advice of Jesus "to come away...and rest for a while" (Mark 6:31), this book will be a useful resource for private spiritual reading.

There are two indexes to make *Anecdotes and Scripture Notes for All Occasions* more useful. As a preacher of God's word, for example, the scriptural index (page 243) will assist you in finding the complementary lectionary text to help form a seed-idea for a homily or a good introduction or conclusion for a homily. The topic index (page 249) will also be valuable in finding a theme associated with the lectionary readings for Mass. The numbers in each index refer to the entry in which the Scripture or topic may be found, not to a page number. Both indexes will be equally helpful to those who teach classes in spirituality or theology and for those involved in pastoral ministry.

Those interested in personal faith formation may use this book as a guide for daily spiritual reading by selecting pertinent themes according to personal interest, the seasons of the liturgical year, or by making selections at random for personal spiritual enrichment. Whether you are a vowed religious, a homebound man or woman, or a busy frequent flyer, you will discover a message of faith, hope, and love throughout these pages, beckoning you to deeper intimacy with the Lord Jesus.

The value of this book and its positive impact on an individual, a small group, or a larger audience will depend on how you will bring your own imagination, know-how, and prayerful disposition to the various selections. You will notice that each story or anecdote is followed by a theological reflection on the story or anecdote. Having spent more than twenty years in pastoral ministry, I know it is important to include not only inspiring stories and appealing anecdotes but also brief reflections to help you use the story or anecdote as a useful catechetical tool.

As you read each selection, you will soon notice that in some cases the story or anecdote and reflection you select is exactly what you were searching for and you will have to do little more than present it. In other cases, you may want to use the story, anecdote, or reflection as a seed or building block in developing a more comprehensive treatment of a theme or subject so as to make your presentation more effective.

As a teacher and preacher of God's holy word, it has always fascinated me how people recall long afterward important aspects of the faith I presented. The reason is because they retained the story or anecdote I used as a backdrop to the important spiritual or theological point I wanted to make. In other words, the story or anecdote served as a catalyst to remind them of the more significant spiritual or theological truth I hoped to communicate. It is my hope and prayer that you will experience the same joy in hearing another say "I remember what you said because...."

May your ministry of God's word be fruitful because of what you present and how you present it.

ACKNOWLEDGMENTS

I am grateful to the Very Reverend Edward C. Puleo and Monsignor Donald M. Endebrock from the Diocese of Metuchen for reading the manuscript of my book, for their reassurance, for their many fine suggestions and fraternal support; to Monsignor James C. Turro and Reverend Benedict Groeschel, C.F.R., for their words of encouragement and support; to Reverend William G. O'Brien of the Diocese of Worcester for his continued friendship and affirmation; to the Very Reverend Douglas Mosey, C.S.B., to my colleagues and my seminarian students at Holy Apostles Seminary, Cromwell, Connecticut, for their constant support and assistance.

I also express my gratitude to Bishop Robert J. McManus of the Diocese of Worcester and to Bishop Michael R. Cote of the Diocese of Norwich, for their continued support and prayerful assurance; to the priests of the Diocese of Worcester and to the parishioners of the parishes where I have served for their fraternal and prayerful support; to the staff at Twenty-Third Publications, and most especially to John van Bemmel, for his care and attention during the editing process in bringing my manuscript to completion.

Finally, I am grateful to my family and friends for their constant love and affirmation, especially my parents, Graham and Margaret Hillier of St. John's, Newfoundland, Canada, to whom I dedicate this book. They continue to be the greatest example of love and fidelity to me, having been married for more than fifty years.

1. SIMON OF CYRENE *Cross, discipleship*

Legend has it that Simon of Cyrene, a stranger who was forced to help Jesus carry his cross (Mark 15:21), became a follower of Christ, then a bishop in the early church, and eventually a saint. We are told that he suffered martyrdom for his faith. Of course, we can't be sure of that, but we do know that his two sons, Alexander and Rufus, became Christians, because Saint Mark mentions them by name in his gospel. How proud they must have been to know that their father actually carried the cross of Jesus. How singularly blessed his sons must have felt that their father actually walked in the Master's footsteps, the dream of every true disciple.

REFLECTION

Simon, who actually walked the way of the cross, sets an example for us to follow. As disciples of Christ, we too must carry the cross. It could be illness, loss of a loved one, poverty, injustice, or misunderstanding. For parents, it might be the non-Christian lifestyle of their children, such as marriages outside the church, or addiction to drugs or alcohol. For the disciple of Christ, it is not just a matter of enduring these crosses, but carrying them for the atonement of one's sins and the sins of others. That is why Saint Paul states in his letter to the Philippians, "For he has graciously granted you the privilege not only of believing in Christ, but of suffering for him as well" (1:29).

2. TURNING AROUND *Discipleship*

There is a legend told of a young man who saw a beautiful young woman walking through a park and followed her. After awhile she turned around and confronted the young man. "Why are you following me?" she asked. "Because," he replied, "you are so beautiful and the instant I saw you I knew I was in love." To this she replied, "But you have only to look behind you to see my younger sister. She is far more beautiful than I." The young man quickly turned around but saw no one. "You are making fun of me," he said to her. She replied, "On the contrary, if you were so madly in love with me, why did you turn around?"

REFLECTION

This legend reminds us of the importance Jesus places on the demands of discipleship. He always requires complete love and trust in him, and in him alone. He wants your love and my love undividedly. "No slave can serve two masters; for a slave will either hate the one and love the other, or be devoted to the one and despise the other. You cannot serve God and wealth" (Luke 16:13). We will serve the Master faithfully if we keep our eyes fixed on Jesus.

3. THE THREE TREES   *Cross, divine love*

There were once three trees that stood in a beautiful forest for a very long time. When they were young, they each had hopes and aspirations concerning their future. Their dreams were noble ones, even though they knew that human beings would probably cut them down some day. One tree hoped to become a cradle for infants. The second wished to be fashioned into a seafaring vessel that would safely transport precious cargo. The third dreamed of being spared so it could stand in the forest majestically pointing to the goodness and beauty of God's creation. One day men came into the forest and cut all three trees down. The first tree was turned into a trough, an open box for livestock feed. This was hardly the future the little tree had dreamed about. The wood of the second tree was used to make a small fisherman's boat, not a sleek cargo ship of the sea. It too was disappointed. Finally, the wood from the third tree was sold to the military, and Roman soldiers fashioned its wood into beams for an instrument of torture and death. Its spirit was crushed when it realized what evil humans would do with its wood. But fortunately God also had dreams for the trees. The wooden farm trough became the cradle it always wanted to be for God's only Son on Christmas night (Luke 2:7). The little fishing boat eventually passed into the hands of a Jewish fisherman named Simon Peter, his brother Andrew, and James and John, who used the boat not only to fish but to transport Jesus during his public ministry (Mark 3:9). The third tree, as you now can guess, was used for Jesus' crucifixion, becoming the sign that will stand forever of God's goodness and love, the cross of Jesus Christ (John 19:17).

REFLECTION

This legend reminds us that whatever our dreams might be, God always has our best interests at heart. Wherever our lives may take us and whatever twists and turns we may experience, God, whose love is unconditional, will never forget or abandon us. "I have loved you with an everlasting love; therefore I have continued my faithfulness to you" (Jeremiah 31:3).

4. THE DOG AND THE FOX
Stewardship, relationship with God

An old legend tells of a hound dog that was unique in the annals of the foxhunt. According to the story, the dog was known as the fastest hound in all Kentucky. The dog loved to run and when it came time for the chase, he scampered to and fro in a manner suggesting that he just couldn't wait to take off after the fox. Ironically, each time he ran he would begin to overtake the fox, but then he would put on an extra burst of speed and run right on past the fox. Those who witnessed the performance reported that they had never seen a picture of such gleeful surprise as when the fox discovered that he was chasing the dog.

REFLECTION

We must ask ourselves whether or not we have been running so hard and fast on our journey through life that we have left the all-important goal behind us. Are we racing aimlessly, dealing "urgently" with matters that are really unimportant, or are we keeping our focus on the things of God, using our time as good stewards to deal with matters that need our urgent attention? This is the heart of Christian stewardship. "Do you not know that in a race the runners all compete, but only one receives the prize? Run in such a way that you may win it" (1 Corinthians 9:24).

5. CANDY CANE
Christmas, Incarnation

To celebrate Christmas a candy maker in Indiana decided to create a candy that would include several symbols of the life of Jesus, so he made the Christmas candy cane with which we are all familiar. He began with a stick of pure white, solid candy; white to symbolize the virgin birth and the sinless nature of Jesus, and solid to be a symbol of the solid rock, the foundation of the church, the firm promises of God, and the firm love of Jesus for all of us. The candy maker made the candy in the shape of a "J" to represent the precious name of Jesus. It also represents the staff of Jesus the Good Shepherd who seeks his sheep who have gone astray. Thinking that candy was too plain, the candy maker added red stripes to represent the nails that held Jesus on the cross and to represent the blood shed by Jesus, giving us the promise of eternal life. Then he added the pungent, bittersweet flavor of peppermint, a gift of spice for a king. The flavor signifies that living as a follower of Christ is sweet and joyful, but at times bitter, or sorrowful.

REFLECTION

Although the candy became known as a candy cane, a meaningless decoration seen at Christmas time, the real meaning is discernable for those with eyes of faith: the wondrous Incarnation and Jesus' unimaginable love for all people, becoming human that we might become divine. "The Word became flesh and lived among us" (John 1:14).

6. THE LEGEND OF LA BEFANA *Christmas, love*

An ancient Italian legend tells of the Magi stopping to ask directions from an old woman, La Befana, who was so awed by their magnificence that she was unable to speak. They invited her to go with them to worship the newborn king, but she could only shake her head. After the Magi left, she suddenly found her tongue and started out to catch them. She never overtook them. But at each place she stopped in her pursuit she left a little gift, hoping that someday she would find the Christ Child. In Italy, therefore, it is not Santa Claus who brings gifts to good little children, but La Befana.

REFLECTION

Like La Befana, we too must follow the Magi in seeking Christ and imitate them in bringing gifts, giving to others as if we were giving to Jesus. The Magi gave special gifts "of gold, frankincense, and myrrh" (Matthew 2:11). We should give the special gift of ourselves, offering our presence to those in need and therefore to Jesus himself (Matthew 25:31–45).

7. SILENT NIGHT *Christmas*

All over the world the Christmas carol Silent Night has become the most beloved of all carols. Here is the story of its origin: On Christmas Eve in 1818 Father Joseph Mohr, the parish priest of Oberndorf, near Salzburg, Austria, was notified that repairs of the church organ could not be finished in time for midnight Mass. This caused great disappointment for the priest and the people since the music for the Mass that the choir had prepared could not be sung. To lessen the disappointment, Father Mohr decided to surprise his parishioners with a new carol. He went to work immediately and wrote three stanzas, the first of which was inspired by the sight of a baby whose ailing mother he had visited earlier in the day. Having finished the text, he brought it to his friend, Franz Gruber, a teacher and organist in the nearby village of Arnsdorf. Gruber composed the tune in a few hours. At midnight Mass, the hushed congregation in the little church heard the first performance of Stille Nacht, performed to the accompaniment of a guitar.

REFLECTION

When one door closes, God has a way of opening up another, if we only place our complete trust in him. The deep disappointment of a broken pipe organ on Christmas Eve for one parish priest in Austria in the early part of the nineteenth century became a blessing for the Christian world from that day forward. Father Mohr could have never imagined that his willingness to use his imagination, experience, and talents, instead of settling for a Mass without Christmas music, would be the origin of a beautiful Christmas hymn sung in every language throughout the world both within and outside the church.

8. IN YOUR HANDS   *Discipleship*

In days of old in a small village an elder used to meet with the people in the village square each year. He spent his time with them, answering their questions and solving their problems. But in the same village there was also a group of young men who were jealous of the prestige and status of this elder. They said, "We'll fix him! We'll make him look foolish in the eyes of the people. That way we will put him down." This was the plan. One of the young men would go before the elder the next night and gently hold out his closed hand. He would say, "Old man, what do I have in my hand?" The old man would correctly guess that it was a small bird. Then he would say, "Is it alive or dead?" If the old man said it was dead, the young man would open his hand and let the bird fly away. If the old man said it was alive, the simple pressure of his thumb on the bird's throat would kill it and when he opened his hand, the bird would be seen as dead. Either way, the poor old fellow would lose. So the following night the plan was put into operation. The young man held out his hand and the old man guessed correctly, "It's a bird." "But is it alive or dead?" There was a delay of about thirty seconds as the eyes of the old man burned into those of the youth. Then he simply replied, "That is in your hands. That is in your hands."

REFLECTION

Concerning our response to the ongoing invitation to become a faithful disciple of Jesus, committed to authentic Catholic living, that is in our hands. That is in our hands. The invitations of Jesus, "Follow me"(Luke 9:23), and "Come and see" (John 1:39) demand a response, yes or no!

9. KNOCK ON WOOD   *Prayer, trust, resignation*

Long ago, pagan belief in Germany and Holland held to the following logic. Johann would meet Hans in the forest and say, "Hey, Hans, I got that horse I wanted, at a good price too!" In a second both men would gasp. Johann would run to the nearest tree and start pounding on it. They believed that the gods lived in trees, and if they heard about any human happiness, they would cause mischief. Johann, realizing his mistake in the listening forest, would knock on the wood of the trees to drive the gods away in the hope that his good fortune would suffer no reversal. Even when it was no longer a custom to literally "knock on wood," the phrase has remained to this day to fulfill the same purpose.

REFLECTION

Have you ever met someone who, when something good happens, starts wondering when things are going to fall apart? Knocking on wood, of course, accomplishes nothing. It is much better to take reasonable steps to avoid disappointment and to pray, "Your will be done" (Matthew 6:10).

10. DA VINCI'S LAST SUPPER   *Primacy of Christ*

We have all seen a picture or painting of the Last Supper. Most famous of them all is the Last Supper by Leonardo da Vinci. The story is told that when da Vinci finished his beautiful painting he called a friend to inspect it. To his good friend da Vinci said, "Now, I want you to give me your honest opinion." The friend exclaimed, "It is marvelous. Look how that cup stands out from the table. Why, it looks as if it were real. I can't take my eyes from it." Instantly da Vinci stepped to the canvass, and with a few bold strokes blotted out the gleaming cup. He explained, "If that cup attracts you in that way, it cannot remain. Nothing, absolutely nothing, must be allowed to distract your attention from the figure of Our Lord. He is the focus of the painting."

REFLECTION

Our faith, our everyday living, must be Christ-centered. The center of our lives must be Jesus, the Son of God and Son of Mary, present in our midst and united with us, interceding with love on our behalf. He is our consolation and strength; he is with us through life as we work to build the kingdom of God as we journey to our heavenly home. "Who will separate us from the love of Christ? Will hardship, or distress, or persecution, or famine, or nakedness, or peril, or sword?" (Romans 8:35).

11. EMPTY THE SEA   *Holy Trinity*

Saint Augustine tells us that he once met a little boy on a beach who had dug a little hole on the sand, and with his little cup, would go to the sea, collect some water, and go back and pour it into the hole. When Saint Augustine inquired what he was doing, the little boy told him he was trying to empty the sea into the hole. Saint Augustine told him how unreasonable it was, and the little boy responded by saying it was no more unreasonable than trying to comprehend the Holy Trinity.

REFLECTION

No one can ever understand the mystery of the Holy Trinity. However, the church helps us understand the truth of the trinitarian God in the words of the Athanasian Creed, "the Father is God, the Son is God, and the Holy Spirit is God and yet there are not three Gods but one God," and in the words pronounced at our baptism, "in the name of the Father and of the Son and of the Holy Spirit." But the word "trinity" is not in Scripture. Beyond this, we are summoned to surrender ourselves to the Blessed Trinity, just as we did on the day of our baptism. In surrendering ourselves to the mystery of God, we actually find ourselves, and we also find the only power that can draw us out of ourselves, out of the stuff of our lives, making an eternal difference.

12. THE OBSTACLE IN OUR PATH
The price of discipleship

In ancient times, a king had a large boulder placed on a roadway. Then he hid himself and watched to see if anyone would remove the huge rock. Some of the king's wealthiest merchants and courtiers came by and simply walked around it.

Many loudly blamed the king for not keeping the roads clear, but no one did anything about getting the big rock out of the way. Then a peasant came along carrying a load of vegetables. On approaching the boulder, the peasant laid down his heavy load and tried to move the rock to the side of the road. After much pushing and straining, he finally succeeded. As the peasant picked up his vegetables, he noticed a purse lying in the road where the boulder had been. It contained many gold coins and a note from the king indicating that the gold was for the person who removed the boulder from the roadway.

REFLECTION

Every obstacle, however big, presents an opportunity to improve one's life and to accomplish what might have seemed impossible. The reward may not be gold coins, but it will be enriching, sometimes beyond measure. Our determination to remain authentic disciples should lead us to meditate on two of Jesus' parables, on the pearl and on the hidden treasure (Matthew 13:44–45).

13. MAKING A DIFFERENCE   *Mission, ministry*

As the old man walked on the beach at dawn, he noticed a young man ahead of him picking up starfish and flinging them into the sea. Catching up with the youth, he asked him why he was doing it. The youth's response was that the stranded fish would die if left until the morning sun. "But the beach goes on for miles and there are millions of starfish," countered the old man. "How can your effort make any difference?" The young man looked at the starfish in his hand and then threw it to safety in the waves. "It will make a difference to this one," he said.

REFLECTION

It is very easy for us to become overwhelmed by our Christian duty to follow Jesus' commands to "make disciples of all nations" (Matthew 28:19), "love your enemies," (Matthew 5:44), "forgive seventy-seven times" (Matthew 18:21–22). These broad commands seems less overwhelming when we begin concretely at home or in the neighborhood by reaching out to make a difference in the life of one person.

14. SPIDER WEB   *Sin*

On a spring morning a spider descended from a tree to a thorn bush in order to build a nice big web for itself between the sprouts and the twigs. A month and a half passed and the spider was living luxuriously because the big web caught an abundance of flies. Soon after, though, the spider was in a very bad mood. The sun did not shine all day and not one solitary fly was caught in the spider's web. In order to pass the time, the spider toured its web and inspected everything to make certain the web was still in good order. It pulled on all threads but it did not find a thing to correct. Suddenly, on the farthest corner of the web, the spider came upon a thread that was quite unfamiliar. The other threads went here and there and had a set purpose, but this strange thread apparently went nowhere. The spider had forgotten that long before as a poor emaciated little baby spider, it had descended on this single thread, and that this thread had been very useful when it was building its house. Now only an empty thread went up into the air with no obvious purpose. "Away with you!" the spider shouted, and with one fierce bite it broke the thread right in the middle. Immediately, the whole web, which had been built so artistically, collapsed completely, and when the spider recovered its senses, it was lying between the leaves of the thorn bush, with the web wrapped around its head like a wet rag.

REFLECTION

Not only are we connected with all other humans and with the earth that has nurtured us, but we are supremely connected with the God who created us and has loved us. We do immeasurable harm to ourselves and make ourselves unhappy at the very moment we forget our origin and break the thread from above. When we sin, we become disconnected from the source of all that is good; we sever, or at least damage, our relationship with God. As someone has observed, "that which we seek is the One who is causing us to seek."

15. THE LION AND THE WILD CAT   *Discipleship, devil*

The African lion and the wildcat look very much alike, yet they are different. An ancient African theory explains it this way. The same lioness gives birth to numerous cubs, some of which are truly lions at heart and some are not. How does the mother lion know which is which? Months after the birth of the cubs, just before they are weaned, the mother lion leaves the den and then, at an unsuspecting moment, she jumps into the den with a terrifying roar as if she were an enemy attacking the cubs. Some of the cubs stand up and fight the presumed enemy, while others flee the den with their tails between their legs. The cubs that hold their ground to face the danger prove themselves to be real lions. Those that run away are mere wild cats, false lions.

REFLECTION

As testing distinguishes a true lion from a false one, so too, testing can distinguish true disciples from false ones. Under the old covenant God subjected his people Israel to testing in the desert, which they failed (Exodus 17:1–7). We see Jesus, whom we are to follow, as the bearer of the new covenant, being subjected to testing in the desert (Matthew 4:1–11). He stood his ground and resisted the devil, thus showing that he is truly the Son of God, who does always the will of his Father.

16. THE BOX IN THE ATTIC *Greed, sharing, stewardship*

There is a story told about a woman who immigrated to the United States from Norway. After she died, her husband found a box in the attic containing a selection of blue dishes that appeared unique and expensive. He called his daughter to come to the homestead to examine the dishes before he discarded them. Opening the box, she found the finest porcelain she had ever seen in her life: hand-painted, obviously irreplaceable, in mint condition, with no evidence of having ever been used. As it turned out, in the region where the woman had been raised, the custom was for the family to select place settings in a particular pattern of hand-painted china to be given as gifts on special occasions. The woman had carefully packed these dishes, put them in a box, and brought them with her many years before when she first came to America. They never again saw the light of day. Even her own daughter was unaware that the precious dishes existed. The woman obviously felt that the dishes were so important to her that she didn't share them with anyone. The precious gift was never used.

REFLECTION

The sin of greed doesn't always involve great wealth. Greed or the lack of generosity takes many forms. The Holy Spirit graciously stands at the door of our hearts, reminding us that God can satisfy our every longing, our every hunger, with his presence. God has given all of us enough to share, but often we hide our most precious treasures and share them with no one. This violates the very concept of stewardship, that whatever we have is only "borrowed" from God. Our possessions are not only for our own benefit, but are to be used for God's kingdom and God's children who are in need. Jesus taught us this, as we see in Matthew 25:14–30.

17. THE BISHOP'S GIFT   *Presence of Jesus*

A church had fallen upon hard times and only five members were left, including the pastor. In the mountains near the church there lived a retired bishop. It occurred to the pastor to ask the bishop if he could offer some advice that might help save the church. The pastor and the bishop spoke at length, but when asked for advice, the bishop simply responded, "I have no advice to give. The only thing I can tell you is that one of the remaining members of the church is the Messiah." Returning to the church, the pastor told the church members what the bishop had said. The five church members pondered the words of the retired bishop. As they did, they all began to treat each other with extraordinary respect on the off chance that one among them might be the Messiah. As time went on, people visiting the church noticed the aura of respect and gentle kindness that surrounded the five members of the small church, and more and more people began to come back to the church. Within a few years, the small church once again became a thriving community, thanks to the bishop's gift.

REFLECTION

In our zeal to be the best in our committees and with our great plans for success, we often take those closest to us for granted and forget that our responsibility for Christian outreach is as close as the persons around the table…if we just take the time to reflect on the presence of Jesus in every one of them. We don't have to think of those we live and work with as the Messiah, but we do have to recognize the presence of Jesus in each person. "Truly I tell you, just as you did it to one of the least of these who are members of my family, you did it to me" (Matthew 25:40).

18. A FIVE AND DIME IDEA   *Risk-taking, Holy Spirit*

When young F.W. Woolworth was a store clerk, he convinced his boss to have a special ten-cent sale to reduce inventory. The sale was a resounding success. This inspired Woolworth to open his own store and price items at a nickel and a dime. Needing capital for such a venture, he asked his former boss for help, but his boss turned him down. "The idea is too risky," he told Woolworth. "There are not enough items to sell for five and ten cents." Woolworth went ahead without his boss's backing, and he not only was successful in his first store, but eventually he owned a chain of F.W. Woolworth stores both nationally and internationally. Later, his former boss remarked, "As far as I can figure out, every word I used to turn Woolworth down cost me about a million dollars."

REFLECTION

We can learn something new and innovative from the most unlikely people. An employer can learn from an employee, a teacher from a student, a parent from a child, the educated from the uneducated. Being open to advice, even when it comes from an unlikely source, is a wise attitude to have. So is openness to taking risks, after prudent consideration of all that is involved. Are we open to the "advice" of the Holy Spirit? Are we open to taking risks for the kingdom of God? "Now we have received not the spirit of the world, but the Spirit that is from God, so that we may understand the gifts being bestowed on us by God. And we speak of these things in words not taught by human wisdom but taught by the Spirit, interpreting spiritual things to those who are spiritual" (1 Corinthians 2:12–13).

19. NEW PIPE ORGAN   *Providence*

In the 1850s, the Know Nothing movement was at its height. Everything Catholic was attacked. A man named Orr, known as the Angel Gabriel, mounted a white horse and, blowing a bugle, went about the countryside inciting people with slander and misrepresentations. Riots, destruction of churches, and even murder resulted from these outbursts. St. Louis Church in Webster, Massachusetts, could thank the arrival of a new pipe organ for its safety, because when the pipes arrived in their long narrow boxes, the rumor spread that guns and ammunition were being stored in the church basement and the place was being turned into a barracks. No further attempt was made to destroy the church building. The Know Nothing movement left town and the church prospered.

REFLECTION

Not only words but signs or actions can be an effective means of communication for the good, even when they are misunderstood.

20. RETURN TO YOUR EVIL HABITS
Repentance, Holy Spirit

In 1951, comedian Red Skelton and a group of friends flew to Europe, where Mr. Skelton was to star in a show. As they were flying over the Swiss Alps, three of the airplane's engines failed. The situation looked very grave and the passengers began to pray. Skelton went into one of his best comic routines to distract them from the emergency as the plane lost altitude, coming closer and closer to the ominous mountains. At the last moment, the pilot noticed a large field between the precipitous slopes and made a perfect landing. Skelton broke the relieved silence by saying, "Now, ladies and gentlemen, you may return to all the evil habits you gave up twenty minutes ago."

REFLECTION

When we receive the abundance of God's grace, especially through the sacrament of reconciliation, or penance, we are not to return to our evil habits but rather, having been transformed by the power of the Holy Spirit, we are to return to our everyday life, challenging others by our words and actions to be instruments of God's love and peace. Saint Peter's call for repentance in Acts (2:38) has echoed through the centuries to the present: "Repent, and be baptized every one of you in the name of Jesus Christ so that your sins may be forgiven; and you will receive the gift of the Holy Spirit."

21. DOING YOUR BEST
Perseverance, gratitude

Long ago, an Irish citizen named Connell was found guilty of murder and sentenced to death. Philip Doddridge, a hymn writer, unsuccessfully tried to prove that the man had been 120 miles away from the scene of the crime at the time it was committed. Granted a last wish, the condemned man asked that on the way to his execution, then a public spectacle, he be allowed to pause outside Mr. Doddridge's home. Kneeling on the doorstep, he cried, "Mr. Doddridge, with every part of me, every hair of my head, every throb of my heart, every drop of my blood, I thank you, for you did your best to save me."

REFLECTION

The hymn writer wanted to save the condemned man but wasn't able to. So often we are able but unwilling to save those who, without our words of encouragement and lives of Christ-like example, are lead astray or left in need. We should never underestimate the influence we have as members of the body of Christ. Our potential for good should make us blanche, make us resolve to do more for God's kingdom.

22. WELCH GRAPE JUICE   *Obedience, God's will*

A young man named Charles E. Welch was accepted to be an African missionary. He reported to New York to make travel arrangements, but learned that his wife would not be able to tolerate the climate. He was heartbroken, but prayerfully returned to his home with great determination to make all the money he could to be used for spreading the word of God throughout the world. His father, Thomas B. Welch, a dentist, had meanwhile been making an unfermented wine for the communion service at his church. The young man, himself a dentist, discontinued his practice of dentistry to give full attention to marketing the grape juice. Taking over the business, he further developed it until the business prospered. The Welch family still manufactures "grape juice." They have given hundreds of thousands of dollars to the work of the missions.

REFLECTION

As noble as our goals may be, God's will for us may surpass even our greatest expectations. It often becomes a question of allowing ourselves to move from what "I desire" to what "God desires of me." Whether we receive abundant blessings for this is quite a secondary matter. As always, Jesus is our model: "I seek to do not my own will but the will of [my Father] who sent me" (John 5:30).

23. MADAME BUTTERFLY, TAKE TWO
Renewal, starting over

In February 1904, Giacomo Puccini's *Madame Butterfly* debuted at the La Scala opera house in Milan. Puccini had high hopes for the work. It starred the best singers of the day, the music was impeccable, and he was the leading figure in Italy's music scene. The composer was so sure of the opera's success that he piled his whole family into the carriage and, for the first time, took them to the premiere of one of his works. But he didn't count on hecklers in the audience, planted by his envious enemies. The breathtaking love duet in the first act was greeted with hissing and booing. At one point, Butterfly's kimono billowed and an audience member yelled out that she was pregnant. The bird calls that greeted the sunrise during the second act brought a cacophony of cock-a-doodle-doos, mooing, and braying. Puccini returned La Scala's fee, pulled the production, and rewrote it.

REFLECTION

Puccini did not settle for second best. After this "failure," he was willing to revise what he previously thought was the finished product. In so doing he made what was good not only better but the best. We too must never settle for second best, but use our talents as well as we can. Our task in life is to always reach high and not live as if we have completed the race. With every new day and every new breath we must seek first the kingdom of God, both within us and around us. We must seek to become perfect, that is, holy, as our heavenly Father is (Matthew 5:48). Every day is the day we must start anew.

24. TAKING TO WATER   *Discipleship*

A Newfoundland dog living with a family in a fishing village was famous for having saved three persons from drowning on three separate occasions. This particular dog was very fond of the water, and he considered any disinclination to it in other dogs as an insult to the species. If another dog was left on the wharf by its owner with the hope that it would follow the boat across the narrow harbor, and if it stood barking and unwilling to take to the water, the old Newfoundland dog would go down to him, and with a satirical growl, as if in mockery, take him by the back of the neck, and throw him into the water.

REFLECTION

Like the reluctant dogs needing a shove, we likewise need others to press us into service at times. Although reluctant at first, with a little boost we just might get the hang of it and wonder why we hadn't moved outside our comfort zone sooner, espe-

cially when tending to the work of God. To stretch ourselves for God, when there is no such thought as "I've done enough," we must become prayerful, reflective, and go into our own kind of desert place and rest awhile in the presence of God. As Jesus counseled the apostles, "Come away to a deserted place all by yourselves and rest a while" (Mark 6:31).

25. 1930 AIRPLANE INSTRUCTIONS
Commandments, love

On May 15, 1930, the first airline stewardesses boarded airplanes with the following set of instructions: 1) Keep the clock and altimeter wound up. 2) Carry a railroad timetable in case the plane is grounded. 3) Warn the passengers against throwing their cigars and cigarettes out the windows. 4) Keep an eye on passengers when they go to the lavatory to be sure they don't mistakenly go out the emergency exit.

REFLECTION

What was once "the law" for those who flew the friendly skies has become not only outdated but humorous. The same can never be said of the ten commandments (Exodus 20:1–17; Deuteronomy 5:1–21), or the "new commandment" of Jesus Christ (John 13:34), that we love one another as he has loved us. God's instruction remains always in effect at all times and in all places.

26. THAT SODA POP
Gluttony

Babe Ruth was enormously popular, a larger-than-life figure in many respects, including his habit of overeating and overdrinking. The most notorious occasion was in the course of preseason training when, on a train ride to New York, the Babe got off at the train station and consumed about twelve hot dogs and eight bottles of lemon-lime soda. Soon afterward he was stricken with "the stomachache heard around the world." For days ominous headlines had his fans across the country fearing he would die. Recovering, Ruth is reported to have said, "That soda pop will get you every time."

REFLECTION

Remember the gospel story of the Rich Man and Lazarus (Luke 16:19–31)? No wonder gluttony is counted among the deadly sins. Overindulgence in drink or food makes us susceptible to becoming cold and callused, unaware and uncaring of those around us who do not have enough. It also causes personal discomfort and unpredictable, serious health problems and social problems. Are not good stewards responsible for the way they use the gifts of God? "So, whether you eat or drink, or whatever you do, do everything for the glory of God" (1 Corinthians 10:31).

27. THE WISE WOMAN'S STONE   *Generosity, gifts*

A wise woman who was hiking in the mountains found a precious stone in a stream. The next day she met another hiker who was hungry, and the wise woman opened her bag to share her food. The hungry hiker saw the precious stone and asked the woman if he could have it. She surrendered it without hesitation. The man left, rejoicing in his good fortune. He knew the stone was worth enough to give him comfort and security for a lifetime. But a few days later he came back to return the stone to the wise woman. "I've been thinking," he said; "I know how valuable the stone is, but I give it back in the hope that you can give me something even more precious. Give me what you have within you that enabled you to give me the stone in the first place."

REFLECTION

It is a big mistake to determine the value of a gift by cost alone. The most precious gifts we have to offer another seldom hold monetary value. The gifts we create are valued more than the gifts we purchase. The greatest treasures we have come from within. They are not costly but nonetheless valuable. Saint Peter offered a lame man something more valuable than money. "I have no silver or gold, but what I have I give you; in the name of Jesus Christ of Nazareth, stand up and walk" (Acts 3:6).

28. THE LORD WILL SAVE
Instruments of God, presence of God

A traveling sales representative found himself caught in a tremendous rainstorm accompanied by thunder and lightening. Within a few hours, the motel in which he was staying flooded. As the water rose, the sales rep began to get anxious but suddenly a rescue party showed up in a truck. "Let's go, mister, get into the truck." "I'll stay here," he responded. "The Lord will save me." An hour later, a second rescue party reached the motel in a boat. "Sir, you better get in. The water is still rising." "No thanks," he said. "The Lord is my salvation." Toward evening, the motel became almost completely under water with flashes of lightening and loud thunder, and the distressed man was clinging to the satellite dish on the roof. A helicopter came with a final plea, "Hey, buddy, get in the helicopter! This is your last chance." "I'm all right," he said, as he pointed toward heaven, "I know the Lord will provide." As the rescuers departed, the satellite dish was hit by lightning, and the man was killed. When he arrived at the pearly gates, he was furious. "What happened?" he shouted. "I thought the Lord would provide!" Within seconds, a gentle voice was heard, "My friend, you were given not only one or two but three chances. I sent a truck, a boat, and a helicopter!"

REFLECTION

God is faithful and aware of our needs, but we have to recognize that God delivers us not usually through miracles, but through others. To believe otherwise is presumptuous. We are the hands of God, instruments God uses for the benefit of humankind. God uses us to build the kingdom of God. For our part, we have to be supple instruments that God can use, open to his will, dedicated to our calling, sensitive to the needs of others. We see this in the prayer attributed to Saint Francis, "Lord, make me an instrument of your peace...."

29. SOCRATES CONDEMNED   *Divine love, wisdom*

When Socrates was tried on charges of corrupting the Athenian youth and sentenced to death by drinking hemlock, his wife, Xantippe, visited him in prison to bewail the jury's condemnation. Socrates sought to comfort her. "They are by their nature also condemned," he remarked. "But your condemnation is unjust!" Xantippe cried. "Would you prefer it," Socrates asked, "to be just?"

REFLECTION

Such a comment by Socrates explains partly why, more than 2400 years later, the world still recognizes his name. For most of us, though, our names will soon be lost from the memory of the world, lingering only for a time between close family and friends. Who will be invoking our names one hundred years from now? Sacred Scripture tells us that God, our loving Father, is the faithful One who will remember us forever: "Can a woman forget her nursing-child, or show no compassion for the child of her womb? Even these may forget, yet I will not forget you" (Isaiah 49:15).

30. HIGH LEVEL COMPLIMENT   *Discipleship, vocation*

In 1402, Italian designer and sculptor Lorenzo Ghiberti was awarded the commission to decorate the baptistry doors of the Duomo in Florence, a project to which he devoted the remainder of his life. "These designs," Michelangelo exclaimed upon seeing them, "are worthy to adorn the gates of paradise!"

REFLECTION

Given the fact that Michelangelo is responsible for the Sistine Chapel and many other masterpieces, his comment about the sculptor's work was a profound compliment. It would be tantamount to Bill Gates complimenting a computer programmer or Walter Cronkite complimenting an entry level news anchor. It would be like God offering the supreme compliment of becoming one of us. "And the Word became flesh and lived among us" (John 1:14), or like Jesus inviting ordinary men and women to become his disciples. "[Jesus] found Philip and said to him, 'Follow me'" (John 1:43). How privileged we are to be Jesus' brothers and sisters, through baptism, co-heirs with him!

31. LIAR, LIAR   *Grace, sin*

Mark Twain loved to brag about his hunting and fishing exploits. He once spent three weeks fishing in the woods of Maine, despite the fact that it was not the state's season for fishing. Relaxing in the lounge car of the train as he started his return journey to New York, his catch refrigerated in the baggage car, he looked for someone to whom he could relate the story of his successful trip. The stranger to whom he began to boast of his sizable catch appeared unresponsive. "By the way, who are you, sir?" inquired Twain. "I'm the state game warden," was the unwelcome response. "Who are you?" Twain nearly swallowed his cigar. "Well, to be perfectly truthful, Warden," he said, "I'm the biggest liar in the whole United States of America."

REFLECTION

Only a man the caliber of Mark Twain could turn a sentence at a moment's notice to dig himself out of jam. Having broken the state law in Maine by "stealing" the state's out-of-season fish, he then imprudently bragged about his expedition and finally decided to lie his way out of the mess. Though a humorous insight into one day of Mark Twain's life, it reinforces the idea that one unrepented sin can lead to another, no matter who you happen to be. The human condition is weak and help-less without God. For this reason we take to heart Saint Paul's words: "[The Lord] said to me, 'My grace is sufficient for you, for power is made perfect in weakness'" (2 Corinthians 12:9).

32. NEAREST THE EXIT   *Salvation*

French dramatist Tristan Bernard won a newspaper competition by providing the best answer to the question, "If a fire broke out in the Louvre in Paris and you could save only one painting, which one would it be?" The expected answers might have been the precious da Vinci's *Mona Lisa* painted about 1505 or Paolo Veronese's irreplaceable *The Marriage at Cana* painted about 1562. Instead Bernard replied, "The one nearest the exit."

REFLECTION

When given the option to save precious and irreplaceable objects we can act ran-domly or selectively. But when to comes to salvation, God has no favorites. Saints Matthew and Luke tell us that Jesus came to save "what was lost" (Matthew 18:14; Luke 19:10). Saint John tells us that Jesus came to "take away the sin of the world" (1:29) and that "the Father sent his Son as Savior of the world" (1 John 4:14). In other words, Jesus came to save all people, of all times and places. God's desire for salvation is universal. "This is right and is acceptable in the sight of God our Savior, who desires everyone to be saved and to come to the knowledge of the truth" (1 Timothy 2:3–4).

33. SO MANY TELEPHONES   *Presence of Jesus*

One day the Israeli Prime Minister Menachem Begin went to the United States to visit President Ronald Reagan On the table in Reagan's office there were several telephones of assorted colors. "Why do you need so many telephones?" asked Prime Minister Begin. President Reagan explained: "The blue one is to call Africa, the red one is for Russia and the communist countries, the green one is for Germany, the yellow one is for China, and so on." "And what about the white one," asked Begin. Reagan explained, "This one I hardly use because it's a direct line to God and unless it's very urgent I never use it because it's a long distance call and very expensive." Six months later President Reagan went to visit Israel. Upon entering Begin's office he noticed only one telephone, which was used constantly. "You have only one telephone," Reagan said. "Well, we're only a small country and don't have as many relations with so many countries as you do," replied Begin. "Which telephone do you use to call God?" asked Reagan. "Oh, this one," Begin says. "We use it every day, but I pay nothing because it's a local call."

REFLECTION

It is always a special joy and privilege to visit religious shrines and holy places around the world and it is easy to understand how some might assume that one's access to God is easier in these spiritual centers, although not through the telephone. This is especially true when we think of places such as the Holy Land and the Vatican. In the faith of Catholics, the joy of privileged access to Jesus is equally available in almost every town and city throughout the world, in the perpetual presence of Christ in every tabernacle in every church around the globe, in the assembly at Mass, in the word of God proclaimed, and in the presiding priest. On top of all that, by faith we know that Jesus is present everywhere, in his body, the church, and in all who are in need (Matthew 25:31–45).

34. DINNER OUT   *Gifts, stewardship*

By her own admission, famous Catholic actress Helen Hayes was not noted for her cooking skills. One day, in an experimental mood, she retired to the kitchen to put the finishing touches on her dinner preparations. "This is the first turkey I've ever cooked," she warned her family. "If it isn't right, I don't want anybody to say a word. We'll just get up from the table, without comment, and go down to the hotel for dinner." Several minutes later she returned to the dining room, where the family had expectantly settled around the table—wearing their hats and coats!

REFLECTION

We should never be surprised when our loved ones seem to know us better than we know ourselves. In the case of Helen Hayes, they knew that her cooking talent was nonexistent. That is not to say, however, that like Helen Hayes, we cannot discover our talents in other areas. As we learn from Saint Paul, "We have gifts that differ according to the grace given to us" (Romans 12:6). What is important is to discover our talents and use them for the greater glory of God.

35. PROMISE TO RETURN   *Second coming*

In 1710, while serving as Kapellmeister to the Elector of Hanover, Georg Friedrich Händel, the famous composer, visited London on a leave of absence and promptly fell in love with the city. Shortly after returning to Hanover, he persuaded the elector to let him visit the city again, promising to return. He did return—nearly fifty years later.

REFLECTION

Handel did return as promised, although after a long absence. Before Jesus ascended into heaven, he also promised that he would return (John 14:3). Many early Christians thought it would be in their lifetimes. Gradually the church came to understand that his return would be delayed. We do not know when the parousia, the second coming of Christ, will occur, but we do know that it will happen. At the Eucharist we acknowledge this belief when we proclaim the memorial acclamation: "Christ has died, Christ is risen, Christ will come again." Also, we acknowledge this belief in the Nicene Creed when we pray, "He will come again in glory to judge the living and the dead."

36. TO FOLLOW HIS EXAMPLE   *Natural law, morality*

When Darius, King of Persia, was on his deathbed, his son Artaxerxes, who wished to follow his example, asked him by what policy he had governed the kingdom for nineteen years. "My son," said Darius, "be assured that if my reign has been blessed with greater success and peace than those of my predecessors, it is because, in all things, I have honored the gods, and done justice to everyone."

REFLECTION

Matters pertaining to justice, as well as related issues of right and wrong find their intrinsic value not only in faith but in the natural law. Long before Jesus walked among us and even before God revealed himself to Moses, humanity already possessed a sense of justice and righteousness. People acted morally before the Ten Commandments. This is what we call natural law, which is a participation in the wisdom of God. We strive to live a moral life not only because God commanded such behavior, but also because the natural law is written within our very beings. We strive to live a moral life because it is the right thing to do.

37. IT BECOMES CLEAR   *The cross, suffering*

Whoever ascends Mount Heroseeta, about thirty miles east of Madrid, will reach a very large granite cross, which stands at the brim of a cliff and dominates the whole *El Valle de los Caidos* (Valley of the Fallen). The view from the cross is magnificent. The valley is lined with trees planted to commemorate those who lost their lives in the Spanish Civil War. Exactly at the altitude of the granite cross is the edge of the fog that is usually very dense, especially during the colder season. One day, a tourist ascended Mount Heroseeta and about halfway up met a farmer and expressed his surprise that he couldn't see much, due to the heavy fog. The farmer replied, "You must go up to the cross; at the cross it becomes clear." The tourist, a mountain climber, full of renewed courage and hope, continued on his way until he reached the cross. There he was able to take in the beautiful valley below. Only at the cross did all of this become clear.

REFLECTION

"Only at the cross did all of this become clear!" In this story we get a very good sense of the Christian vocation, which always includes the cross. The Israelites experienced suffering from the very beginning of their existence as a people. They discovered that their covenant with God did not protect them from suffering. We are no different from them. We too try to escape suffering and sorrow. So often we place much credence and hope in the ability of technology to solve all our problems and ease all our sufferings. Jesus teaches us that suffering has meaning only when it is viewed in relationship to his cross. Saint Paul puts it this way, "I consider that the sufferings of this present time are not worth comparing with the glory about to be revealed to us" (Romans 8:18).

38. A MATTER OF LIFE AND DEATH
Love, compassion

In 1783, a poor woman in Dungannon, Ireland, went to a house where oatmeal was sold, and offered to exchange much needed clothing for some oatmeal for herself and her four children. The shopkeeper's wife refused to let the poor woman have any of the oatmeal. That night she had deep regrets and told her husband about the poor woman, adding that she feared the family was in distress. The husband got out of bed instantly, and hurried to the poor woman with some oatmeal but it was too late. She was dead in her wretched cabin with the children crying around her!

REFLECTION

Virtues are forever important, but love is held up as the most important of all the virtues (1 Corinthians 13:13). We may think of compassion in much the same way. There may be times when others will take advantage of our kindness and exploit our good will, but to refuse those in need is to risk not only their health and well-being but God's judgment on us as well.

39. KEEPING GOOD COMPANY   *Simplicity, detachment*

Mohandas (Mahatma) Gandhi gave a lecture to a gathering of Indian princes, exhorting them to give up their money and possessions and embrace a life of poverty and simplicity, imitating his own severe lifestyle. One by one his distinguished audience slid out until there was nobody left except, as Gandhi afterward said, "God, the chairman, and myself." After another few minutes the chairman himself melted away. "Poor fellow," observed Gandhi, "he must have been very uncomfortable in that strange company."

REFLECTION

Being in the company of God can be uncomfortable because God is always challenging us to rise above ourselves and live in a way that only God can expect, becoming more like Jesus. We can, with God's grace-filled presence, accept his gentle invitation to embrace such a life. "God is able to provide you with every blessing in abundance" (2 Corinthians 9:8).

40. DO NOT LAY UP WEALTH   *Poverty of spirit, lifestyle*

An ancient philosopher named Aristippus was shipwrecked. All his earthly possessions sank into the sea, but he managed to reach the shore safely. The local people, out of respect for the philosopher's great knowledge, presented him with gifts equaling the value of what he had lost. Deeply moved, Aristippus wrote: "Do not lay up wealth that swollen seas can swallow. Labor only for knowledge, the indestructible good, which not even a shipwreck can take away."

REFLECTION

Many possessions may be taken from us, but if we live the life of Jesus Christ, we can never lose our most precious treasures, because we possess them deep within ourselves. One insightful person observed that only when we don't have anything do we realize that God is everything. "Take care! Be on your guard against all kinds of greed; for one's life does not consist in the abundance of possessions" (Luke 12:15). We are also cautioned that our heart will always be where our riches are (Luke 12:34).

41. $80,000 IN PENNIES   *Money, values*

In Dillonvale, Ohio, Louis Staffilino's savings filled forty garbage cans, weighed thousands of pounds, and took four days to deliver by truck to the bank. The seventy-year-old bar owner had been saving pennies for sixty-five years. By the time he decided to cash them in, he had eight million of them—$80,000. He also had something he didn't particularly care for, publicity. People from all over the world called to know more about Staffilino and his penny stash.

REFLECTION

Benjamin Franklin, who once said "a penny saved is a penny earned," would never have imagined the number of pennies one person could actually collect over many years. Ironically, with the high cost of living, many people today don't even count loose change as having much value anymore. Considering that one man over several decades collected eight million pennies, one might wonder what else might be worth saving: How many acts of kindness? How many prayers? How many Masses? How many rosaries? How many sacrifices for others? "Where your treasure is, there your heart will be also" (Matthew 6:21).

42. IRS VISIT   *Stewardship*

An IRS inspector visited a church and asked to see the pastor. He went to his office and said, "Father, I believe a member of your parish, Mr. Ludlow, stated on his tax return that he has donated $100,000 to your church. Tell me, Father, is this correct?" The priest answered, "Yes, he will."

REFLECTION

Any monetary gift to a parish is always gratefully accepted with the firm assumption that the gift is given in the spirit of good stewardship, out of love for God and his church. As a member of the body of Christ, each parishioner is to determine how much to give and where to direct one's resources. Thus, we speak of the faithful steward of God's good gifts. "Each of you must give as you have made up your mind, not reluctantly or under compulsion, for God loves a cheerful giver" (2 Corinthians 9:7).

43. A DONKEY, ROOSTER, AND LAMP
Providence, trust

There is an old story told of Rabbi Goldstein who took a trip to a strange land and brought with him a donkey, a rooster, and a lamp. Since he was a Jew, he was refused hospitality at the village inns, so he decided to sleep in the woods. He lit his lamp to study the holy books before going to sleep, but a fierce wind came up, knocking over the lamp and breaking it. The rabbi decided to turn in, saying, "All that God does, God does well." During the night some wild animals came along and drove away the rooster, and later thieves stole the donkey. Goldstein woke up, saw the loss, but still proclaimed easily, "All that God does, God does well." The rabbi then went back to the village where he had been refused lodging, only to learn that enemy soldiers had invaded it during the night and killed all the inhabitants. He also learned that the soldiers had traveled through the same part of the woods where he lay asleep. Had his lamp not been broken he would have been discovered. Had not the rooster been chased, it would have crowed, giving him away. Had not the donkey been stolen, it would have brayed. So once more Rabbi Goldstein declared, "All that God does, God does well!"

REFLECTION

Submitting to God's will may be very difficult, but it does have its benefits if only we place our complete trust in God, even when we don't know the final outcome. God's care for us exceeds our imagining, even when all the "evidence" seems to say otherwise.

44. GANDHI'S SHOES   *Possessions, love*

As Mohandas Gandhi stepped aboard a train one day, one of his shoes slipped off and landed on the track. He was unable to retrieve it because the train was moving. To the amazement of one of his companions, Gandhi calmly took off his other shoe and threw it along the track to land close to the first. When his companion asked him why he did this, Gandhi smiled. "The poor man who finds the shoe lying on the track," he replied, "will now have a pair he can use."

REFLECTION

When we practice virtue and not just talk about it, we can acquire the clarity of mind and heart to give spontaneously, even when we may never know who the recipient of our gift might be.

45. ROCKING WITH ME   *Time, stewardship, love*

There was once an elderly, despondent woman in a nursing home. She wouldn't speak to anyone or request anything. She merely existed, rocking back and forth each day in her creaky old rocking chair. The old woman didn't have many visitors. But from time to time a concerned and wise young nurse would go into her room. She didn't try to speak or ask questions of the old woman. She simply pulled up another rocking chair beside her and rocked with her. Months later the old woman finally spoke. "Thank you," she said. "Thank you for taking the time to rock with me."

REFLECTION

Time is such a valuable gift to give. Contrary to the conventional wisdom in our culture, we need not always speak or be active to share our time and to be present to someone in need. As the verse goes:

I have only just a minute,
only sixty seconds in it,
forced upon me, can't refuse it,
didn't seek it, didn't choose it,
but it's up to me to use it,
I may suffer if I lose it,
give account if I abuse it,
just a tiny little minute,
but eternity is in it.

46. PARALYSIS   *Judging*

A young student at a university was able to move around only with his wheel-chair. Although a homely sort, he was very friendly and outgoing and enjoyed great respect of the other students. One day a classmate asked the cause of his paralysis. When he explained it was from birth, the classmate questioned him further, "How can you face the world so confidently and cheerfully with such an affliction?" He replied, "Oh, the disease affected my limbs, not my heart."

REFLECTION

Many are tempted to make judgments about others only by what they see external-ly, ignoring the interior, the character and disposition of the person. It's much more rewarding, and honest, to get to know the whole person instead. The one before us just might be a stranger waiting to be a friend.

47. THE BEST PART   *Spiritual values*

In a poor inner-city parish, a young missionary nun received a monetary gift from a benefactor and used it to hire a bus to take the local children to a park for an afternoon of hot dogs, swimming, balloons, and ice-cream. On the ride home, she asked little Maria what she enjoyed most that day. The child respond-ed immediately, "The best part was when you put your arm around me on the way to the bus and kept me safe."

REFLECTION

We often seek new things or experiences to bring joy to others and to ourselves. We soon come to realize, however, that true joy is found not in material things but in spiritual things. Safety, love, compassion, forgiveness, and care all help move us toward interior joy. Our Lord once said, "Come to me, all you who are weary and are carrying heavy burdens, and I will give you rest" (Matthew 11:28). Freedom from sin is the true source of joy and peace of soul. Centuries ago Saint Augustine in his book Confessions *expressed it this way: "You have made us for yourself, Lord, and our hearts are restless until they rest in Thee."*

48. GOD'S WIFE?　　　　*Compassion, sins of omission*

It happened in New York City on a cold December day. A little barefoot boy about ten years old was standing before a shoe store on Broadway, peering through the window, and shivering with cold. A woman approached the boy and said, "My little fellow, why are you looking so intently in that window?" "I was asking God to give me a pair of shoes," was the boy's reply. The woman took him by the hand and went into the store, and asked the clerk to get a half dozen pairs of socks for the boy. She then asked if he could give her a basin of water and a towel. He quickly brought them to her. She took the little fellow to the back of the store and, removing her gloves, she knelt down, washed his little feet, and dried them with a towel. By this time the clerk had returned with the socks. Placing a pair upon the boy's feet, she then purchased a pair of shoes and gave them to him. She patted him on the head and said, "No doubt, my little fellow, you must feel more comfortable now." As she turned to go, the astonished lad caught her by the hand, and looking up in her face, with tears in his eyes, asked, "Are you God's wife?"

REFLECTION

A missed opportunity can sometimes be a sin of omission. We pray sometimes during Mass, "I have sinned through my own fault, by what I have done and what I have failed to do." This can mean not only an opportunity to help a person in need, but an obligation to do so. But an opportunity taken can instill profound faith and hope we may never have known we were capable of having. As someone once said, "I am only one. But I am one. I cannot do everything. But I can do something. And by the grace of God, what I can do, I will do!" Saint Paul, of course, knew of the divine empowerment he enjoyed: "I can do all things through him who strengthens me" (Philippians 4:13).

49. FIND ME ANOTHER SEAT
Love, racial bias, discipleship

On an overseas flight from Johannesburg years ago, a middle-aged, white South African woman found herself sitting next to a black man. She called the flight attendant over to complain. "What seems to be the problem, Madam?" asked the attendant. "Can't you see?" she said. "You made me sit next to this black man. Find me another seat!" "Please calm down, Madam," the stewardess insisted. "The flight is very full today, but I'll check to see if we have any seats available." The woman gave a snooty glance at the black man beside her. A few minutes later the stewardess returned with information, which she delivered to the woman, who stared at the people around her with an arrogant grin. "Madam, unfortunately, as I suspected, economy is full. However, we do have one seat in first class." The stewardess continued. "It is most extraordinary to make this kind of upgrade, however, and I had to get special permission from the captain. But, given the circumstances, the captain felt that it was outrageous that someone should be forced to sit next to such an obnoxious person." The flight attendant then turned to the black man and said, "So, if you'd like to get your things, sir, your seat is ready for you in first class." At this point, the surrounding passengers stood and gave a standing ovation as the black man walked up to first class.

REFLECTION

Our duty as Christian disciples is to be always on guard against not only a prejudice against those with whom we are familiar, but against those we do not even know. If we were less inclined to unjustly criticize and made an effort to look for the inherent good qualities of those with whom we live, work, and meet by chance, we would be surprised to find many strangers waiting to be friends. We must make an effort not to be blind to the essential worth of every person. To do this would be to divorce ourselves from the love that Jesus demanded and that Saint Paul writes is paramount among the virtues (1 Corinthians 13:13).

50. WORLD OF SMILES
Learning from others, joy, discernment

While working at the cash register in a gift shop, a young college student saw an elderly couple come in with their granddaughter in a wheelchair. The cashier looked closely at the girl, perched on her chair; she had no arms or legs. The child was wearing a little white dress with red polka dots. As the couple wheeled her up to the counter, the college student turned her head toward the girl and gave her a wink. As she took the money from the child's grandparents, she looked back at the girl, who gave her a beaming smile. All of a sudden the child's disability was gone and all the young student saw was this beautiful girl, whose smile was just breathtaking and almost instantly gave the college student a completely new sense of what life was all about. She took the young cashier from being a poor, unhappy college student into her world of smiles, love, and warmth. Several years later as a successful business person, the once unhappy college student continued to be inspired by this chance encounter years before, and whenever she became discouraged, she remembered the little girl and the remarkable lesson about life that the child taught her that day.

REFLECTION

If we keep the eyes of our hearts wide open, moving beyond stereotypes, we can learn the greatest lessons from those we least expect to influence us. Even those who are often seen as a burden can be a blessing for us.

51. SPECIAL OLYMPICS   *Values, compassion, solidarity*

In 1976, at the Seattle Special Olympics, nine contestants assembled at the starting line for the 100-yard dash. At the gun, they all started out, not exactly in a dash, but with a relish to run the race to the finish and win. All, that is, except one little boy who stumbled on the asphalt, tumbled over a couple of times, and began to cry. The other runners heard the boy cry. They slowed down and looked back. Then they all turned around and went back. One girl with Down's Syndrome bent down and kissed him and said, "This will make it better." Then all nine linked arms and walked together to the finish line. Everyone in the stadium stood to applaud, and the cheering went on for several minutes.

REFLECTION

We can read books, listen to the directions others give, or practice regularly to learn the rules of a sporting event—or of life. The most valuable lessons we learn in life, however, often come spontaneously. In the end, it really doesn't matter who wins the race, but what we do on the way to the finishing line. It's the journey that matters, not only the destination.

52. SOMEONE TO UNDERSTAND
Judging, compassion

There was a sale on puppies at the pet store. One little boy went to the store and asked, "I would like to buy a puppy. How much do they cost?" "One hundred dollars," was the salesman's response. The boy continued, "I only have fifty dollars. I heard there's one puppy with a bad leg. How much does he cost?" "You wouldn't want him," responded the salesman. "That one will never walk perfectly." Pulling up the leg of his pants, the child exposed a brace on his leg. "I don't walk so well either. I think that's just the puppy I want. He'll need someone to understand him for a long time till he gets used to it. I did."

REFLECTION

Whom do we identify with in the story? The boy who had compassion for the dog because he had a similar disability and thought he would better understand its disability? Or the salesman who downplayed the dog's value because of a walking problem and who must have been embarrassed by his implicit judgment of anyone with a physical defect? Because every person is made "in [God's] image" (Genesis 1:27) and is the object of God's love, there is an inherent value in every person, whatever physical drawbacks there may be.

53. DIED FOR YOU
Love of Jesus, redemption

It has been said that when the body of President Abraham Lincoln lay in state in Cleveland, Ohio, a poor black woman made her way to the casket and held her child up to see the president. She said to the child, "Take a long, long look, honey; that man died for you."

The advice of one poor woman spoken to her child is important advice for every human being who ever lived or who ever will live when contemplating the death of Jesus on the cross, "Take a long, long look…that man died for you." "For I handed on to you as of first importance," Saint Paul writes, "what I in turn had received: that Christ died for our sins in accordance with the scriptures" (1 Corinthians 15:3).

54. FARMER FLEMING *Love, generosity*

His name was Fleming, and he was a poor Scottish farmer. One day, while trying to eke out a living for his family, he heard a cry for help coming from a nearby bog. He dropped his tools and ran to the bog. There, mired to his waist in black muck, was a terrified boy, screaming and struggling to free himself. Farmer Fleming saved the lad from what could have been a slow and terrifying death. The next day, a fancy carriage pulled up to the Scotsman's sparse surroundings. An elegantly dressed nobleman stepped out and introduced himself as the father of the boy the farmer had saved. "I want to repay you," said the nobleman. "You saved my son's life." "No, I can't accept payment for what I did," the farmer replied. At that moment, the farmer's own son came to the door of the family hovel. "Is that your son?" the nobleman asked. "Yes," the farmer replied proudly. "I'll make you a deal. Let me take him and give him a good education. If the lad is anything like his father, he'll grow to be a man you can be proud of." And that he did. In time, the farmer's son graduated from St. Mary's Hospital Medical School in London, and went on to become known throughout the world as the noted Sir Alexander Fleming, the doctor who discovered penicillin. Years afterward, the nobleman's son was stricken with pneumonia. What saved him? Penicillin. The name of the nobleman was Lord Randolph Henry Spencer Churchill. His son's name was Winston Churchill.

In most cases we never know the results of a simple, or even heroic, act of kindness, or if anyone will even know about it. The decisions and circumstances that come together to influence people and events, because of an act of love, are most often beyond our reach. From time to time, however, God gives us a glimpse of how far-reaching one act of generosity can be. Such is the case in this story.

55. DO THE SAME   *Effects of love*

Several years ago a very poor family of five boys and three girls had little wealth, but much love and great faith. As poor as they were, the mother consistently gave each week to St. Peter's Church. She couldn't give much, but it was sacrificial. The oldest boy was an intelligent young man hoping to be a doctor, but he knew such a career was far beyond the reach of his family. One day the family doctor came to the house to treat two of the children. The mother told the doctor about her son's ambition and he asked her to send the young man to his office. There, he told the young man, "I will pay your way through medical school on one condition, that when you become a physician, you do the same for another dedicated and needy person. Let him promise to do the same, but always remind him that this has to be a secret between him and his beneficiary."

REFLECTION

Only God knows how many dedicated and needy students became physicians thanks to this dedicated mother who consistently made her sacrificial offering to the church, and to the visiting physician who was willing to place his confidence in the ambition of one young man. Thanks to the faithfulness of this mother and the unselfish act of the doctor, the world itself was given a brighter future. Whatever we do in God's name, God will never forget it or let it go unrewarded. As Saint Paul observes, "He scatters abroad, he gives to the poor; his righteousness endures for ever. He who supplies seed to the sower and bread for food will supply and multiply your seed for sowing and increase the harvest of your righteousness" (2 Corinthians 9:9–10).

56. THE OTHER SIDE   *Value of life*

The famous book *The Other Side of the Mountain* by E.G. Valens, which was later made into a movie, told the story of a young woman, a champion skier, who had an accident that paralyzed her. What she had valued most in her life was her ability to be a champion skier, but she had not thought much about the value of her life. The unfortunate accident taught her that life has value only if you first appreciate it in yourself. Though never able to walk again, a rebirth of self took place when she began to place a high value on her person and also taught others to value themselves.

Value for the human person is measured not by what we do but by who we are. It is the realization that the flesh-and-blood person is not somehow less human or less deserving of dignity because of a disability. This realization does not always come easily. Sometimes it takes a dramatic life-changing event to help a person come to this truth. It was that way with the young champion skier who in losing her life, as she saw it, gained it in a way she could never have imagined.

57. DADDY IS DRIVING   *Providence, trust*

While driving to his mother's house in a far-off state, the father decided it was necessary to drive day and night, to get to their destination on time. His young daughter was scared when night came and asked, "Where are we going, Daddy?" "To your grandmother's house," came the reply. "Have you been there before?" "No," came the answer. The child continued, "Do you know the way?" The father assured the child, "Don't worry, dear, we will get there safely." The child persisted, "Where are we going to eat if we get hungry before we get there?" "We can stop at a restaurant if we are hungry." "Do you know if there are restaurants on the way?" "Yes, there are." "Do you know where?" "No, but we will be able to find one." After an entire night of questions, the second night came and went without questions. The father thought his child might have fallen asleep, but when he looked he saw that she was awake and was just looking out the window calmly. He couldn't help wondering why she was not asking any more questions. "Susan, do you know where we are going?" "Grandma's house in Florida," came the response. "Do you know when we are going to get there?" "No." "Then why aren't you asking me any more questions?" "Because, Daddy, you are driving and I know we will get there safely."

REFLECTION

"Because, Daddy, you are driving and I know we will get there safely." The words of a young child can strengthen us when questions and fears arise in our journey with God. Our loving Father, who is in control of our lives, will lead us safely to heaven, providing for all our needs along the way, as long as we trust him—"Your heavenly Father knows that you need all these things" (Matthew 6:32)—and fol-

low his will—"Not everyone who says to me, 'Lord, Lord,' will enter the kingdom of heaven, but only one who does the will of my Father in heaven" (Matthew 7:21).

58. BE THANKFUL   *Sin, optimism*

Matthew Henry, the famous Protestant Scripture scholar, was once accosted by thieves and robbed of his money. He wrote in his diary: "Let me be thankful, first, because I was never robbed before; second, because, although the thieves took my all, it was not much; and, third, because it was I who was robbed, not I who robbed."

REFLECTION

Matthew Henry had the wisdom to recognize that it is better to be the victim of sin than to sin. He saw in this an example of finding something good in an unfortunate situation. The short journal entry teaches us that there really is a silver lining, even when we are victimized. The challenge is for us to discover it.

59. A LESSON   *Forgiveness, sacrament of penance*

There is a story told of a rancher and a homesteader in the Old West. The homesteader had suffered several years of crop failure due to bad weather. Desperate, he decided to steal one of the cows from the neighboring ranch to provide food for his starving family. Unfortunately, he was caught in the act. The rancher said to his hired hands, "String him up; it will teach him a lesson." When the rancher died several years later he came before God to be judged. Remembering his treatment of the homesteader, the rancher feared the worse punishment. God said, "Forgive him; it will teach him a lesson!"

REFLECTION

God loves us individually, as though there was no one else to love. As we hear so often, "God's love is unconditional." That's why God gives us the gift of the sacrament of penance, or reconciliation. To receive God's forgiveness through the sacrament we should be sorry for the sin, repent, resolve not to repeat it, perform the penance, and receive absolution. Then we will be once again grace-filled to continue on our heavenly journey.

60. DEO VOLENTE   *Trust, openness to God's will*

Some years ago a priest used to be in frequent correspondence with a friend in another part of the country. He noticed that in his friend's letters he would often place the letters D.V. after some of his sentences. He would write, "Mary is in the hospital but should be out in a couple of weeks, D.V." or "We are planning a trip to Lourdes next summer D.V." or " John will graduate from college next May, D.V." The priest never could figure out what the D.V. stood for, so he asked his friend. He answered that D.V. was an abbreviation for the Latin words *Deo Volente*, God willing.

REFLECTION

It was the friend's custom to use these letters to express his resignation to God's will in making his plans, a faith-filled custom. We cannot go too far wrong when we place our total selves at God's disposal. All our hopes and dreams, plans and yearnings depend ultimately on the graciousness of the One who loves us more than we can ever imagine. We submit ourselves always to God's holy will "on earth as it is in heaven" (Matthew 6:10).

61. HEAVY POTATOES   *Forgiveness*

A teacher once told each of her students to bring a clear plastic bag and a small sack of potatoes to school. For every person they refused to forgive, they were to remove a potato, write on it the name of the person they refused to forgive, and place it in the plastic bag. Some of their bags were quite heavy. They were then told to carry this bag with them everywhere for one week, putting it beside their bed at night and on the school bus, next to their desk at school, and even to the movie theater and the playground. The hassle of lugging this around with them made it clear what a weight they were carrying spiritually, and how they had to pay attention to it all the time in order to not forget it or leave it in embarrassing places.

REFLECTION

This is a great image for the price we pay when we keep our pain and bitterness bottled up inside us by refusing to forgive. Too often we think of forgiveness only as a gift to the other person. Clearly it is a great gift for ourselves as well.

62. IMPORTANT LESSON   *Humility, respect*

During the second month of nursing school, a professor gave the students a quiz. One of them was a conscientious student who had breezed through the questions, until she read the last one, "What is the first name of the woman who cleans the school?" Surely, this was some kind of joke. Everyone knew that the cleaning woman was tall, dark-haired, and in her fifties, but they did not know her name. The student handed in her paper, leaving the last question blank. Just before class ended, one student asked if the last question would count toward the grade. "Absolutely," said the professor. "In your careers, you will meet many people. All are significant. They deserve your attention and care, even if all you do is smile and say hello." The conscientious student later commented, "I've never forgotten that lesson. I also learned her name was Dorothy."

REFLECTION

In our efforts to achieve success we can often forget that people are more important than things. Every person is of value. Jesus insists, "It will not be so among you; but whoever wishes to be great among you must be your servant, and whoever wishes to be first among you must be your slave" (Matthew 20:26–27).

63. INTERIOR WEALTH   *Spiritual values, wealth*

During the Great Depression, there was a man who owned a sheep ranch in Texas but did not have enough money to continue making mortgage payments. Like many others in those days, he was forced to live on government subsidies. Each day as he tended his sheep he worried about how he was going to pay the bills. Sometime later a seismographic team arrived at the ranch suggesting that there might be oil on his land. After a lease was signed, they tested the land and at 1115 feet a huge oil reserve was struck. Subsequent wells revealed even more oil than the first and the ranch owner owned it all. He had been living on relief, yet he was a multimillionaire. He owned all that oil with its tremendous potential, yet he did not realize it.

REFLECTION

The same can be said of us. We so often look outward toward others, whether they are friends, neighbors, associates, or famous personalities, and observe the appar-

ent good fortune that they enjoy. We sometimes feel that our lives are substandard when we place ourselves next to others. Yet, we possess the greatest treasure of all, living as "children of God in Christ Jesus" (Galatians 3:26).

64. HOW I CAN SEE?   *Experience, wisdom*

In the movie *Driving Miss Daisy*, a wealthy white dowager criticizes the eyesight and the driving ability of her aging black chauffeur named Hoke, to which he responds, "How do you know how I can see, lest you look out my eyes?"

REFLECTION

The comment made by the chauffeur rings true. Isn't this the great and holy desire of Christian parents, that their children may be able to see through their eyes? They have the experience, training, and wisdom to make important decisions that are based not on how "I feel" or "what I want to do," but on what Christ desires of me.

65. STILL SMILING   *Love of others, common good*

When Pedaretus, the Spartan, missed the honor of being elected one of the three hundred who held a distinguished rank in the city, he went home extremely well satisfied, saying he was overjoyed to find that there were three hundred men in Sparta more honorable than himself.

REFLECTION

Whatever the shortcomings that Pedaretus might have had, jealousy was certainly not among them. He thought of the prosperity of Sparta, not just his own. Do our desires go beyond ourselves? Do we rejoice in the good fortune of others? Do we nourish a life of prayer that enables us to wish for and work toward the well-being of others? How do we really know we are living the life of faith—the Catholic faith—that God has so generously blessed us with?

66. TEAMWORK   *Body of Christ*

Things were not working out for the young teenager who wanted to play on the football team. Every time he came home from practice he was battered and bruised. When the practice season began, the coach knew he would never make the team, but the boy worked hard and went to practice faithfully, so the coach placed him on the team roster as a substitute. In the final game of the season the coach decided to let him play. They won the game by a narrow score and when the referee brought them the football, the coach asked the team, "Who should receive this important symbol of our winning season?" Every player called out the name of their teammate who had worked so hard but had played in only the final game. As one teammate said, "He's the one who made us a team."

REFLECTION

Being a member of the team is not just a good thing, it's everything. When we apply this to the church, we realize quickly how important it is to be on God's team as members of the body of Christ (Colossians 1:24). No matter who we are or the role we play as members of the mystical body of Christ, each of us has an indispensable part to play in the social, liturgical, and educational life of the parish (1 Corinthians 12:4–12).

67. PRACTICE MAKES PERFECT   *Spirituality*

Lucille Ball was a lithe and inventive physical comedian, and her famous slapstick bits, such as trying to keep up with a candy assembly line or stomping grapes in an Italian wine vat, were widely celebrated. She was far more than a clown. Her elastic face could register a whole dictionary of emotions; her comic timing was unmatched; her devotion to the truth of her character never flagged. She was a tireless perfectionist. For one scene in which she needed to pop a paper bag, she spent three hours testing bags to make sure she got the right size and sound. Careful preparation and practice were the key to her success.

REFLECTION

None of us can arrive at sound spiritual practice without careful preparation and ongoing practice. The rhythm of prayer and virtuous living does not come spontaneously. It takes time, effort, and much focused energy; it often involves many disappointments and failures along the way. But if we keep our attention fixed on Christ—putting on the mind of Christ—it is possible, although difficult, to reach heights that may surprise us.

68. WITHOUT BLOODSHED — *Nonviolence, pro-life*

When Edward the Confessor had entered England from Normandy in the eleventh century, ready to give the Danes battle in order to recover his kingdom, one of his captains assured him of victory, adding, "We will not leave one Dane alive." To this Edward replied, "God forbid that the kingdom should be recovered for me, who am but one man, by the death of thousands. No. I will rather lead a private life, unstained by the blood of my fellow men, than be a king by such a sacrifice." Then he broke up his camp, and retired to Normandy, until he was restored to his throne without bloodshed.

REFLECTION

In the spirit of Isaiah 2:4 ("Nation shall not lift up sword against nation, neither shall they learn war any more"), Edward set clear limits to what he would tolerate to achieve his goals. He would not allow bloodshed to be the price of regaining his kingdom, placing more value on the lives of others than on his throne.

69. FIRM BELIEVER — *Jesus, knowing Jesus*

There was a young father who had converted to the Catholic faith. At every opportunity he talked about Jesus. One day an atheist neighbor challenged him with this question, "Do you really know anything about Jesus?" "Yes, I do," replied the convert. "When was he born?" asked the atheist. The new Christian was not exactly sure. Then came another question, "How old was Jesus when he died?" Again he could give no answer. In fact, he had feeble and even incorrect answers for most of his neighbor's questions. Finally the godless one exclaimed, "See, you don't know very much about him, do you?" "I guess I know very little," replied the convert, "but I do know this: Two years ago I hit rock bottom; two years ago I was a drunkard; two years ago I was hopelessly in debt; two years ago my wife seldom smiled; two years ago my children feared my footsteps. But today I am a sober man. Today I am out of debt and even making payments on a new home. Today my wife smiles often. Today my children run to greet me. All this Jesus has done for me. That much I do know."

REFLECTION

The young convert did not know many facts about Jesus, but he "knew" Jesus and had a relationship with Jesus! Implicitly, he knew: "This is eternal life, that they may know...Jesus Christ" (John 17:3). Our faith is believable not because we are able to quote Scripture or the catechism or the words of a saint or church documents. Our faith is most believable when the manner in which we treat others is unbelievable. He may not have been able to tell the atheist everything Jesus did or said in the gospels, but he could show him by his life that faith in Jesus made all the difference in the world.

70. BECOMING CATHOLIC   *Body of Christ, conversion*

Samuel S. Haldeman was a distinguished scientist, author, naturalist at the University of Pennsylvania and founder of the National Academy of Science. His love for the natural sciences was so intense that he studied, taught, and lectured on many aspects of natural history until his death. He became a convert to Catholicism. When his friends and colleagues asked why, he replied, "The study of bugs!" He pointed out that in his study he always found head and members working together as one body. Professor Haldeman reasoned that if God created the tiniest of creatures with such unity of purpose and function, he would likewise give his church a unity so that its head and members could function as one body. What Haldeman's scientific reasoning demanded, he found realized in the Catholic Church.

REFLECTION

Dr. Haldeman's expertise and love for the sciences allowed him to be a leader in his field, cementing his place in the history of science. But for the non-scientific world, Samuel Haldeman also means a great deal. His conversion places him in the company of countless men and women down through the centuries who found their path to union with God in the Catholic Church. Among those are Saint Elizabeth Ann Seton, Venerable John Henry Newman, and, in our own day, Dr. Scott Hahn and his wife Kimberly, Rev. Richard John Neuhaus, Thomas Merton, and Cardinal Avery Dulles.

71. A TERRIBLE CROSS   *The cross of Jesus, self-denial*

There is a story told about a young man who had a terrible cross to bear. He decided that he would ask the Lord if he could trade his cross for another cross. The Lord gave him the opportunity to look at the other crosses that were available. He made his way around a large room filled with many crosses. He saw large crosses, small crosses, rugged crosses, crosses of every shape and size. Finally, he found one that seemed to suit him. It didn't seem to be as heavy as the others and he knew that this cross would not be as difficult to bear as the others. So he gladly embraced it. As he left, he thanked the Lord that he had found a more suitable cross. And the Lord responded, "But that's the cross you came with."

REFLECTION

No one can live the Christian life without the cross, and the cross we have fits us. "If any want to become my followers, let them deny themselves and take up their cross and follow me" (Matthew 16:24). Everyone has losses, problems, uncertainties, and worries. Sometimes our faith is tested. We are called upon constantly to bear the cross of Christ and in so doing to be faithful and to trust in God. We should never lose hope or rely on our own schemes to get through life, but trust the love and mercy of God totally. Why? Because, as Saint Paul tells us, we who "belong to Christ Jesus" (Galatians 5:24), must bear our crosses as he bore his.

72. POVERTY   *Spiritual values, detachment*

One day a father and his rich family took his young son on a trip to the country to show him how poor people live. They spent a day and a night on the farm of a very poor family. When they got back from their trip, the father asked his son, "How was the trip?" "Very good, Dad!" "Did you see how poor people can be?" the father asked. "Yeah!" "And what did you learn?" The son answered, "I saw that we have a dog at home, and they have four. We have a pool that reaches to the middle of the garden, and they have a creek that has no end. We have imported lamps in the garden, and they have the stars. Our patio reaches to the front yard, and they have a whole horizon." When the little boy was finished, his father was speechless. His son added, "Thanks, Dad, for showing me how poor we are!"

R E F L E C T I O N

It all depends on how we look at things, doesn't it? If we have faith, love, friends, family, health, peace of mind, we have everything. We can't buy any of these things. If we had all the material possessions we can imagine, if we are spiritually bankrupt, we have nothing. Another way of looking at it: It is only when we have nothing but God that we realize that we have everything.

73. TO LIVE WITH NOTHING   *Compassion, detachment*

Dr. John Coleman, president of Haverford College in Pennsylvania from 1967 to 1977, wanted to experience what it means to live with nothing. After he lived as a homeless person in the streets of New York City, he wrote: "I walk much more slowly. I no longer see a need to beat the traffic light. Force of habit still makes me look at my wrist. But there's no watch there and it wouldn't make any difference if there were. The thermometer has become much more important. I go back to the heated grate on 47th Street. The man who was there last night is already in place."

R E F L E C T I O N

Some might argue that this experience of Dr. Coleman was rather artificial because he planned the circumstances under which he became "homeless," and he knew that in the end he would return to the comfort of his own home. True. Still, his experience brought to a new level the old Sioux Indian prayer, "Great Spirit, help me never to judge another until I have walked a mile in his moccasins." He is also more likely to be moved to action on behalf of the homeless.

74. KEEPING VIGIL   *Faithfulness, children of God*

The Marquis of Worcester, England, had a poodle that was taken from the grave of its master, a French officer who fell at the battle of Salamanca and was buried on the spot. This dog remained on the grave until he nearly starved, and even then was removed only with difficulty, so faithful was he to his master, the French officer.

A pet's faithfulness and loyalty gives us much reason to be very optimistic about God's faithfulness. If the unintelligent creature is faithful to and loves its master, how much more should we be to the Creator of the universe who made us "in the image of God" (Genesis 1:27)?

75. SPIRIT OF THE MASTER   *Discipleship*

There was a young man who was the son of a famous woodcarver. This woodcarver could make fabulous and intricate things out of a simple piece of wood, and his fame was known throughout the land. When his son came of age and had to choose a profession he became a woodcarver. So the young man picked up a piece of wood and began to whittle. He worked for a week, but just could not produce the beautiful pieces of art his father made. So, he thought to himself, "Perhaps if I use the wood that my father uses, I can create the carvings he does." So the boy took some of his father's wood and began to carve again. After another week of hard work he still couldn't get the same results as his father. So he thought, "Perhaps if I use the same tools that my father uses, I can create beautiful art." So the boy went to his father's workshop, took his tools, and began to carve once again. Another week went by without positive results. Finally the boy became so frustrated that he ran to his father in a rage and said, "Father, I don't understand. I am your son, your very flesh and blood. I've used your wood and your tools and still I cannot create the masterpieces you do!" His father smiled, looked at him and said, "My son, it is not the master's blood or wood or tools you need. It is the spirit of the master you need!"

REFLECTION

We can be imitators of our greatest heroes. We can even imitate Jesus, the greatest of all, as we go about performing the corporal works of mercy (feeding the hungry, giving water to the thirsty, clothing the naked, sheltering the homeless, visiting the sick, visiting those in prison, burying the dead) and the spiritual works of mercy (converting the sinner, instructing the ignorant, counseling the doubtful, comforting the sorrowful, bearing wrongs patiently, forgiving injuries, praying for the living and the dead). But if we do not have a personal and intimate relationship with Jesus, if we have not put on Christ (Romans 13:14), we will never find the intense satisfaction of discipleship experienced by the saints who had the spirit of the Master.

76. THE VASE   *Cross, suffering, redemption*

A little girl went into a gift shop and began to speak to a ceramic vase. "You are so beautiful and I want to buy you!" And the vase said, "Ah, but you know, I wasn't always beautiful." Instead of being surprised at a vase talking to her, the little girl simply asked the vase what it meant. The vase explained, "Originally, I was a soggy, ugly, damp, lump of clay. They put me on a wheel and started turning the wheel until my head became dizzy. Then they started to poke and prod, and it hurt. I cried, 'Stop!' But they said, 'Not yet.' At long last, they did stop the wheel and put me into a furnace. It became hotter and hotter until I thought I could no longer stand it, and I cried out, 'Stop!' But, they said, 'Not yet.' Finally they took me out of the furnace and someone started to put paint on me and the fumes from the paint made me ill. It made my head swim and I cried out, 'Stop!' But they said, 'Not yet.' When at long last they had finished painting, they put me back into the furnace and it was hotter than before. And I cried out, 'Stop!' And they said, 'Not yet.' Finally, they took me out of the furnace, and after I had cooled down, they placed me on a table in front of a mirror. I remembered myself as a soggy, damp, lump of clay. When I looked at my image in the mirror, I lost my breath and I said in amazement, 'I am beautiful.' And then I knew that it was only the pain that I went through that made it this way."

REFLECTION

Like the vase, we too must experience the pain of our trials and sufferings at one time or another. These crosses may be due to ill health, financial problems, the loss of loved ones, the burden of caring for sick family members, the difficulty of living with someone, misunderstandings, and so on. If we accept these crosses in imitation of Christ and offer them for our salvation and that of others, we not only grow in greater holiness and love of God but we also share in Christ's redemptive plan. "Are you able to drink the cup that I drink?" Jesus asks us (Mark 10:38).

77. BEING NEEDED   *Compassion*

A nurse escorted a tired, anxious young man to the bedside of an elderly man. "Your son is here," she whispered to the patient. Suddenly the old man's eyes opened. He was heavily sedated because of the pain, and he dimly saw the young man standing outside the oxygen tent. He reached out his hand, and the young man tightly wrapped his fingers around it, squeezing a message of encouragement. All through the night the young man sat holding the old man's hand, offering gentle words of hope. The dying man said nothing as he held his son's hand tightly. As dawn approached, the old man died. Then the young man went to notify the nurse. While the nurse did what was necessary, the young man waited. When she had finished her task, the nurse began to say words of sympathy to the young man when he abruptly interrupted her. "Who was that man?" he asked. The startled nurse replied, "I thought he was your father." "No, he was not my father," he answered. "I never saw him before in my life." "Then why didn't you say something when I took you to him?" asked the nurse. He replied, "I knew he needed his son, and his son just wasn't here. When I realized he was too sick to tell whether I was his son or not, I knew how much he needed me."

REFLECTION

This story reminds us of the story of the Good Samaritan in which the importance of loving and helping our neighbor in need is illustrated. "Who is my neighbor?" (Luke 10:29) the lawyer asks Jesus in the gospel account. Our Lord responds, "The one who showed him mercy" (Luke 10:37). My neighbor is any person who is in need. As well, Christ considers done to himself what we do to the least of his brothers or sisters. It is only by having a healthy prayer life that we can begin to imitate the Good Samaritan and see Jesus in others.

78. VALUE OF THE PICTURES   *Spiritual treasures*

An old Scottish woman lived in the most impoverished conditions. Years before, her son had emigrated to America. There he had become a very successful businessman but had never found time to return home to visit his mother. One day a friend sat talking with the old lady in her sparsely furnished cottage. "Doesn't your son ever send you money to help with your needs?" she inquired. "No," the woman shook her head sadly. "He does write me nice letters, though. And he sends me the most interesting pictures!" The listener was annoyed, realizing that the son was quite wealthy. But instead of speaking her mind, she simply said, "May I see the pictures?" The aged mother proudly brought them out of a drawer. To her visitor's amazement, they were not pictures at all. They were bank notes from America amounting to thousands of dollars.

For decades, the Scottish mother had been needlessly living in poverty. The problem was that she did not know the value of those "interesting pictures" of the presidents of the United States. She owned the money, but she did not possess or appreciate it. She didn't understand its value. If only we really knew on our spiritual pilgrimage what riches of our Christian heritage we possess and do not appreciate.

79. A CHILD'S HONESTY   *Human solidarity, compassion*

In days of old there was a nobleman traveling in Edinburgh, Scotland, who was approached by a little ragged boy begging for alms. The man told the child he had no loose change, so the boy offered to go get change. The nobleman, in order to get rid of the young pest, gave the boy a piece of silver, and the boy ran off to get change. On his return, he could not find the man and in fact watched for several days in the place where he had received the money. Some time later, the nobleman happened again to pass that way. The boy accosted him again, and put the change he had procured into his hand, counting it with great exactness. The nobleman was so pleased with the child's honesty, that he placed him in school, with the assurance of providing for him.

R E F L E C T I O N

As the story illustrates, the materially poor may well be rich in terms of moral character and personal integrity. The little ragged boy reminds us of the image of the hungry woman, man, or child struggling to survive in every age and country, wearing only the wrappings of their poverty. Such images should painfully remind us of our human solidarity with all people, including the poor, and what we might do to improve the circumstances of anyone in need. Do we have to ask, "Lord, when was it that we saw you hungry…" (Matthew 25:37)?

80. EASTER STORY
The Passion, redemptive suffering, the cross

Many years ago, on Princess Street in Edinburgh, Scotland, one of the window displays caught the eye of a rather well-dressed gentleman. He found himself gazing at a moving depiction of the scene on Calvary, that first Good Friday. The painting showed Jesus stretched out on the cross with his sorrowing mother, Mary, and the beloved disciple, John, standing nearby. It had been a very long time since the gentleman had allowed any religious thoughts or sentiments to enter his mind and touch his heart. For some reason, the artist's portrayal of the crucifixion, however, had sparked the remembrance of long-forgotten truths, and he became troubled. Suddenly, he became aware of someone standing at his side. He looked down and saw a small boy in tattered clothes who was also looking intently at the crucifixion scene. The child turned to the gentleman and spontaneously began to explain the picture and its meaning. "That's Jesus on the cross, sir. He was nailed there, with a crown of thorns on his head. Too bad because he was such a kind and gentle man. He healed the sick and helped so many people. And that's his mother and friend looking at him." The young lad then asked the man, "Do you know, sir, that Jesus died for us because he loved us and wanted us to love one another?" As the child spoke, the well-dressed gentleman felt a lump rise in his throat and tears well up in his eyes. The story of Calvary, so long forgotten, as well as the sight of the poor boy bothered him. Everything seemed all too real, and he felt overwhelmed. And so, he turned away quickly from the window and began to walk down the street. But before he had gotten very far, he felt some tugging at his jacket. It was the little boy again, now out of breath from running after him. In all innocence, the child blurted out, "Sir, you don't have to be sad. I forgot to tell you the best part of the story. It changes everything. You know Jesus who was crucified? Well, he's alive. On Easter Sunday, God raised Jesus from the dead."

REFLECTION

The passion of Jesus Christ is a vivid account of human deprivation and suffering at the hands of Jesus' contemporaries. It leaves us at a loss for words because the worst of humanity was at work in this descriptive record of his death. Death struck and left its mark. But our faith reminds us that the tomb bears within itself the seed of new life. "Unless a grain of wheat falls into the earth and dies, it remains just a single grain; but if it dies, it bears much fruit" (John 12:24). The cross cannot be restrained from its own triumph!

81. STREET SWEEPER   *Stewardship*

Martin Luther King, Jr., had this to say: If a man is called to be a street sweeper, he should sweep streets even as Michelangelo painted, as Beethoven composed music, or as Shakespeare wrote poetry. He should sweep streets so well that all the hosts of heaven and earth will pause to say, "Here lived a great street sweeper who did his job well."

REFLECTION

Whatever our task in life, however great or mundane, we should approach it as our unique contribution to the benefit of humankind, using all our ability and talent to make God's good earth a better place to live. Saint Paul's words about the diversity of gifts in the church may be applied to our civic society as well (1 Corinthians 12:4–12).

82. WILLING TO LIVE   *Discipleship, ministry*

During the Civil War, President Abraham Lincoln had a strapping athletic young man as his secretary. In those days before office machinery, such a man would literally be doing a good deal of writing and other clerical work. This particular man was not happy about it. He wanted to get out where the action was, on the battlefield. He wanted to go and do great things for his country. He was quite willing to die if necessary. So he kept on complaining about the work he was doing, when he could be in uniform confronting the enemy. After hearing the usual complaint one day, Lincoln stared at him, stroked his beard with his hand, and said in a philosophical way, "Young man as I see it, you are quite willing to die for your country, but you are not willing to live for it."

REFLECTION

The advice President Lincoln offered is applicable to the Christian life. We often contemplate the lives of the saints, especially those martyrs who died for the faith. In our spiritual zeal, we commit ourselves even to die for our faith. A more pressing question might be, "Am I willing to live for it?" Some might say that that would be even harder than dying for it.

83. TWO BILLS   *Tithing, stewardship*

One day, a one-dollar bill and a one-hundred-dollar bill got folded together and began talking about their life experiences. The one-hundred dollar bill began to brag, "I've had a great life," he said. "I've been to all the big hotels. Donald

Trump himself used me at his casino. I've been in the wallets of Fortune 500 board members. I've flown from one end of the country to the other! I've even been in the wallet of two Presidents of the United States." In awe, the one-dollar bill humbly responded, "Gee, nothing like that has ever happened to me…but I've been to church a lot!"

REFLECTION

Financial support and generosity to the parish are not always a priority for many regular parish members. The fact, as we know, is that the parish and the church at large depend on the financial support of all the faithful to continue its ministries. Without continued support, performing the work of the church, God's work, would be impossible. Giving generously to the church of one's time, talent, and treasure is not a matter of charity but a matter of justice. It is never a good sign when parishioners dig into their pockets and contribute whatever happens to fall out. Unfortunately, these people often belong to the faithful majority that might be called "the dollar club." Isn't it ironic that so many give so little to the one who has given them everything? The challenge for the good steward is to give not from one's surplus but, like the widow in the gospel, to give from one's livelihood (Luke 21:3–4).

84. THE WILL TO PREPARE   *Advent*

A famous football coach once rebuked a confident player who said that their team would win because it had the will to win. "Don't fool yourself," said the coach. "The will to win is not worth a nickel unless you have the will to prepare."

REFLECTION

We often associate the word "preparation" with the season of Advent as we prepare not only for the birth of Jesus in Bethlehem but also for his coming into our hearts and everyday life, and again in glory. Preparation is what the life of discipleship is all about, before, during, and after the Advent season. We "wait in joyful hope" not as passive observers, but as full participants, taking our rightful place within the community of the church as brothers and sisters of Jesus. "Come, Lord Jesus" should be our prayer, in season and out of season (Revelation 22:20).

85. TOO MANY OPTIONS
Discipleship, baptism, abortion

In our technical world, our lives are drowning in options that consume our time. Even watching television may be a giant undertaking because it seems to take fifteen minutes to go through all the 197 channels trying to choose what to watch. If we shop for spaghetti sauce, we have to choose from a dozen brands. The sad truth is that we have become "prisoners of options."

REFLECTION

Although some options in modern living may border on the ridiculous, having them is not always bad. Worse than options is the sad truth that we often assign equal value to the choices we have. Making decisions must always be responsible and legitimate. To use the example of abortion, it can never be a correct, moral choice. The question of choice, by definition, suggests that the outcome would be a valuable one. We may have options concerning how we are to live out the details of discipleship, but what options do we have if Jesus invites us through baptism to follow him in fidelity? Only two: to accept whole-heartedly, or not to accept. What will our R.S.V.P. be?

86. CHURCH MEMBERS
Baptism, parish, conversion

Parishioners can be divided into five types of bones: 1) Wishbones: those always wishing for better things, but never willing to work and pray for them. 2) Jawbones: the gossiping kind that keep the parish in turmoil. 3) Funny bones: like the bone in the elbow that throws a person into a tizzy when it is hurt; they are touchy, wear their feelings on their sleeves, and are always talking about leaving the parish. 4) Dry bones: scrupulously faithful but as dead as fossils. 5) Backbones: the spiritually sound and faithful ones who support the mission of the church and keep the body of Christ standing.

REFLECTION

The mission of every parish is to be all-embracing toward all people, despite the shadow side of humanity. Whatever the type of parishioner, all have been baptized into Christ and must be constantly on the road of conversion, in the process of becoming God-centered and ever more faithful to their calling. "As many of you as were baptized into Christ have clothed yourselves with Christ" (Galatians 3:27).

87. TOO CLOSE   *Catholic Church, renewal, spirituality*

A visitor to New York City asked a passerby to show him the Empire State Building. The New Yorker took the tourist two blocks from where they had just been, then pointed in the direction from which they had just come. "There it is," said the New Yorker. "Why didn't you tell me that when we were there?" asked the tourist. "Because you were too close to see it," replied the New Yorker.

R E F L E C T I O N

Being Catholic is not only an experience of the church, Jesus, God, creation, and more, it also depends on how we relate to them. But like the visitor to New York, we are sometimes too close to the reality of our Catholic faith to properly appreciate it. Sometimes we have to "stand back" and see the larger picture. Put another way, we have to see Jesus again for the first time, the church, God, and so on. We can gain this fresh view and take in the larger picture though prayer, reading and reflection, conversation, perhaps even a retreat. Like the Empire State Building, the magnificence of our Catholic faith can sometimes only be fully appreciated when we see it in its greater fullness and splendor. Only then perhaps will we know that we have found "the pearl of great value" (Matthew 13:45–46).

88. SECRET OF SUCCESS   *Experience, failure, fidelity*

A local reporter asked a bank president to state in two words what the secret was to his success. "Right decisions," came the answer. "And can you state in one word how you make right decisions?" asked the reporter. "Experience," came the answer. And finally the reporter asked, "In two words, how did you get experience?" "Wrong decisions," responded the bank president.

R E F L E C T I O N

Although it doesn't always come easy, almost everyone hopes and even prays for success in life. It should come as no surprise, however, that success comes only after our experiences of mistakes and detours. All the more, we should pray constantly for a much more noble pursuit, which is being faithful in our relationships, the true success. Mother Teresa of Calcutta said it well, "We are called not to be successful but to be faithful." Saint Barnabas in Acts 11:23 exhorted the disciples in Antioch, and us, "to remain faithful to the Lord with steadfast devotion."

89. BEFORE YOU ACT   *Decision making, discernment*

Before you speak, listen. Before you write, think. Before you spend, earn. Before you invest, investigate. Before you criticize, wait. Before you pray, forgive. Before you quit, try. Before you retire, save. Before you die, give.

REFLECTION

Lengthy books and articles have their place and lengthy homilies are also useful. But simple advice may often be the best. A single word or phrase can become the seed that blossoms into a long and fruitful nature walk, a reflective stroll along the beach, a heart to heart with an old friend, or a holy hour before the Blessed Sacrament, in preparation for an important decision.

90. GOOD MANAGEMENT   *Social justice, leadership*

H. Gordon Selfridge founded the world's largest department store, in London. He achieved success by being a leader, not a boss. Here is his own comparison of the two types of executives:

The boss drives his men; the leader coaches them.

The boss depends upon authority; the leader, on good will.

The boss inspires fear; the leader, enthusiasm.

The boss says "I"; the leader, "we."

The boss fixes the blame for the breakdown; the leader fixes the breakdown.

The boss knows how it is done; the leader shows how.

The boss says "Go"; the leader says "Let's go!"

REFLECTION

"Being a leader, not a boss," is a management philosophy that serves parish administration well. It is also a very acceptable model for good management in a just society. Such a philosophy of management echoes the teaching of Rerum Novarum, *the famous 1891 encyclical of Pope Leo XIII on capital and labor, which states: "The rights and duties of the employers, as compared with the rights and duties of the employed, ought to be the subject of careful consideration....Among the several purposes of a society, one should be to try to arrange for a continuous supply of work at all times and seasons" (58). The encyclical continues, "Every one should put his hand to the work which falls to his share" (62).*

91. CALL IN SICK   *Sin, dishonesty*

A ski resort was promoting an ad campaign for midweek skiing. A billboard on Route 91 near Springfield, Massachusetts, read, "Go ahead. Call in Sick!" The ski resort took the billboard down after being inundated by protests, particularly from management groups who called the advertising immoral and "an affront to any citizen with a basic sense of decency."

REFLECTION

Temptation raises its ugly head in the most unlikely places. The ski resort went beyond promoting its business and publicly suggested that people act dishonestly. Just as people, places, things, and events can be catalysts of profound blessing, they can also be occasions of temptation and sin.

92. HELEN KELLER'S VISIT   *Faith*

The *New Yorker* (June 16, 2003) carried a story about Helen Keller's 1932 visit to the Observation Tower of the Empire State Building. "I will concede that my guides saw a thousand things that escaped me from the top of the Empire Building," she later wrote, "but I am not envious. For imagination creates distances and horizons that reach to the end of the world. It is as easy for the mind to think in stars as in cobblestones. Sightless Milton dreamed visions no one else could see. Radiant with an inward light, he sent forth rays by which mankind beheld the realms of Paradise....There was the Hudson—more like the flash of a sword blade than a noble river. The little island of Manhattan, set like a jewel in its nest of rainbow waters, stared up into my face, and the solar system circled about my head!"

REFLECTION

When we talk about sight, we ordinarily assume we are talking about eyesight. Helen Keller teaches us that our ability to see goes far beyond our eyesight. We see not only with our eyes but also with our imaginations. Our imaginations are a great gift from God. Jesus teaches us to also see with eyes of faith. As someone said, "I would rather walk in the dark with God than go alone in the light; I would rather walk with [God] by faith than walk alone by sight."

93. SHORT TIME   *Spirituality, saints*

Despite concern about Ronald Reagan's age (69) when he ran for the presidency in 1980, he won by a wide margin, becoming the oldest president ever elected. During a televised debate with his opponent Walter Mondale in the next campaign for reelection, Mondale asked Reagan whether he was too old to serve another term. "I'm not going to inject the issue of age into this campaign," he astutely replied. "I am not going to exploit, for political gain, my opponent's youth and inexperience."

REFLECTION

A long life is not required to attain holiness, but a certain intensity of life is. It may be said of three saints who died young—Aloysius Gonzaga, Maria Goretti, and Therese of Lisieux—that they lived a long life in a short time.

94. HE NEVER LIVED   *Morality, Christian living*

There was a very cautious man who never romped or played,
who never drank or even smoked or kissed a pretty maid.
So when he passed away, his insurance was denied,
for since he never lived, they claimed he never died!

REFLECTION

Although this man may have missed out on his life insurance benefits, greater benefits awaited him beyond this world. It is often true that the value of our lives is measured by our willingness to participate in sinful practices. Those who embrace virtuous, disciplined living are often seen as not really living life to the fullest. "Get a life," people say. Nothing could be further from the truth. To really live is to live in and for Christ. It means making the decision for Christ not just once, but every day. Living for Christ is not always easy, but it is something we must strive to do all the days of our lives.

95. SUBSTITUTE NEWSPAPER CARRIER

Pets, creation

A New York newspaper carrier was stricken ill and unable to deliver his newspapers. His son took his place but not knowing specifically where the papers were to be delivered, he took for his guide the dog that had usually accompanied his father. The animal trotted on, ahead of the boy, and stopped at every door where the paper was to be left, without making a single omission or mistake.

REFLECTION

Using a little imagination and ingenuity, the boy made a potentially impossible task seem almost effortless. What made this successful was not the assistance of a neighbor or friend but of a faithful pet. We sometimes underestimate the value and usefulness of the creatures that God has given us for our enjoyment and comfort. This did not go unnoticed by many of the saints and by many popes. Pope Benedict XVI loves cats and other animals. In a 2002 German newspaper interview, the then Cardinal Joseph Ratzinger said animals are our "companions in creation." All animals, as all creation, are entrusted to our stewardship. Saint Francis of Assisi always comes to mind when we think about the place of pets in creation.

96. PERSPIRATION AND INSPIRATION   *Scripture*

A young medical student had to take an examination in therapeutics. The professor asked, "What remedies can be used to induce perspiration?" The young student responded, "Sudorific flowers, hot water, and warm blankets." "Let's suppose," the examiner continued, "that the patient doesn't perspire with these remedies." At that point the student began to perspire and said, "In that case, if the patient couldn't perspire, I would ask him to come here and sweat out this exam with me."

REFLECTION

There are times when we least expect it that circumstances inspire new insights to unsolved problems, moral questions never before raised. This is especially true concerning matters of faith and morals. Nowhere in Scripture do we find the now familiar terms, such as the Holy Trinity, Incarnation, in vitro fertilization, or embryonic stem cell research. Yet, we are able to use our natural reason, coupled with a reflection on the word of God, to offer an explanation on these matters of human and religious concern. The church in every age relies on circumstances to inspire new insights to problems previously left unanswered or even unthought of.

97. IMPRISONED BY NATURE   *Humility, vanity*

A friend once encouraged Plotinus, a Roman philosopher, to have his portrait painted. He refused. "It is bad enough to be condemned to drag around this image in which nature has imprisoned me," he explained. "Why should I consent to the perpetuation of this image?"

REFLECTION

The message here could be the virtue of humility or the sin of excessive vanity. In humility one may not want his likeness painted, photographed, or otherwise duplicated or mass produced because life should never be about "me" but about Christ who lives through me. To repeat the sentiment of John the Baptist, "He must increase, but I must decrease" (John 3:30). On the other hand, if the reluctance to have one's image reproduced is a matter of vanity, this is a different matter. We are each made in God's holy image, as we are, each unique from the moment of conception, each uniquely beautiful, and for that we must be full of gratitude.

98. A BETTER PERSON   *Faith*

A young student approached the famous French scientist and philosopher, Blaise Pascal, and declared, "If I had your brains, I would be a better person." Pondering the depth of that statement, Pascal paused momentarily before replying, "Be a better person, and you will have my brains."

REFLECTION

According to the Hebrew way of thinking, the heart, not the brain, is the seat of the intellect and emotions. Following the logic of Pascal, virtuous living would have a positive impact on our intelligence. Being an intelligent person does not necessarily imply being religious and faithful, but being faithful would lead us to make intelligent decisions.

99. DESIRE TO BE CATHOLIC   *Evangelization*

An elderly man was in his hospital room and the head nurse came to his bedside to get some information for his medical chart. Among the questions she asked was, "What is your religious preference?" The elderly patient stared at the nurse and said, "I'm so glad you asked me that question. I've always desired to be a Catholic, but no one ever asked me. You're the first one to ask."

REFLECTION

We need not have all theological expertise or have reached great heights in the spiritual life to begin to fulfill Jesus' command to evangelize: "Go therefore and make disciples of all nations, baptizing them in the name of the Father and of the Son and of the holy Spirit, and teaching them to obey everything that I have commanded you" (Matthew 28:19–20). Our most important role may be to simply extend an invitation or make a suggestion and allow Jesus to do the rest.

100. VALUE — *Human value, pro-life*

Attempting to make an important point about values, the speaker began by holding up a 100-dollar bill. When the speaker asked, "Who would like this $100 bill?" Hands among the 500 people started going up. He announced, "I am going to give this $100 to one of you but first, let me do this." He proceeded to crumple the 100-dollar bill. He then asked, "Who still wants it?" Still, the hands were up in the air. "Well," he replied, "What if I do this?" And he dropped it on the ground and started to grind it into the floor with his shoe. He picked it up, now all crumpled and dirty. "Now who still wants it?" Hands continued to be raised. Finally, he spilled some coffee on it and tore the corners. "Who wants it now?" Still, the hands were up in the air.

REFLECTION

We easily understand that the value of money does not change regardless of the changes it might undergo. If only we would view the value of the human person in the same way and appreciate the inherent dignity and beauty of each.

101. NO MALE PALLBEARERS — *Vocation, single state*

An elderly woman died recently and, having never married, she requested that there be no male pallbearers. In her handwritten instructions for her memorial service, she wrote, "They wouldn't take me out while I was alive. I don't want them to take me out when I'm dead."

REFLECTION

Each and every one of us is called by God to respond generously to his call, whether that is marriage, the priesthood, religious life, or the single state. People are not meant to embrace the single state by default, but rather by discerning God's providence in the circumstances of their life. Sacred Scripture is full of single men and women who present a positive view of the single state. Examples of those working for God while embracing the single state include: Elijah (1 Kings) who was a bold prophet and servant of God; Naomi (Ruth 1–4) who showed great faith as a widow; Hagar (Genesis 21:12f), whom God cared for as a single mother; and Saint Paul (Acts 9:20), who dedicated his life to bringing the gospel to others. Jesus, of course, is the perfect example of a single person living out his vocation.

102. CREMATED AND SCATTERED
Aging, respect for the dead

A woman from New York was getting her affairs in order. She prepared her last will and testament and made her final funeral arrangements. As part of these arrangements she met with her pastor to talk about what type of funeral service she wanted. She told her pastor she had two final requests. First, she wanted to be cremated, and second, she wanted her ashes scattered over Bloomingdale's. "Bloomingdale's?" the pastor inquired. "Why Bloomingdale's?" "That way," she explained, "I know my daughter will visit me at least twice a week."

REFLECTION

The sad truth is that many older people can no longer assume that their children will be supportive and be present as they grow older. Gone are the days, as well, when parents who are dying can take comfort in the fact that their children will visit the cemetery to show their love for them, recall their times together, express their gratitude, and pray for them. The excuse is often, "I'm just too busy." We have become a society too busy to visit the resting place of a loved one, but not too busy to go shopping or dining out or participate in such other activities. Becoming self-centered will always distance us from virtuous living.

103. BANKING ON TIME   *Time, stewardship*

Imagine a bank that credits your account each morning with $86,400. It carries over no balance from day to day. Every evening the bank deletes whatever part of the balance you failed to use during the day. What would you do? Draw out every cent, of course. Each of us has such a bank: time. Every morning, it credits you with 86,400 seconds. Every night it writes off, as lost, whatever you have failed to invest to good purpose. It carries over no balance. It allows no overdraft. Each day it opens a new account for you. Each night it burns the remains of the day.

REFLECTION

"Time is of the essence," says the adage. The gift of time keeps on giving. However, whether we use it or abuse it is totally in our hands. From the perspective of faith, time is to be cherished. The Liturgy of the Hours, *for example, illustrates by its very title the dignity with which the church values time. Practicing good stewardship means using time well; it is a matter of conscience. Scripture reminds us, "For everything there is a season, and a time for every matter under heaven: a time to be born, and a time to die; a time to plant, and a time to pluck up what is planted; a time to kill, and a time to heal; a time to break down, and a time to build up…" (Ecclesiastes 3:1–8).*

104. PRECIOUS TIME   *Time, stewardship*

Distance is no longer a serious obstacle because of the means of travel we have. But time remains unconquerable. It cannot be expanded, accumulated, bought, mortgaged, hastened, or retarded. It is one thing completely beyond our control. Use it well—it will never return, and soon may stop arriving.

REFLECTION

Someone once said, "A great part of life is spent in doing evil, the greatest part in doing nothing, and nearly the whole of it in doing what one should not do." How sad it is to waste this precious treasure. What shall we do with this precious gift? We are to make good use of it so as to increase not only in age, but in the grace of God and doing the work of God. With every new breath and every new moment in life, we have a new opportunity to grow in greater love and service of God. If only we could believe that this hour is the "hour of the Lord" and must not be used for any other purpose but for God and his praise, and for our salvation. "With the Lord one day is like a thousand years, and a thousand years are like one day" (2 Peter 3:8).

105. DROP THE PENNY   *Trust, detachment*

The Reverend Billy Graham told the story of a little child who was playing one day with a very valuable vase. He put his hand into it and could not withdraw it. His father also tried to extract the boy's hand, but all in vain. They were thinking of breaking the vase when the father said, "Now, my son, make one more try. Open your hand and hold your fingers out straight as you see me doing, and then pull." To their astonishment the little fellow said, "Oh no, Father. I couldn't put my fingers out like that, because if I did I would drop my penny."

REFLECTION

We are so busy holding on to the world's worthless penny that we cannot accept the true liberty of the children of God. Our task is to drop the least significant impediment from our hearts. We must let go, as they say, and let God. We must surrender to God and let God have his way in our lives. To do that, we have to trust God.

106. PRECIOUS TIME   *Service, love, ministry*

There is a story told of a very attractive young nun working in a leper colony in the tropical heat of West Africa. A journalist was visiting the colony and stood there amazed watching the young nun bathing the wounds of a leprosy victim. "I wouldn't do that for $10,000," said the journalist. "Neither would I," said the nun, "but I do it for love."

REFLECTION

We do not serve our brothers and sisters simply because it might help us to get to heaven. We do it because it's the right thing to do. We do it for love, in response to the love Jesus showed us, and in imitation of Jesus' example at the Last Supper: "If I, your Lord and Teacher, have washed your feet, you also ought to wash one another's feet" (John 13:14).

107. INSIDE JOB　　　　　　　*Spirituality, discipleship*

The Bay of Naples in Italy is the habitat of a jellyfish called Medusa and a snail of the nudibranch variety. When the snail is small, the jellyfish will sometimes swallow it and draw it into its digestive tract. But the snail is protected by its shell and cannot be digested. The snail fastens itself to the inside of the jellyfish and begins to eat it, from the inside out. By the time the snail is fully grown, it has consumed the entire jelly fish. If this was a crime, it would be what is called an "inside job."

REFLECTION

Many of us are like the jellyfish, and have our own snail that eats at us from the inside. Our snail may be alcohol, anger, insecurity, depression, worry, greed, sex, pride, or some other trait. Slowly, it grows and begins to gnaw at us. Eventually we are consumed from the inside. So, what's eating you? What impediment or attachment is distracting you from your work as a disciple of Jesus?

108. JESUS, THE DOOR　　　*Repentance, Good Shepherd*

A tourist in the Middle East observed with interest how a middle-aged shepherd drove all his sheep into a sheepfold. The fold was an enclosed wall with only one opening. The tourist noticed that there was no door or gate on the opening. He remarked to the shepherd, "Aren't you afraid of wild beasts getting in there?" "No," replied the shepherd, "because I am the door. When the sheep are in for the night, I lie down across the doorway. No sheep can get out except over my body and no wolf or thief can get in except over me."

REFLECTION

This story of the shepherd reminds us that the image of Jesus the Good Shepherd would be meaningless unless we placed ourselves into the mindset of shepherds in the Middle East. The image of the Good Shepherd, brought to life when we consider the role of the shepherd in the field of sheep, suggests that we too may wander away, ignoring and even harming our relationship with Jesus. He reminds us in the parable of the lost sheep of his desire to save us: "Which one of you, having a hundred sheep and losing one of them, does not leave the ninety-nine in the wilderness and go after the one that is lost until he finds it? When he has found it, he lays it on his

shoulders and rejoices.... 'Rejoice with me, for I have found my sheep that was lost.'
Just so, I tell you, there will be more joy in heaven over one sinner who repents than
over ninety-nine righteous people who need no repentance" (Luke 15:4–7).

109. CHARLIE CHAPLIN   *Discipleship*

Charlie Chaplin once entered a Charlie Chaplin look-alike contest in Monte
Carlo, Monaco. In the final round, he came in third.

REFLECTION

One might wonder if Jesus suddenly showed up and entered a similar event, would
anyone recognize him? Would others recognize the presence of Jesus in us?

110. THE LEAST PROMISING
Relationship with God, spirituality

Many years ago in France, an election was held to decide who was the most distinguished Frenchman. Louis Pasteur was chosen. Ironically, although Pasteur
was one of the founders of modern medicine, his grades as a child were in no
way impressive. One of his early teachers wrote of him: "He is the meekest, the
smallest, and least promising pupil in my class."

REFLECTION

Although others may evaluate us in such superficial ways, God knows us to the core
of our being, better than we know ourselves, and looks much deeper, into our heart.
God sees our potential for good, sees us as we are. Certainly God judges, but always
with compassion and mercy because "God is love" (1 John 4:16).

111. AN UNUSUAL DEFENSE   *Repentance, judgment*

In 1821, a French citizen was being arraigned for a capital offense. He pleaded
in his defense that, having been born at the commencement of the French
Revolution, he had been indoctrinated by all its harmful principles and had
never been able to distinguish between good and evil. The court disregarded the
plea and the man was convicted and sentenced to six years in prison.

REFLECTION

Such a defense reminds us of the condition which each of us will face on Judgment Day when, as Saint Paul tells us, "For all of us must appear before the judgment seat of Christ, so that each may receive recompense for what has been done in the body, whether good or evil" (2 Corinthians 5:10). On that day we will stand before God, without a list of excuses for our sins of commission or omission. We will have only the realization that God was present for us if we had called upon him and repented of our unfaithfulness.

112. PRESSURE   *Relationship with others*

Pressure correctly and cautiously administered can be of great value. For example, white diamonds emerge from black coal after undergoing intense pressure over millions of years.

REFLECTION

Pressure, correctly and cautiously applied, can be a good thing. Presence, on the other hand, being there for someone, is most often more valuable and effective. We must always strive to be more of a presence than a pressure in dealing with others.

113. COMPASS PLANT   *Discipleship, obedience*

On the plains of America, there grows a strange flower called the compass plant. Its petals always point toward the north, just like the magnetic needle on a compass. Too much sunshine or even a rain storm or any other change of weather cannot prevent it from pointing north. Hikers who have lost their bearings can find their way again through the compass plant, and are never disappointed when they follow its direction.

REFLECTION

No one will be disappointed in following the simple directions of Mary, the mother of Jesus: "Do whatever he tells you" (John 2:5), or of Jesus, "I seek to do not my own will but the will of the one who sent me" (John 5:30). Jesus has told us, his disciples, to live and love as he did. We are to work to establish the kingdom of God, a kingdom of justice, love, and peace.

114. FRED ASTAIRE   *Judging*

Attracted to Hollywood as a young dancer, Fred Astaire submitted himself for the usual screen test. The verdict has become part of film history: "Can't act. Slightly bald. Can dance a little."

REFLECTION

Contrary to popular belief, first impressions are not always reliable. This was good news in the case of Fred Astaire, fortunately enabling others to discover who he really was and what he was capable of doing. This "second look" eventually gave millions of people many years of fine entertainment. In most cases, it is wise to take our time before passing judgment.

115. FACING FAILURE   *Aging, failure*

Failure is something all of us must face in our lives. Abraham Lincoln knew firsthand what failure meant. In 1832, he was defeated for the legislature in Illinois. In 1831, his business failed. In 1832, he was defeated for the legislature. He had a second failed business in 1833, and it took him seventeen years to pay back the debts accumulated in this venture. In 1836, he suffered a nervous breakdown. He was defeated for Speaker in 1838. He was defeated for Elector in 1840. In 1843, he lost the nomination for Congress. He tried to get a job with the U.S. Land Office and was turned down. In 1848, he again lost the nomination for Congress. In 1855, he was defeated for the Senate. In 1856, he lost the nomination for vice president. Stephen Arnold Douglas beat him for a senate seat in 1858. Finally, in 1860, he was elected President of the United States.

REFLECTION

Similar success stories born on the heels of repeated failure have been noted in other interesting lives. Harland (Colonel) Sanders founded Kentucky Fried Chicken when he was sixty-five years old, and Estelle Getty became a familiar television character in The Golden Girls *when she was in her sixties. The point is this: Age should never be an excuse to allow dreams or obligations to go unfulfilled. This is all the more important in matters of faith. It is never acceptable, because of advanced age, to put off or ignore returning to the Catholic Christian faith or converting to it, or going to confession, or participating at the Eucharist, or beginning a special ministry, or otherwise carrying out God's will. It's never too late to make a new decision for God.*

116. MIND READING?   *Jesus, spirituality*

Think of a number between one and ten. Then multiply that number by two, add ten, and divide the result by two. Finally, subtract the number initially thought of. The result will be five. It works every time.

REFLECTION

A miracle? The ability to read another's mind? No. Just simple mathematical logic. Fascinating, yes, but in no way close to the wondrous gift of Jesus Christ in our lives. This is the thought of Saint Paul, who wrote, "I regard everything as loss because of the surpassing value of knowing Christ Jesus my Lord" (Philippians 3:8). With Jesus Christ as the center of our lives, every breath and every action becomes a grace-filled moment, which is always miraculous.

117. THE BUS DRIVER   *Jesus, spirituality*

A bus driver was going down a street. He went right past a stop sign without stopping. He turned left where there was a "No Left Turn" sign. Then he turned the wrong way into a one-way street. And yet, he didn't break a single traffic law. Why not? Answer: The bus driver was on his day off, and he was walking.

REFLECTION

We too must look at things differently in matters of faith and really "think outside the box." We may look at our challenge and responsibility as disciples to live and die and rise with Christ daily and wonder, "How can I do it all?" We will discover the answer, borrowing the words of the angel to Mary, when we acknowledge that "nothing will be impossible with God" (Luke 1:37).

118. BROOM CLOSET   *Ministry of words*

On a door in one of the government buildings in Washington, D.C., a visitor read the following: Room 4573 General Services Administration Region 3 Public Buildings Service Buildings Management Division Utility Room

Custodial. When she asked an attendant what all this meant, he briskly responded, "Broom Closet."

REFLECTION

The nonsense written on the broom closet door is laughable. Words, of course, are meant to communicate, not to confuse, to help, not to hurt. From the first word that was "spoken" when the eternal Word of God "became flesh and lived among us" (John 1:14), to the words we use to build up the body of Christ—to comfort, advise, entertain, forgive, admonish, and instruct—we know that words, which can also hurt, are precious tools to use carefully, in a constructive way.

119. UPSIDE DOWN YEARS   *Jesus*

The year 1961 was special in a rather odd way. The number 1961 reads the same way upside-down as it does right side up. And, a little more than a hundred years ago, there was another upside-down year. It was 1881. Can you figure out what the next upside-down year will be? Answer: There won't be another upside-down year for more than four thousand years. The next one will be the year 6009.

REFLECTION

When we compare our world today with the world of 1961, one can argue that we now live in a world that really seems upside-down. What will the world look like in four thousand years? Will the world still exist, or will the second coming of Christ be a past event? If we could visit the world of 6009, would we find a place penetrated by Jesus' presence, or a world that has turned its back on him? The way we live today will influence that far-off time.

120. WHY WORRY   *Fear, worry*

40% of the things I worry about will never happen, for anxiety is the result of a tired mind.

30% concerns old decisions that can't be altered.

12% centers on criticisms, mostly untrue, made by people who feel inferior.

10% is related to my health, which worsens while I worry.

8% is legitimate, showing that life does have real problems that may be met head on.

REFLECTION

We are too often consumed by worries and concerns that never seem to material-ize? Winston Churchill said, "When I look back on all these worries, I remember the story of the old man who said on his deathbed that he had a lot of trouble in his life, most of which never happened." Jesus said it best, "Are not five sparrows sold for two pennies? Yet not one of them is forgotten in God's sight. But even the hairs of your head are all counted. Do not be afraid; you are of more value than many sparrows" (Luke 12:6–7). He also told us many times not to fear: "Take heart, it is I; do not be afraid" (Mark 6:50).

121. SLEEP LANGUAGE   Faith, readiness to learn

In English, we say, "I didn't sleep a wink." The equivalent in the African language Xhosa translates, "When dawn broke, I was looking through yesterday's eyes."

REFLECTION

One of the greatest challenges of our time is not simply to look, but rather "to see" through yesterday's eyes, that is, with eyes of experience and faith. Such seeing com-municates lessons we've learned through failures and accomplishments. It's the kind of wisdom that parents want to instill in their children. It calls for an open mind and a willingness to learn. On the other hand, if we understand this kind of sight to mean "being preoccupied with the past" to such an extent that we are unable to live fully in the present or look to the future, we would do well to follow the advice of Blessed Junipero Serra, "Always look forward and never look back."

122. THE MARRIAGE ACT OF 1670
Pro-life, abortion, women

In 1670, the British Parliament under King Charles II passed the following remarkable legislation: "Be it resolved that all women, of whatever age, rank, profession, or degree; whether virgin maids or widows; that shall after the pass-ing of this Act, impose upon and betray into matrimony any of His Majesty's male subjects, by scents, paints, cosmetics, washes, artificial teeth, false hair, Spanish wool, iron stays, hoops, high-heeled shoes, or bolstered hips, shall incur the penalty of the laws now in force against witchcraft, sorcery, and such like misdemeanors, and that the marriage, upon conviction, shall stand null and void."

REFLECTION

We see in this marriage act of 1670 that women were treated as property. It was not only a matter of attitude or culture, but also a matter of law. Thus we see a whole segment of the population whose basic human rights and dignity as human persons were unjustly violated, simply because of who they were. The biology of it! In our own day another segment of the population is legally treated as property. They have their basic human rights and dignity as human persons unjustly violated. Under current law, death is legally acceptable for the most innocent of human beings. The "civilized" world calls this abortion.

123. DIFFICULT LANGUAGE   *Mysteries of faith*

We polish the Polish furniture.
He could lead if he would get the lead out.
A farm can produce produce.
The dump was so full it had to refuse refuse.
The soldier decided to desert in the desert.
The present is a good time to present the present.
The dove dove into the bushes.
I did not object to the object.
The insurance for the invalid was invalid.
The bandage was wound around the wound.
They were too close to the door to close it.

REFLECTION

These clever sentences demonstrate the intricacies of the English language. It is near impossible to explain these grammatical nuances, especially to a person who is learning English as a second language. Within the mysteries of the Catholic faith, we find even greater and more complex intricacies such as the mystery of the Holy Trinity, the Incarnation, the Resurrection, the Ascension, and transubstantiation. Think of these mysteries, and religious mysteries in general, not just as subjects we can't understand, but as subjects that we can learn more and more about.

124. AN EXPERIMENT   *Conversion*

In the cold winter of 1839 in Woburn, Massachusetts, Charles Goodyear was experimenting with various quantities of rubber and sulphur, attempting to discover what effect heat would have on the mixture. He carelessly dropped some of the mixture on a hot stove and was surprised to discover that the rubber became hard. In that instant there was a great discovery. Further experiments proved that rubber when treated with sulphur before it is placed over heat, will always harden. This process is called vulcanizing rubber. Goodyear's discovery resulted in a rubber product that would wear well and not be greatly affected by temperature.

REFLECTION

Important discoveries can be made under unlikely circumstances. Conversion stories—discoveries—of those who journey into the church often occur under strange circumstances as well. For the non-believing Augustine, it meant visiting a cathedral one day to hear a sermon by Saint Ambrose. For Rabbi Israel Zolli, the chief rabbi of Rome during the pontificate of Pope Pius XII, it meant being inspired by the depth of love exemplified by the Holy Father. For the Anglican John Henry Newman, it meant recognizing the Catholic Church as the home of the real presence of Jesus in the Eucharist.

125. FOR BIRDS AND ANGELS   *Nature of God*

Protestant bishop Milton Wright was discussing philosophy with a college professor. The bishop's opinion was that the millennium was at hand, because everything about nature had already been discovered and all useful inventions had already taken place. The professor politely told the bishop that he was mistaken. "Why in a few years," he said, "we'll be able to fly through the air." "What a nonsensical idea," Bishop Wright said. "Flight," he assured the professor, "is reserved for the birds and the angels." Ironically, it was Bishop Wright's sons, known as the Wright brothers, Wilbur and Orville, who later launched the first manned powered flight.

This short encounter between Milton Wright and the professor may be "the greatest irony of ironies." Contrary to Wright's strong conviction about inventions and flying machines, his own sons pioneered the invention of what would greatly influence human history. It is a good reminder for parents generally to abstain from absolute statements in matters beyond their limited horizon or beyond their control. We are reminded, too, to be cautious about making absolute statements concerning God. Who are we to limit the God of surprises? As Saint Luke reminds us, "Nothing will be impossible for God" (Luke 1:37).

126. THREE CITIES   *Heaven, purgatory*

Visiting the Holy Land means visiting the State of Israel. Tel Aviv is considered the cultural and amusement center, while Haifa is considered the industrial center, and Jerusalem, the religious center. Citizens of Israel like to say that they have three cities: the playing city (Tel Aviv), the praying city (Jerusalem), and the paying city (Haifa).

REFLECTION

As followers of Christ, we are, or will be, citizens of three cities: the city of God (heaven), the city of humankind (the world), and the city of hope (purgatory).

127. STOPPED WATCH   *Spirituality*

A professor at the university entered this problem into a very sophisticated computer: "I have the choice between two watches: one is broken and irrevocably stopped. The other loses one second every twenty-four hours. Which one should I buy?" The computer's reply: "Buy the one that is stopped, because it indicates the correct time twice every twenty-four hours; the other does only once every 120 years."

REFLECTION

Using a broken and stopped watch, although correct twice a day, would be nonsense. It's one thing to be precise; it's another to use common sense. This is a lesson we should learn especially in our day-to-day Catholic Christian lives. We are not meant to be walking computers or robots, but living and breathing and thinking examples of what it means to be Christ in the world, all of the time and not just twice a day, like a stopped watch.

128. COURAGE OF CONVICTIONS
Sin, absolutes, immorality

Abraham Lincoln delivered a great speech at his famous senatorial campaign in Springfield, Illinois. The convention before which he spoke consisted of a thousand delegates. His speech was carefully prepared; every sentence was guarded and emphatic. It has become known as "The Divided House" speech. Before entering the hall, Lincoln stepped into the office of his law partner and locked the door, so that their conversation might be private. He read one of the opening sentences, "I believe this government cannot endure permanently, half-slave and half-free." His partner remarked that the sentiment was true, but suggested that it might not be good policy to utter it at that time. Mr. Lincoln replied with great firmness, "No matter about the policy. It is true, and the nation is entitled to it. The proposition has been true for six thousand years, and I will deliver it as it is written."

REFLECTION

In every age, there are certain objective truths that stand the test of time and cannot be diluted or compromised. The issue of slavery was a hot button issue during Lincoln's time. In our day, so-called hot button issues include abortion, embryonic stem cell research, homosexual "marriage," and euthanasia. At all times and in all places, the moral response to these matters is to reject them as objectively immoral and sinful. There can never be a circumstance where something which is by its very nature immoral can suddenly be deemed moral. This does not mean that we reject those who commit such acts. Our challenge is always to love the sinner even when we hate the sin.

129. NOTHING BEYOND, EVERYTHING BEYOND
Death

Before Christopher Columbus set sail and discovered the new world, there was a sign at Gibraltar with these words, *Ne plus ultra*, meaning "Nothing beyond."

After Columbus discovered the new world, the sign had to be changed. The *Ne* was rubbed out, thus making it read, *Plus ultra* or "Everything beyond."

REFLECTION

Before Jesus was raised from the dead, the claim of death was Ne plus ultra, *or "Nothing beyond." But after it, death's claim was empty. Because of Christ's resurrection, we can now place on every grave marker the inscription,* Plus ultra. *As Saint Paul makes very clear in his letters, including 1 Corinthians 15:54, death has been conquered once and for all in Christ Jesus.*

130. EXECUTIONERS WANTED
Death penalty, forgiveness

As in Denmark, the punishment for capital crimes in Iceland was beheading. The problem was that for many years no one could be found who would undertake the office of executioner. It was necessary to send the very few who had been sentenced to death to Norway, where the sentence was carried out.

REFLECTION

What civilized person would ever want to be employed as an executioner? So much for a civilized form of justice, which can never be achieved without mercy.

131. HANG HIM
Death penalty, forgiveness

In 1785, an Indian murdered a man in Pittsburgh. After a confinement of several months, the chief of his nation, the Delaware, was invited to be present at the proceedings and see how the trial would be conducted, as well as to speak on behalf of the accused. The chief instead sent the following letter to the civil officers: "Brethren! You inform us that a member of our nation who murdered one of your men at Pittsburgh is shortly to be tried by the laws of your country, at which trial you request that some of us may be present. Brethren! Knowing this man to have been always a very bad man, we do not wish to see him. We therefore advise you to try him by your laws, and to hang him, so that he may never return to us again."

So much for family ties. So much for being innocent before proven guilty. So much for hearing the evidence. So much for an opportunity to repent. Unlike the harsh response of the Delaware chief, God offers opportunities for repentance and forgiveness through the church. Justice is always a part of God's mercy. No matter the extent of one's sins, with every new breath there is a new opportunity to repent and return to God in a loving, covenantal relationship.

132. LAST MINUTE SWITCH
Justice, death penalty, abortion

In the 1660s, an eloquent preacher, a cobbler of New York, killed an Indian. The colonists, determined not to lose his fine preaching, tried him in the usual manner and found him guilty. On the day of the execution, however, they took a poor old weaver, who had long been bedridden, from his bed, and hanged him instead of the real offender.

REFLECTION

There are times in our present culture when we become increasingly frustrated by our justice system where evil things are sometimes designated as good, while things good are seen as evil. Isaiah condemned such a policy: "Ah, you who call evil good and good evil" (5:20). This is especially the case with life matters, such as abortion, the death penalty, and embryonic stem cell research. Often we think of days gone by when things were better. The fact is, as we see in our anecdote, that the justice system has always been burdened with unfair practices. In this case, we discover one criminal case where swift justice is denied and swift injustice is inflicted. We need to begin seeing justice as God sees it, not as the world has repackaged it. If we don't see the difference, we are bound to pay a huge price. Such unethical decisions can take us farther than we want to go, keep us longer than we want to stay, and cost us more than we want to pay.

133. MY CONVERSION · Conversion

Eve Lavalliere was a famous French actress and comedian who was very well known in the theater. She once said, "I will be four on June 19, the anniversary of my conversion. The rest of my life doesn't count because it was such a mess."

REFLECTION

Not unlike the twentieth century and our present one, the nineteenth was marked by many conversions to the Catholic faith. Our present age chronicles famous and interesting examples of individual conversion stories on The Journey Home, *a television program hosted by convert Marcus Grodus on the Eternal Word Television Network. Most of us also know others, both within our families and parishes, who are not so famous. One famous nineteenth-century conversion to Catholicism in England was that of the Anglican clergyman, John Henry Newman. Another is Eve Lavalliere, who lived in England during the lifetime of Cardinal Newman. If she lived in our own day, she would have certainly made an appearance on* The Journey Home. *Her conversion would be tantamount to the conversion of someone like pop singer Madonna.*

134. DYING LANGUAGES   *Baptism*

The world's 6,000 languages are dying off quickly, and experts predict that up to half of them will probably become extinct during the next century. Satellite television, cellular telephones, and the Internet all allow people to communicate with each other instantly all over the world, and all drive the need for languages that many understand. Scientists estimate that in prehistoric times, humans probably spoke between 10,000 and 15,000 languages.

REFLECTION

The study of languages and linguistics is always a fascinating venture. We learn so much about the history and circumstances surrounding the lives of countless people and cultures. In the beginning, however, there was a common language and culture that served as a source of unity for people. With original sin came sin and death, as well as alienation, which sparked new languages and customs. With the new Adam, Jesus, came a new source of unity. Our most important source of unity is not language or custom, but a common baptism in Jesus Christ. Saint Paul tells us much about this signal event in our life: We have put on Christ; we have died with Christ to rise with him (Romans 6:1–14).

135. END THE PREGNANCY   *Abortion*

One doctor said to another, "About the termination of a pregnancy, I want your opinion. The father had syphilis. The mother had tuberculosis. Of the four children born, the first was blind, the second died, the third was deaf and dumb, the fourth also had tuberculosis. What would you have done?" "I would have ended the pregnancy," said the second doctor. "Then you would have murdered Beethoven," stated the first.

REFLECTION

We should never assume that intelligent and enlightened minds include enlightened hearts. In our age of sophistication we desperately need a conscience that is informed. As Pope John Paul II correctly pointed out, "The cemetery of the victims of human cruelty in our century is extended to include yet another vast cemetery, that of the unborn." The prophet Isaiah asked the question many centuries ago, "Can a woman forget her nursing-child, or show no compassion for the child of her womb?" (49:15).

136. THE IRONY OF ROBESPIERRE
Abortion, gift of life

Robespierre, the famous leader of the French Revolution, was noted especially for bringing about a reign of terror. On May 30, 1791, he spoke in the National Assembly in favor of abolishing the death penalty. Ironically, there hardly ever was an individual who showed less regard for human life, or shed blood with such indiscriminate profusion.

REFLECTION

More than 200 years later, the irony continues as politicians and government leaders from all over the world strongly oppose capital punishment and yet hold little regard for innocent human life by aggressively promoting abortion, including the gruesome act of partial birth abortion, as well as embryonic stem cell research, involving the destruction of human life in its earliest stages. The Catholic Catechism *(2256) teaches us that, as citizens, we are "obliged in conscience not to follow the directives of civil authorities when they are contrary to the demands of the moral order. 'We must obey God rather than men' (Acts 5:29)."*

137. TWELVE DAYS OF CHRISTMAS
Faith, catechizing

It has been said that a well-known English Christmas carol, The Twelve Days of Christmas, is more than a repetitious tune with pretty phrases and strange gifts. From 1558 to 1829, the Catholics in England were not permitted to practice their faith. During this period, The Twelve Days of Christmas was written as a catechism song for young Catholics. The hidden meanings of the song's gifts were intended to help the children remember lessons of their faith. For example, the true love mentioned in the song refers to God. The "me" who receives the gifts is every baptized person. The partridge in a pear tree is Jesus Christ. Jesus is symbolically presented as a mother partridge that feigns injury to decoy predators from her helpless nestlings. The meaning of the other symbols are: two turtle doves: the Old and New Testaments; three French hens: faith, hope and charity; four calling birds: the four gospels; five golden rings: the first five books of the Old Testament, which give the history of humanity's fall from grace; six geese a-laying: the six days of creation; seven swans a swimming: seven gifts of the Holy Spirit; eight maids a-milking: the eight beatitudes; nine ladies dancing: the nine fruits of the Holy Spirit; ten lords a-leaping: the ten commandments; eleven pipers piping: the eleven faithful disciples; twelve drummers drumming: the twelve points of belief in the Apostles Creed.

REFLECTION
The Twelve Days of Christmas reminds us of the extent to which our ancestors went to preserve the authentic faith of the church. We each have a role to play in preserving it, enriching it by our study and spirituality, and passing it on to posterity.

138. CELEBRATING CHRISTMAS   *Christmas*

In 1659, the General Court of Massachusetts enacted a law making any observance of December 25 a penal offense. People were even fined for hanging decorations. That stern solemnity continued until the nineteenth century, when the influx of German and Irish immigrants undermined the Puritan legacy. In 1856, the poet Henry Wadsworth Longfellow commented: "We are in a transition state about Christmas here in New England. The old Puritan feeling prevents it from being a cheerful, hearty holiday; though every year makes it more so." In that year, Christmas was made a legal holiday in Massachusetts, the last state to uphold Cromwell's philosophy.

REFLECTION

Newspaper clippings from the 1920s indicate that Christmas Day continued to be a regular workday in many towns throughout Massachusetts. Not only should we be grateful that we can celebrate Christmas without government or employer interference, but we should resolve to celebrate Christmas as originally intended, to recognize the supremely joyful event of God becoming human so that we might become divine.

139. BABYSITTER PROBLEMS   *Family Life*

A first-grade catechist asked her class why Joseph and Mary took Jesus with them to Jerusalem. A small child replied, "They couldn't get a babysitter."

REFLECTION

The environment in which families live may change down through the ages, including the need for babysitting services, but the basic virtues to be practiced by the family remain the same. As for the family of Joseph and Mary, they did all they could to protect their Child. When Herod began looking for the Child Jesus to destroy him, "Joseph got up, took the child and his mother by night, and went to Egypt" (Matthew 2:13–14). What parent wouldn't do the same? The church reminds families that they must be holy. This is their main purpose as a family, to nourish one another by prayer and example and to encourage one another in the way of the Lord. Parents have a special responsibility to provide for the religious education of their children.

140. IMAGE OF GOD   *Image of God*

A little girl was meticulously drawing a picture with her new box of crayons as her dad looked over her shoulder. "What are you drawing, sweetheart?" "I'm drawing a picture of God." "But sweetheart, nobody knows what God looks like." She looked at her dad and replied, "They will in a minute."

REFLECTION

We have never seen God but we love him. We do not completely understand the mystery of God as three persons, each unique, and yet, only one God, but we believe it. We believe what the Catechism of the Catholic Church *teaches us: "The Trinity is One. We do not confess three Gods, but one God in three persons….The divine persons do not share the one divinity among themselves but each of them is God whole and entire….The divine persons are really distinct from one another….He is not the Father who is the Son, nor is the Son he who is the Father, nor is the Holy Spirit he who is the Father or the Son. They are distinct from one another" (253–254).*

141. ETERNAL LIFE   *Afterlife*

A medical doctor who volunteered as a parish catechist asked, "What must we do in order to get to heaven?" "We must die," responded one boy. "Very true," replied the doctor, "but what must we do before we die?" "We must get sick and send for you," responded the child.

REFLECTION

But what kind of life after death do we believe in? Heaven? Hell? Purgatory? At one time or another most of us have felt like the poet Tennyson, "Ah, Christ! That it were possible. / For one short hour to see. / The souls we loved, that they might tell us. / What, and where they be!" Of course, Jesus spoke often about eternal life with God. Saint Paul also teaches us, "no eye has seen, nor ear heard, nor the human heart conceived, what God has prepared for those who love him" (1 Corinthians 2:9).

142. 20,000 LEAKS   *Education, Image of God*

Five-year-old Mark couldn't wait to tell his friend about the movie he and his family had watched on television, *20,000 Leagues Under the Sea.* The scenes with the submarine and the giant octopus had kept him wide-eyed. In the middle of telling the story, Mark's father interrupted and asked, "What made the submarine sink?" With a look of incredulity Mark replied, "Dad, it was the 20,000 leaks!"

REFLECTION

We can never assume how a child thinks or how a child sees the world. The way a child interprets his or her own experience is often unique and sometimes rather humorous, to us. This can be said of a child's experience of faith as well. As we seek to teach children the ways and mindset of Jesus, we should never assume what they perceive or actually understand concerning faith and religion.

143. ANGELS MADE DEVILS   *Evil*

The young religious Sister asked her third graders, "Who made the angels?" Little Timothy answered immediately, "God made the angels." "And who made the devil?" asked Sister. There was silence for a few seconds until Anna answered, "God made the angels and then some of the angels made devils out of themselves."

REFLECTION

The child's answer is correct. Evil came into existence not by the will of God, but through the will of those who turned away from God. God created all things good, including the angels and humanity. It was the creature, not the Creator, who fell in love with evil and opened the floodgates to sin and death.

144. PARENTAL INFLUENCE   *Example*

In the cartoon series entitled *For Better or For Worse*, there was a particular episode featuring a little girl named Elizabeth who was playing with her dolls in the backyard. She had them all lined up and was lecturing them on their behavior and the things they had to do. While all this was going on, Elizabeth's mother was watching her through a window. Suddenly the father entered the room and observed his wife monitoring little Elizabeth's actions. He asked, "What are you doing, watching Elizabeth play?" The mother answered, "No, I'm watching myself!"

REFLECTION

Imitation is the finest compliment we might receive. When another imitates us for the good, it is likely that there is something virtuous and godly that we are teaching. How especially proud a parent must be when their child imitates the good words or actions of a parent. But we are also capable of setting an example that others may imitate that may not be for their good, as we are reminded in Matthew 18:6: "If any of you put a stumbling block before one of these little ones who believe in me, it would be better for you if a great millstone were fastened around your neck and you were drowned in the depth of the sea."

145. KNOW YOU SOONER   *Jesus, spirituality*

A grandmother was telling her little granddaughter what her own childhood was like. "We used to skate on a pond. I had a swing made from a tire that hung from a tree in our front yard. We rode our pony. We picked wild raspberries in the woods." The little girl was wide-eyed as she listened. At last she said, "I sure wish I'd gotten to know you sooner!"

REFLECTION

For many of us, we could say the same when reflecting on our relationship with Jesus. Knowing what we know now, and who Jesus is, and feeling the way we do about all he has done for us, would that we had gotten to know the Lord sooner. But starting today, we can get to know him better. There are DVDs to watch, books to read, retreats to make, conversations to hold, moments of meditation, and so on.

146. MADE IN CHINA   *Creation*

The first-grade CCD teacher explained to her class in great detail how God created everything out of love. "God made not only the moon and the sun and the stars," she explained, "but also the trees and the flowers and the animals and all of us human beings. In fact, God made everything." One of the children returned to class the following week and told the teacher, "God didn't make everything. My mom said that half of what we have at home was made in China."

REFLECTION

We know that God is the ultimate source of all things, even the things with Made in China stamped on it. The Catechism *(290) reminds us, "In the beginning God created the heavens and the earth: three things are affirmed in these first words of Scripture: the eternal God gave a beginning to all that exists outside of himself; he alone is Creator (the verb "create" always has God for its subject). The totality of what exists (expressed by the formula "the heavens and the earth") depends on the One Who gives it being."*

147. YOU BE JESUS   *Presence of Jesus*

A mother was preparing breakfast for her children, Jimmy, 5, and Billy, 4. The boys began to argue over who would get the first pancake. Their mother saw the opportunity for a moral lesson. "If Jesus were sitting here, he would say, 'Let my brother have the first pancake. I can wait.'" Jimmy turned to his younger brother and said, "Billy, you be Jesus!"

REFLECTION

Inviting others to be Jesus is one thing, being Jesus to others in the caring ways we act is another. And seeing the presence of Jesus, the face of Jesus, in the annoying person, the smelly, the overbearing, even an enemy is still another challenge. When we are at our best, we are Jesus to others, seeing Jesus in others, and our words and actions should inspire others to do the same. We are all Christophers, Christ-bearers.

148. PLEASE DON'T SHOVE   *Free will, providence*

A little girl was running as fast as she could trying not to be late for religion class. As she ran, she prayed, "Dear Lord, please don't let me be late! Dear Lord, please don't let me be late!" While she was running and praying, she tripped on a curb and fell, getting her clothes dirty and torn. She got up, brushed herself off, and started running again. As she ran she once again began to pray, "Dear Lord, please don't let me be late…but please don't shove me either!"

REFLECTION

The Spirit of God, God's providence, is always moving us in the direction of life and love and faith. God continues to encourage and direct us, to invite us to deeper spirituality, a deeper relationship with him. But God will never force us or manipulate us, or "shove us." God will always allow us to make our decisions not in fear, but in freedom. God may not keep us from falling when we choose to run, but will not abandon us if we do. His mercy is everlasting.

149. LIKE MOTHER, LIKE DAUGHTER
Grace at meals, gratitude

A mother invited some people for dinner. At the table, she turned to her six-year-old daughter and asked, "Would you like to say the blessing?" "I don't know what to say," the child replied. "Just say what you hear Mommy say," the mother said. The little girl bowed her head and said, "Dear Lord, why on earth did I invite all these people to dinner?"

REFLECTION

Art Linkletter has told us for decades, "Kids say the darnedest things." How embarrassed the mother must have been. It underlines the importance of a standard grace for all family members to learn, such as the traditional grace: "Bless us, O Lord, and these your gifts, which we are about to receive from your bounty, through Christ our Lord. Amen." Parents may teach variations of this as the children get older. The custom of saying grace at meal time is very beneficial, instilling a sense of gratitude. God, the author of life, is also life's nourisher and sustainer. Our blessed Savior expressly teaches us to pray, "Give us each day our daily bread" (Luke 11:3).

150. GOD IS WATCHING   *Presence of God*

The children were lined up in the cafeteria of a Catholic elementary school for lunch. At the head of the serving table was a large pile of apples. A teacher made a note, and posted it on the apple tray: "Take only one. God is watching." Moving further along the lunch line, at the other end of the table was a large pile of chocolate chip cookies. A child had written a note, "Take all you want. God is watching the apples."

REFLECTION

Contrary to the child's note, God's view is broader than that. God watches over us always, as a Father would. Our Father, whose love is faithful and never-ending, knows when we are hurting, knows our heartaches and grieving, and never stops watching over us. Do we neglect to acknowledge God's abiding presence and care? Do we ever question whether God is present with us always and in all ways? Do we ever reflect on it and thank God for it?

151. EATING BEFORE I WAS BORN   *Eucharist*

The sister was chiding her younger brother at the dinner table for making a grab for the biggest piece of apple pie. "Why do you always reach for the largest piece, Billy?" she asked. "Don't you think I ought to have that one?" "Nope," he countered, "you were eating pie five years before I was born."

REFLECTION

Like sleep, we can never "save up" our food intake and use it at a future moment. We need a constant supply of nourishment and sleep to sustain us. The same can be said of the Eucharist; it should be constant nourishment.. No matter how many times we have celebrated Mass and received Holy Communion, there will never be a time in our lives when we have received our fill of the Bread of Life. Reread John 6:48–58. We must receive Jesus in the Eucharist on a regular basis to sustain us as we journey through life, laboring to bring about the kingdom of God.

152. REACHING HEAVEN   *Heaven, resurrection*

The catechist asked the children in her class, "If I sold my house and car, had a big garage sale, and gave all my money to the church, if I took care of my sick neighbor every day, would I be with God in heaven?" "No," the children answered. "If I lived a life of love, and prayed often, would I go to heaven?" Again, the answer was "No." "Well," she continued, "then how can I go to heaven?" In the back of the room, a six-year-old boy shouted, "You gotta be dead!"

REFLECTION

The most obvious step in reaching a goal is the one we often take for granted. To drive our cars, for example, we need gasoline. If we are to go for a swim in a pool, we take it for granted that the pool is filled with water. When we live good, holy and Christ-like lives, we believe that God, who loves us and desires our intimate union, will raise us up after we take our last breath (2 Timothy 4:8).

153. MARRIAGE QUESTIONS   *Marriage, sacrament*

When asked about marriage, some fourth graders commented. "You got to find somebody who likes the same stuff. Like if you like sports, she should like it that you like sports, and she should let you watch games on TV." A second said, "A man and a woman promise to go through sickness and illness and diseases together." A third child pointed out, "No person really decides before they grow up who they're going to marry. God decides it all way before, and you get to find out later who you're stuck with."

REFLECTION

As Jesus was present at the wedding at Cana, he is also present in every marriage, enriching and sanctifying the union of the couple in the sacrament. This is summed up in the title of a book by Fulton Sheen long ago, Three to Get Married. *The* Catechism of the Catholic Church *(1601) underlines the purpose and meaning of marriage: "The matrimonial covenant, by which a man and a woman establish between themselves a partnership of the whole life, is by its nature ordered toward the good of the spouses and the procreation and education of offspring; this covenant between baptized persons has been raised by Christ the Lord to the dignity of a sacrament."*

154. SEE THE ANGEL   *Angels*

Kerri's thirty-year-old father was killed in a car accident. Later that week, her father's friend brought her something special to show her, a beautiful figure of an angel, two feet tall, named Noel. The figure wore a white fur dress, with gold-trimmed lace wings. When plugged in, a star would light up and the angel would wave her arms back and forth and gently turn her head from side to side. Kerri gasped at its beauty and admired it, and finally said goodbye to Noel. A few days later her father's friend received a homemade card from Kerri, which ended with the words, "Thanks for letting me see the angel."

REFLECTION

Like Kerri, all of us need to "see the angel" in our lives. Angels are a truth of faith (Catechism, 328) and Scripture has many references to them. They are described as pure spirits and personal, immortal beings with intelligence and free will. God created the angels to praise and worship him in his presence (Revelation 5:11, 7:11). In the gospel, Jesus speaks of our guardian angels. "Take care that you do not despise one of these little ones; for, I tell you, in heaven their angels continually see the face of my Father in heaven" (Matthew 18:10). An angel, which means "messenger," also interacts in the world, serving as messengers of God, rendering justice, or providing strength and comfort. We should daily call upon our guardian angels to help us, especially in times of difficulty or hardship.

155. DEAD DOG *Heaven, death, pets*

The parents were desperately trying to console their child, "You know, it's not your fault that your dog died." The little boy was despondent. His father continued to try to console him. "You know that he's probably in heaven right now with God." The child responded, "What would God want with a dead dog?"

REFLECTION

The ability to distinguish between the destiny of a family pet and the destiny of a human being is generally understood by those who have progressed in the spiritual life. Some people, though, believe that the family pet will also be part of the new heaven and new earth, safe one day in heaven.

156. THE HIGH ROAD *Discipleship, faithfulness, justice*

When discussing the song "The Bonnie Banks o' Loch Lomond," a country teacher asked his pupils for an explanation of the line, "Yu'll tak' the high road and I'll tak' the low road." One boy answered, "One was going by air and the other by bus."

REFLECTION

The lyrics themselves also suggest that one was taking the highway or express lane while the other was taking the local road. For those who contemplate the words in the context of faithful discipleship, the high road is always the correct route. When we take the high road in the moral life we know that, although it may have its own demands and difficulties, we will have no regrets in the end. The high road connotes faithfulness, justice, and the way of Christ.

157. COLD SOUP *Faith development, learning from others*

While preparing dinner one evening, a mother asked her five-year-old son what he had for lunch at their neighbor's house earlier in the day. After thinking a bit, the boy replied, "Cold soup." Unable to get any more information out of him, the mother was left in the dark as to what cold soup really was. She continued preparing the family meal. As the boy watched, he suddenly blurted out, "That's what I had at the babysitter's!" His mother was preparing chili!

REFLECTION

What is interesting about this story is the analytical skill of the boy. Realizing that "chilly" means "cold," he concluded that the chili was obviously cold soup. His conclusion was wrong but his reasoning was right. We see here a child's ability to analyze personal experiences. More important, we recognize that parental guidance is needed to help a child reach correct conclusions. To the degree that this is important for normal learning and ordinary human development, how much more essential is it in matters of spiritual development pertaining to matters of our Catholic faith?

158. CATHOLIC HOME — Sacramentals, faith development

After the baptism of his baby brother, little Johnny sobbed uncontrollably all the way home from church. His father asked him three times what was wrong. Finally, the boy responded, "The priest said he wanted us brought up in a Christian home, but I want to stay with you guys."

REFLECTION

One would hope that the child in this story was unfamiliar with the terminology and simply misunderstood what a "Christian home" meant. It is another matter not to be able to identify one's own home as Christian because Christ and other signs of faith are not evident. It has been said that the family is a garden and that whatever is planted in it will grow. Upon entering a Catholic home, a visitor should see a crucifix or sacred image as a sign that Christ is central in the life of the family. Mealtime should always begin with a prayer of thanksgiving, and children should at an early age have the habit of prayer at different times of day. More and more, families are returning to the practice of praying together, becoming part of the ordinary rhythm of family life.

159. NO DANGER OF THAT
Confession, faith development

A policeman passing by caught little Tommy stealing an apple from the outdoor fruit stand. "You know, my lad," he said to Tommy, "people who start stealing small things end up stealing bigger things. The next thing you'll be robbing banks." "There's no danger of that," replied Tommy. "By the time I get out of school all the banks are closed."

REFLECTION

The responsibility of parents, teachers, police officers, and others is to plant in youth a desire to make good, moral decisions. This must especially be reinforced at home. We should not be too quick to overlook undesirable behavior in young children. If we constantly dismiss inappropriate behavior in children as "cute," they may equate this with being good. Pope Pius X was correct when he promoted early confession in his decree Quam singulari *in 1910. He correctly situated the sacrament of penance for children at the age of discretion so that a child's sins, which orient the child self-ward, rather than God-ward, toward love of self rather than love of neighbor, could be properly directed at an early age.*

160. COME ON IN   *Baptism, ministry*

A ten-year-old boy named Freddie wanted to be Saint Joseph in the school Christmas pageant. Instead, the teacher cast Freddie as the landlord. Freddie objected loudly, but to no avail. When the pageant was presented, Mary and Joseph knocked on the inn door and asked the innkeeper, Freddie, if he had a room for them at the inn. Freddie smiled and said, "Sure, lots of room. Come on in!"

REFLECTION

Cooperation is everything in preparing for and performing a play. We might say that cooperation is everything in preparing for and performing our role as disciples of Christ. We gather together in a community of faith to be empowered to penetrate the world around us. This gathering "in the name of the Father, and of the Son, and of the Holy Spirit" and this scattering, "Go in peace, the Mass is ended," is at the heart of Catholic ministry. Everyone has a calling, by virtue of baptism, to make visible in some way the presence and lordship of Jesus Christ in the church and in the world. This is not a matter of personal piety or personal agenda, but a divine commission to be leaven in the world. How do you exercise your ministry as a member of the church?

161. YOU ARE DUST   *Death, resurrection*

When the young boy arrived home from his faith formation class, his mother was preparing lunch. "Mommy, is it true that before you're born you are just dust and after you die you go back to being dust?" "That's right son, why?" "Well that's what they said at class today." The mother directed the child, "Run upstairs now and wash your hands. Your snack will be ready soon." About ten minutes later the boy came down and asked again, "Is it true that before you're born you are just dust and after you die you go back to being dust?" Once again his mother nodded, "Yes, son." The little boy looked at her and said, "Then you better get up to my room quick, because something under my bed is either coming or going."

REFLECTION

Our faith teaches that we have been created from nothing and our bodies will return to "nothing"—natural elements of the earth—before the final resurrection of the body. To use the words for the imposition of ashes on Ash Wednesday, "Remember you are dust and to dust you will return" (see Genesis 3:19).

162. WHERE IS GOD?   *Presence of God*

Three brothers who lived in a small town always seemed to get into trouble, so one day their mother called the parish priest and asked if he would talk to her sons and give them some spiritual advice. The priest called in the youngest one first. He asked, "Where is God?" The little boy started to look around the room so the priest asked him again. The boy started to look under things and on top of shelves. The priest kept asking, "Where is God?" The little boy finally left the room and told his older brothers, "We're in trouble!" "Why?" the brothers asked. "Because God is missing and they think we have something to do with it," the boy answered.

REFLECTION

Over the centuries, the worst of humanity has caused great death and destruction, wars, and, in recent years, roadside bombings. People recklessly destroy the environment, exterminate fellow humans both before and after birth. Outright godlessness has prevailed for years in many places. The sole constant is God, whose love and presence is constant. God cannot change (Numbers 23:19; 1 Samuel 15:29;

Psalm 102:26–27; Malachi 3:6; Romans 11:29; Hebrews 6:17–18; James 1:17), be manipulated, or become subject to another's rule. Much can be taken from us, but God can never be snatched from us, unless we willingly surrender him.

163. CHRISTMAS   *Mary*

Just before Christmas, the young child found a can of imitation snow spray and, wanting to make his own contribution to the decorations for the festive season, sprayed the following letters across the wall for all to see: "M-A-R-Y C-H-R-I-S-T-M-A-S."

REFLECTION

The child was correct in that there could never be Christmas without Mary. Through the angel Gabriel, Mary said yes to God—"Here am I, the servant of the Lord; let it be with me according to your word" (Luke 1:38)—and gave birth to Jesus.

164. GOD'S QUARTER   *Stewardship*

Johnny was going off to church one Sunday morning with several of his friends. His mother gave him two quarters. "One is for you and one is for God," she said. As Johnny and his friends walked along, he was flipping one of the quarters up in the air and catching it, over and over. Finally, he missed it and it rolled down a sewer. "Oops!" he said. "There goes God's quarter!"

REFLECTION

It seems that we learn quite early how to justify our actions and decisions for our own benefit. Such is the fallout from our inclination to selfishness. But the good Christian steward understands correctly that whatever we have, the first fruits of our labor go to God and not simply the leftovers (Leviticus 27:30). Our life is to be characterized by sacrificial giving.

165. SAME OLD STUFF   *Eucharist*

"Mom, what are we having for supper?" a little boy asked. "Leftovers," answered the mother. "Oh, you mean SOS," observed the boy. "What do you mean by SOS?" asked the mother. "SOS" her son explained, "Same Old Stuff."

Some use this terminology, when they try to justify not embracing their faith in practice, for example, by not going to Mass. The fact is that we can never describe celebrating the Eucharist as SOS. The celebration of the Eucharist is above all else the sacrifice of Jesus we continue to offer to the Father, which is always happening in the present. Certainly, we remember this once-for-all event (see Hebrews 9:25–26) as a past event, but we also cherish it as a present event where none other than Jesus Christ participates in this supreme act of worship.

166. REALLY THERE
Real presence, faith formation

A mother gave a crucifix to her daughter and said, "Now tell me, what's the difference between the figure of Jesus on the crucifix and the presence of Jesus in Holy Communion that you receive at Mass?" The child answered, "When I look at the figure of Jesus on the crucifix, I see an image of Jesus but he is not really there. When I look at the host at Mass, I do not see Jesus but he is really there."

REFLECTION

Children can teach us much about the Master. But first, the wise teacher, preacher, or parent must, like Saint John the Baptist, announce not themselves, but Jesus Christ: "Here is the Lamb of God who takes away the sin of the world" (John 1:29). Our aim is to teach our children well by helping them fix their eyes solely on Jesus Christ and on his message of justice, inclusiveness, peace.

167. SIGN OF LOVE
The cross, love

A priest once went to visit a class of second-grade children after they had just finished their religion lesson. One little girl, quite excited about what she had just learned, immediately asked, "Father, do you know the greatest sign of love?" The question surprised him. She was obviously looking for a very specific answer. The priest was being tested and felt very uneasy. Hesitantly, he said, "Well children, when I really love someone I want to embrace them with both arms." Right away every head in the classroom began to shake from side to side. "No, Father." Then they all stretched out their arms and one girl pointed to the wall behind the priest, to the cross. Then he knew what their gesture meant.

REFLECTION

The cross is the greatest sign of God's love because Jesus stretched out his arms on the cross as the ultimate sign of total love. A human gesture of love is often the embrace, and we read how Jesus would embrace little children (Luke 18:15–17). But Jesus Christ, human and divine, showed us how much he loves us, by stretching his arms out on the cross.

168. SPIRITUAL NEEDS   *Dying*

They had been married more than forty years and are a joy to be around because they are very much in love with each other. But when the husband had major surgery, the days that followed were very difficult for him. He woke from surgery and was unable to return to sleep as he became agitated, anxious, and tired; he grew worse by the hour. The medical staff gave him medication to help him sleep and to numb the pain, but things just went from bad to worse. During the second night without sleep he began to hallucinate and became paranoid from the medication. Thinking he was in danger he unhooked the IV and other medical equipment and left his room in an attempt to return to the ICU where he thought he would be safe. The nurses caught him and returned him to his bed. When the family was told of his state of mind, his wife went to his bedside to keep vigil. She was at a loss as to how to calm him down, so she asked him what he needed. He needed her, he said. So when the nurses left the room, she took off her shoes and climbed into the bed next to him and held him and prayed with him and an hour later he was asleep. He slept for twelve hours.

REFLECTION

The doctors were skilled and the nurses were compassionate, but they could only do so much for him. They could not bridge the gap that would take away his fear and panic. They could not get into his world and get close to him in the way he needed. But his wife could. Their marital union was obviously love-giving and life-giving, which is what Christ had in mind when he raised marriage to the dignity of a sacrament. This is precisely what Genesis 2:24 referred to. No wonder it was quoted by Jesus in Matthew 19:5 and by Saint Paul in his letter to the Ephesians (5:31). The "two become one flesh" in many ways. It includes the sharing of thoughts and dreams, joys and sufferings, hopes and fears, successes and failures. This is a "great mystery" according to Saint Paul.

169. ABSOLUTE FORGIVENESS   *Forgiveness*

A priest was giving the final sacraments to a woman who was dying, but, it turned out, she refused to forgive her estranged husband. The priest advised her, "Now, Bridget, before you die, I'm going to call Patrick in here. Give him your hand and tell him that you forgive him." Bridget replied, "No way, Father, Never! What he has done to me and my children! He ruined my life, wrecked it." The priest persisted, "You know, Bridget, it's very important for you to forgive Patrick before you die." Reluctantly she consented. "All right, call him in." She had her face to the wall as he pleaded for her forgiveness. Weakly she extended her hand to him and said, "Okay, I love you and I forgive you, but if I live…."

REFLECTION

A condition for forgiveness? True forgiveness, as God's is, isn't conditioned. We forgive or we don't forgive. Our forgiveness must be absolute if we seek to extend the forgiveness that Jesus offers and expects of us (Luke 6:37). Certainly we will expect different behavior in the future. We cannot condone sin either, but we should never write the person off. Like Jesus, we must be willing to distinguish between the sin and the sinner.

170. LINE UP   *Heaven, marriage*

Just outside the gates of heaven there were two lines of men. Over one was written "Men Who Were Bossed by Their Wives," and the other read "Men Who Weren't Bossed by Their Wives." There was a big line for the first one, but then the angel in charge of checking the names in the book of life saw one man in the other line. He asked him why he was in that line. The man replied, "My wife told me to stand here."

REFLECTION

There is only one line into heaven, and among the duties of loving husbands or wives is to help their spouse by word and example to be worthy of God's eternal presence, living the sacrament of matrimony day in and day out in loving kindness and forgiveness. In fact, we should keep the thought of heaven before us, always mindful of the richness of heaven for those who live holy lives. If we remain faithful to Christ, we can joyfully proclaim, "The Lord is my light and my salvation.…I believe that I shall see the goodness of the Lord in the land of the living" (Psalm 27:1, 13).

171. RELATIVE OF YOURS? *Marriage*

A husband and wife drove for miles in silence after a terrible argument in which neither would budge. Finally, the husband pointed to a mule in a pasture. "Relative of yours?" he asked. "Yes," she replied, "by marriage."

REFLECTION

Couples may easily forget that each one needs the other as they journey together to final, intimate union with God in heaven. Why do some couples make marriage a power struggle, when it is a mystery—an ongoing sacrament, modeled on Christ's love for his church—to be treasured and worked out together? Reflect on Ephesians 5:25–33 for an inspired description what a marriage should be.

172. DATE TO REMEMBER *Baptism, conversion*

The wife was accompanying her husband on a business trip. He carried his laptop with him and the security guard at the airport metal detector asked him to open his computer case. It was locked and the guard waited patiently as the embarrassed husband struggled to remember the combination. Finally he succeeded and his wife later asked him, "Why were you so nervous?" He confessed, "The numbers are the date of our wedding anniversary."

REFLECTION

We should have the important dates of life fixed in our memory: wedding, births, retirement, deaths of loved ones, and the like. But we very often overlook the dates of other important events in our lives, such as the date of our baptism, or of our conversion to Christ. One spiritual person always celebrated the anniversary of her baptism because that is when she was "born again" (John 3:3).

173. HOUSEHOLD CHORES *Family life, body of Christ*

There was a husband who always teased his wife about her lack of interest in household chores. One day he came home with a gag gift, a refrigerator magnet that read, "Martha Stewart certainly doesn't live here." The next day he found the magnet holding up a slip of paper that read, "Neither does Bob Vila."

REFLECTION

When we least expect it, our attempts at good humor may serve as an incentive for another to point out our shortcomings. Saint Paul (1 Corinthians 12:4–30) likened the functions of various parts of the body contributing to the overall good of the organism to the roles that Christians have in the church, each contributing in a supportive, unique way to the health of the faith community. So too in a marriage each spouse has their agreed upon roles to carry out for their mutual benefit and the growth of their marital relationship.

174. JUST CHECKING   *Prayer*

A parishioner at a parish function one Sunday afternoon once observed a couple she knew who were married about sixty years. She noticed that they spoke hardly at all because they learned to communicate nonverbally over the years. She watched the wife touching her husband Joseph, holding his hand, touching his shoulder, glancing at him from time to time. Afterward the woman said, "That's beautiful, Maria. I noticed you were so attentive to your husband during Mass!" Maria replied, "Well, you know, Elizabeth, I was just checking to see if he was still breathing!"

REFLECTION

People who know and love each other don't need to speak all the time. Some couples who have been married a long time sometimes don't speak at all. The husband or wife might just look at the other to determine what the other is thinking! They are content in each other's presence. In a similar way, when we pray, we don't always have to use words. We can contemplate the mystery, the majesty, the depth of God's love for us—or think nothing at all, just being comfortable in God's presence.

175. DAY DREAM   Revelation, dreams

After she woke, a woman told her husband, "I just dreamed you gave me expensive diamond earrings with a matching necklace for Valentine's Day. What do you think it means?" "You'll know tonight," he countered. That evening, her husband came home with a package and gave it to his wife. Delighted, she eagerly opened it and found a book entitled *The Meaning of Dreams*.

REFLECTION

Christians and Jews have in their Scriptures long valued the content of dreams and acknowledged God's use of them. Dreams, visions, prophetic calls, angelic visitations, prophetic narratives, and indirect references to this phenomenon comprise roughly one-third of the Bible. The most powerful biblical examples are of warning. We recall the story of Joseph sold into slavery by his brothers following his dreams (Genesis 37:5–36). At Christmas we remember the angel of the Lord appearing to Joseph in a dream, to direct him to care for his wife, Mary, and the coming child, Jesus (Matthew 1:18–25). Later he is warned in a dream to escape the infanticide of King Herod (Matthew 2:19–23). We must be careful not to limit the ways in which God may communicate with those God loves.

176. THE OLDER, THE BETTER
Development of doctrine, faith

Novelist Agatha Christie's second husband, Max Mallowan, was a distinguished archaeologist who made a name for himself excavating in Mesopotamia, present-day Iraq. On her return with her husband from the Middle East, Miss Christie was asked how she felt about being married to a man whose interest lay in antiquities. "An archaeologist is the best husband any woman can have," she said. "The older she gets, the more interested he is in her."

REFLECTION

We might say something similar about the church and our common faith. The older they get, the more interested we are. Why? Because with the passage of time we are able to understand more clearly what the church teaches and why, what the church has believed over centuries, how its understanding of Sacred Scripture or Sacred Tradition may have shifted to some degree. This is what the famous convert, Cardinal John Henry Newman, meant when he referred to the development of Christian doctrine. This essentially means that, although the core of doctrine does not change, our ability to more correctly understand it and express it more precisely can, with the passage of time, be fine tuned as we learn more from ancient documents.

177. FOR YOUR WAKE   *Matrimony*

Patrick had been ailing for such a long time and his wife, Bridget, kept coming in each day and asking, "Patrick, how do you feel today?" Patrick would respond day after day, "Not so good." In the meantime, Bridget was fully aware of the practice in Ireland of getting things ready for the wake and funeral. The food has to be cooked. There are a lot of people coming. Things have to be prepared. So Bridget came into the bedroom one morning, "Patrick, how are you doing this morning?" Patrick responded, "You know, I'm feeling a little better this morning, let me sit up…in fact, I feel so good I think I can eat something. What do I smell in the kitchen? Smells like ham. Give me a bit of that ham, Bridget." Bridget responded, "Absolutely not! That's for your wake."

REFLECTION

We should never hurry a spouse (or anyone) out of this world, as it seems Bridget was trying to do. Those who are married are called to be loyal to each other and serve one another until natural death. In fact, the two ministers of the sacrament of marriage are the man and the woman. The priest or deacon serves as the church's official witness to the sacrament. The man and woman minister the sacrament to each other and pledge their love, fidelity, and service for the rest of their lives.

178. WHICH TOOTH   *Suffering, discipleship*

A woman and her husband rushed into the dentist's office. The woman said, "I want a tooth pulled. I don't want gas or Novacaine or any other such thing because I'm in a big hurry. Just pull the tooth as quickly as possible." "You're a brave woman," said the dentist. "Now, show me which tooth it is." The woman turned to her husband and said, "Open your mouth and show the dentist which tooth it is, dear."

REFLECTION

Scapegoating goes back to the book of Genesis (3:12). It's very easy for us to be courageous when we volunteer others to bear the suffering. In terms of Christian discipleship, the measure of being an authentic disciple is being willing to move forward in faith ourselves, holding ourselves responsible for what we do or say or believe, regardless of what the sacrifice might entail.

179. TAKE A WALK   *Marriage, humility, physical fitness*

An old man was celebrating his one hundredth birthday and everybody compli-
mented him on how athletic and well preserved he appeared. "I will tell you the
secret of my success," he said. "I have been in the open air day after day for some
seventy-five years now." His audience was impressed and asked how he managed
to keep up his rigorous fitness regime. "Well, you see, my wife and I were married
seventy-five years ago. On our wedding night, we made a solemn pledge. Whenever
we had a fight, the one who was wrong would go outside and take a walk."

REFLECTION

*It is quite possible that this man was truly humble. Humility is not a pose, but is a
recognition of truth. It does not mean the beautiful woman should pretend she is
homely or the intelligent man pretend he is stupid. It never means pretending that
we are less than we are. Rather, humility means recognizing even our achievements
for what they are: accomplishments through the gifts we have been given, but for
which we accept the responsibility of using them for the benefit of others. It means
recognizing that even our greatest achievements are an insignificant and inadequate
return for all that God has given us. Jesus pointed out its importance, "Whoever
becomes humble…is the greatest in the kingdom of heaven" (Matthew 18:4).*

180. MARRY AGAIN   *Marriage, God's will*

There's a story told of the dying husband who wanted to show his great love, his
generosity, his kindness to his wife. So he said, "Listen, dear. I want you to marry
again. I don't want you to think of me. You have your own happiness to look
forward to. I tell you what…I want you to give all the suits I have in my closet
to the new man when you find him." The wife responded, "But Bob you wear a
size 46. He's a 38."

REFLECTION

*We take away from God's control the kind of life we have committed ourselves to
when we refuse to follow his will and seek instead our own selfish agenda. Married
love does not stop when one of the spouses becomes ill or poor. "In sickness and in
health, " "for richer or poorer" means just that. Such a perspective of faithfulness
may seem outrageous to the world, but when a couple promises love and commit-*

ment, they do so trusting that God will provide. Married life must always include Christ at the center of that life. Just as marriage is a sign of God's faithful love for us, it must also reveal our love for God and each other. To seek another when the spouse is ill or no longer appealing not only leads to the sin of adultery, whereby the spouse is betrayed, but also betrays the One who is the center of the sacrament of matrimony, namely, Christ (Exodus 20:14; Mark 10:11; Romans 13:9).

181. GOOD NEWS, BAD NEWS
Marriage, family life, communication

A father came home from a very bad day at work and said to his wife, "I've had a bad day. If you have any bad news, keep it to yourself." She replied, "Fine, no bad news. Now for the good news: Three of our four children didn't break an arm today."

REFLECTION

Communicating is one thing; how we communicate is another. We learn from this encounter that it is possible to share the same news in a positive or a negative way. The problem in our present world is not one of communication; we have more methods and vehicles of communication than ever before. The present challenge is to communicate in a manner that is positive, hopeful, and constructive. Talent knows what to do; tact knows how to do it. Jesus was the greatest of all communicators because his living word was proclaimed in an uplifting and beneficial way, and it is our responsibility to do so today.

182. GET YOUR MOTHER   *Marriage*

An Amish boy and his father were visiting a mall for the first time. They were amazed by almost everything they saw, but especially by two shiny, silver walls that could move apart and back together again. The boy asked his father, "What is this, father?" The father responded, "Son, I have never seen anything like this in my life, I don't know what it is!" While the boy and his father were watching wide-eyed, an old woman in a wheelchair rolled up to the moving walls and pressed a button. The walls opened and she rolled between them into the small room. The walls closed and the boy and his father watched small lighted numbers above the walls light up. They continued to watch the numbers light up in the reverse direction. Then the walls opened up again and a beautiful twenty-four-year-old woman stepped out. The father's eyes lit up as he turned to his son and said, "Quick! Go get your mother."

REFLECTION

Amazing make-overs have become commonplace on television, but technology has-n't mastered this within the time frame of an elevator ride. The story doesn't tell us whether the man's wife ever showed up, but if she did, the man would have come to the realization that he had to deal with his wife as she was. And that's the case for all of us. Husbands and wives must deal with each another in the present, as they are, not as it used to be or as it might be.

183. FIXED INCOME   *Marriage preparation*

"Darling," said the awestruck man to his new bride, "now that we are married, do you think you will be able to live on my small income?" "Of course, dear, no trouble," she said. "But what will you live on?"

REFLECTION

Prior to receiving the sacrament, couples are required not only to closely examine their finances but several other components of married life as well, including compatibility, health issues, sexuality, children, philosophy of life, and, of course, faith and spirituality. There are frightening statistics concerning the high percentage of divorces, as well as the increasing lack of respect for the dignity of this very important relationship. It is crucial that couples understand the nature of the sacrament and the high regard placed on it by Jesus and the church. Like all the sacraments, the most important one present in this sacrament is Jesus. Saint Paul holds the sacrament in such high regard that he compares the love between husband and wife to the love Christ has for the church (Ephesians 5:25–30). Jesus reaches back to Genesis and reiterates the teaching by stating that those who marry "are no longer two, but one flesh. Therefore what God has joined together, let no one separate" (Mark 10:6–9).

184. SALT AND PEPPER   *Marriage, anger*

One morning a husband and his wife were preparing breakfast. She was at the stove cooking bacon and eggs. When they sat down together to eat, the husband casually reached over, took the salt and pepper shakers, and doctored up his eggs. Immediately his wife exploded, "Don't do that! I salted and peppered those eggs while they were frying!" The husband replied, "Why on earth would you do that? Everyone knows you salt and pepper food at the table." "No," his wife insisted, "you salt and pepper food while it's cooking." They went back and forth: "At the table!" "While it's cooking!" "At the table!" "While it's cooking!" Finally, one of them eventually broke down and started laughing. Here they were, two caring adults, arguing about salt and pepper.

REFLECTION

Ordinary events in life can become moments of misunderstanding, silly arguments, and hurt feelings. Ideally, such moments should never occur in the lives of married couples, but they do. Couples are bound to each other (Matthew 19:6; Mark 10:9) and need to be there for each other, caring for each other because life's journey taxes one's strength and can also bite hard into one's morale. There is much to be said about not letting the sun set on one's anger without first reconciling following an argument, no matter how trivial the argument. "Be angry but do not sin; do not let the sun go down on your anger" (Ephesians 4:26).

185. IN HEAVEN   *Heaven, stewardship*

An eighty-five-year-old couple, married almost sixty years, died together in a car crash. They had been in good health, mainly due to the wife's interest in health food and exercise. When they reached the pearly gates, Saint Peter took them to their mansion which was decked out with a beautiful kitchen and master suite complete with a Jacuzzi. As they "oohed and aahed" the old man asked Peter how much everything was going to cost. "It's free," Peter replied. "This is heaven." Next they went to survey the championship golf course. There were golfing privileges every day and each week the course changed to a new one, duplicating the great golf courses of the world. The old man asked, "What are the green fees?" Peter replied, "This is heaven; you play for free." Next they went to the clubhouse and saw the lavish buffet lunch with the foods of the world laid out. "Well, where are the low fat and low cholesterol tables?" the old man asked. Peter explained, "That's the best part. You can eat as much as you like of whatever you like and you never get fat or sick. This is heaven." With that the old man went into a fit of anger. Peter and the man's wife both tried to calm him down, asking him what was wrong. The old man turned to his wife and said, "This is all your fault. If it weren't for your blasted bran muffins, I could have been here years ago."

REFLECTION

We should never seek ways to rush ourselves or our loved ones out of this world. There is much work to be done to build the kingdom of God. At the same time, we should always be mindful that no one lives here forever. Before we take our last breath, we must do all we can to care for our bodies since we will have to give an account of ourselves to Christ and "receive recompense for what has been done in the body, whether good or evil" (2 Corinthians 5:10). It is a matter of stewardship, talking care of our health, which God has loaned us, so that we may do his work on earth for as long as we can.

186. HOME   *Spirituality*

The famous G.K. Chesterton was so preoccupied that he frequently forgot to keep appointments. He relied on his wife in all practical matters. Once on a lecture tour he sent her the following telegram: "Am in Birmingham. Where ought I to be?" She wired back: "Home."

REFLECTION

As a matter of spiritual reflection, we should ask the question often, "Where am I in my journey to the Father? In my relationship with Jesus?" "Where ought I to be?"

187. PRAYER REQUESTS   *Prayer*

The married couple, both sixty years old, were celebrating their thirty-fifth anniversary. During their celebration an angel appeared and congratulated them, granting them each one prayer request. The wife wanted to travel around the world. The angel made the necessary arrangements immediately and suddenly the wife had tickets in her hand for a world cruise. Next, the angel asked the husband what he wanted. He said; "I wish I had a wife thirty years younger than I am." So the angel immediately granted the husbands request and with the snap of a finger the husband was suddenly ninety years old.

REFLECTION

There is, of course, an obvious place for prayer of petition in our lives. Jesus acknowledged this when he told us to pray the Our Father (Matthew 6:9–12). But he also reminds us to trust God, that "your Father knows what you need before you ask him" (Matthew 6:8). If we believe in the power of prayer, then it is very important, as this story indicates, that we are very specific in our prayer requests. The anecdote also tells us that our prayer life should be other-oriented as well.

188. WRONG DIRECTION   *Spirituality*

An elderly man was driving down the interstate highway when suddenly his cell phone rang. Answering, he heard his wife's voice urgently warning him: "Henry, I just heard on the news that there's a car going the wrong way on the highway. Please be careful!" "Honey," said Henry, "it's not just one car. It's hundreds of them!"

REFLECTION

Driving in the right direction on a highway is not just a good thing but everything. The same can be said of the direction we follow in life. If we are on the wrong course, away from Christ, "the way, and the truth, and the life" (John 14:6), there will be dangerous spiritual consequences for the individual, and our actions can have disastrous effects on countless others as well.

189. FOUR-LETTER WORDS   *Marriage*

As soon as the newlyweds returned from their honeymoon, the young bride called her mother, who lived in another state. "How did everything go?" her mother asked. "Oh, mother," she began, "the honeymoon was wonderful! It was so romantic and we had a terrific time. But on our way back, Fred started using really horrible four-letter words I have never heard before. You've got to come get me and take me home. Please, Mother!" The new bride continued to sob over the telephone. "But, honey," the mother asked, "what four-letter words?" "I can't tell you, mother, they're too awful! Come get me, please!" "Darling, you must tell me what has gotten you so upset. Tell me what four-letter words he used." Still sobbing, the bride said, "Words like dust, wash, iron, cook."

REFLECTION

There are other four-letter words, and better words too. These include love, good, kind, holy, and pray. When a married couple understands how to be loving and faithful, how to exemplify goodness and kindness, how to grow in greater holiness and be people of prayer, then the ordinary things, such as household tasks, will take care of themselves.

190. ADAM AND EVE AND BOBBY   *Marriage*

In one of their religion classes the kindergarten children were told how God created everything, including people. Bobby was especially attentive when the teacher explained how Eve was created out of one of Adam's ribs. Later in the week his mother noticed him lying down on the sofa. Thinking he was ill, she asked, "Bobby what's the matter?" Bobby responded, "I have a pain in my side. I think I'm going to have a wife."

REFLECTION

A wife coming into being from a man's rib (Genesis 2:21–23) is a figurative way of speaking. For better or for worse, the long-standing practice of meeting, dating, and falling in love is the norm in our society. The key to any successful marriage is to always make sure that God is the center of the relationship between husband and wife, that they are supporting each other on the journey to union with God. Adam and Eve were not united with God, and the consequences were deadly.

191. NO LAST WORDS   *Dying*

An Irish family moved from Dublin to Boston. One of the sons later moved to Chicago. When the father died in Boston, the son in Chicago called his brother in Boston and asked, "What were fathers' last words?" The answer came back, "Father had no last words. Mother was with him till the end."

REFLECTION

It is not flattering to suggest that the wife always had the last word, but just perhaps the wife in this story did, because she may have been helping her husband to prepare for death and assisted him with prayer and other words of comfort, including her expression of love for him. The "last words" that matter most, of course, even if they are not vocal, are those of the dying person, expressing faith in God, repentance for sin, and love of God.

192. ARRIVED   *Death*

A newly married couple decided to go to Florida for a long weekend, but because they both worked it was hard to coordinate their schedules. They decided that the husband would go a day early, and his wife would join him the following day. On arriving in Florida, the husband e-mailed his wife but accidentally mistyped her address and sent it off without realizing it. Meanwhile, a widow had just buried her husband, who had just died from a heart attack. The widow checked her e-mail, expecting notes of condolences from relatives and friends, but instead found this:

To: My Darling Wife

From: Your Loving Husband

Subject: I've Arrived!

I've just arrived and have checked in. I see that everything has been prepared for your arrival tomorrow. Looking forward to seeing you then! Hope your journey is as uneventful as mine was. (P.S. Sure is hot down here!)

REFLECTION

The moment of death for each of us remains a secret known to God alone, but when we might die should never be a cause of fear. Although thought of the unknown may instill a sense of apprehension, we should be confident that death will bring us to God, because God has been with us in life, in how we have lived.

193. CHECK OR CASH   *Stewardship*

There was a man who worked all of his life and saved all of his money. He was a real miser and loved money more than just about anything. Just before he died, he said to his wife, "Now listen, when I die, I want you to take all my money and place it in the casket with me. I want to take my money with me to the afterlife." His wife promised she would. Soon after, the man died. He was laid out in the casket and his wife was sitting nearby with her friend. Following the funeral, just before the casket was closed, the wife said, "Wait just a minute!" She approached the casket with a shoe box and placed it near her husband's feet. Then the casket was closed. Her friend said, "I hope you weren't crazy enough to put all that money in the casket." "Yes," the wife said, "I promised and I would never go back on my word. "You mean to tell me you put more than $150,000 in the casket with him?" "I sure did," replied the wife. "I got it all together, put it into my account and wrote him a check and put in the shoe box.

REFLECTION

Like personal gifts and talents "put under the bushel basket" (Mark 4:21), money buried is money that loses its value, as well as its purpose. As faithful stewards, we have to invest our time, talents, and treasure, the many gifts on loan from God, in a way that is not just for our own benefit, but for those in need, for building the kingdom of God. We will have to account for how we used what we have received.

194. WATCH OUT   *Death*

At the end of the funeral service for a woman, the pallbearers carried the casket out and accidentally bumped into a wall, jarring the casket. Suddenly they heard a faint moan. Opening the casket, they found the woman was still alive. She lived for ten more years and then died. A funeral was again held at the same church, and at the end of the ceremony the pallbearers again carried the casket out. As they were walking, the husband told them, "This time, watch out for the wall!"

REFLECTION

In the gospels there are accounts where one who has died is given a new opportunity to live: Lazarus (John 11:44), as well as the daughter of Jairus (Mark 5:41–42) and the son of the widow from Nain (Luke 7:14–15). We won't have a similar opportunity. We will experience only one death and we have our whole life to prepare for it. It will be our passage to the fullness of life with God. The liturgy for the Order of Christian Funerals reminds us that "at death life is changed, not taken away."

195. PUBLIC MOURNING   *Marriage*

The man placed some flowers on the grave of his dearly departed mother and started back toward his car when his attention was diverted to another man kneeling at a nearby grave. The man seemed to be praying with profound intensity and kept repeating over and over again, "Why did you have to die? Why did you have to die?" The first man approached the grief-stricken man and said, "Sir, I don't wish to interfere, but your grief is more than I've ever seen before. For whom do you mourn so deeply? A child? A parent?" The grief-stricken man took a moment to collect himself, then replied, "My wife's first husband."

REFLECTION

There was obviously trouble at home and the grief-stricken man placed the blame at the feet of the first husband. His prayer may have included the refrain, "If you hadn't died, I would not have married your wife." The cemetery visit that day reveals a man who uses the deceased husband as a scapegoat for problems of his own making, trying to avoid responsibility for what he has done or neglected to do.

196. ASKING FOR HELP   *Humility*

A father asked his son Jimmy to go out to the backyard and get rid of the rocks that had accumulated over the years. So Jimmy went outside and did as his father had asked. He worked for countless hours removing rocks of all sizes but there was one rock that Jimmy just couldn't move. He tried rolling it and even tried to put it in his red wagon so he could wheel it away. He finally gave up and went back to his father and said, "I did as you asked, but there was one big rock I just couldn't move and I tried everything." The father responded, "No, you didn't try everything." "Yes, I did," the boy protested. And again the father said, "No, you didn't. You didn't ask me to help you."

REFLECTION

When we attempt to solve our problems alone and find we cannot, we miss the opportunity to seek the assistance of another, who might be just as willing to help us as we would be to help him or her. Much might be accomplished if only we look beyond ourselves for a solution and ask another for a helping hand. Asking for help when the need is present might be an opportunity to develop a friendship. If we have difficulty doing this, we should ask ourselves why. Is it pride or shyness?

197. TRAGEDY OR BLESSING   *Providence, suffering*

Years ago in Scotland Mr. and Mrs. Clark worked hard and saved money to emigrate to the United States with their nine children. After many years, they had finally saved enough. They acquired their passports and made reservations for the whole family on a new ocean liner. They were filled with much anticipation and excitement, but seven days before their departure a dog bit the youngest son, and, because of the possibility of rabies, the family was unable to make the trip to America. The father shed tears of disappointment and cursed both his son and God for their misfortune. Five days later, the tragic news spread throughout Scotland that the Titanic had sunk taking 1500 lives with it. The Clark family was to have been on that ship, but because of a dog bite they were left behind in Scotland. When Mr. Clark heard the news, he hugged his son and thanked him for saving the family. He thanked God for saving their lives. What at first seemed a tragedy turned into a blessing.

REFLECTION

Although we may not always understand what happens, things may happen for a reason. Sometimes with the passage of time, this becomes evident.

198. GOING TO HEAVEN   *Witness, discipleship*

Two young boys spent every afternoon after school with their grandparents. They were quite active and frequently got into mischief. On such occasions the grandmother patiently spoke with the boys and encouraged them to be kind to each other so they would "make Jesus happy and go to heaven." However, the grandfather grew weary of the boys' misbehavior and frequently yelled, bellowed, and screamed at them. One day the grandmother overheard her two grandsons talking in the living room. The older said, "Scott, you're not going to go to heaven because you keep acting bad." The younger replied, "Who cares? I'll be in hell with grandpa." When this account was recounted to the grandfather, he was shocked!

REFLECTION

Our words and actions really speak volumes, especially in a family setting. It is so easy to make an impression on others, particularly younger family members. Parents and grandparents must teach their children, above all, by example. That's how we best love our children and prepare them to live lives of love, imitating Jesus. With the help of God, we help others to become genuine disciples of Jesus by the example we give. That is a major ministry we perform all during our life. "By this everyone will know that you are my disciples, if you have love for one another" (John 13:35).

199. TO BE LIKE YOU   *Witness*

The young boy turned to his father and said, "When I grow up I'd like to be good, strong, and handsome like Superman, but if I can't, I'd like to be like you."

REFLECTION

Don't we often exclude from our list of superheros those who are closest to us and most heroic? Jesus was underappreciated (and worse), and they said of him, "Can anything good come out of Nazareth?" (John 1:46). Philip's reply to Nathaniel's question was "Come and see." We must open our eyes and appreciate those around us, their virtue and integrity, their witness of gospel values.

200. PARENTHOOD   *Witness, scandal*

The life history of parents may be described as follows: "They bear children, bore teenagers, and board newlyweds."

REFLECTION

The greatest gift parents can give their children, in addition to faith and gospel-based witness, is love. They witness well when they show their children their love for each other. Children can't be taught to love the way they are taught mathematics or reading in the classroom. Rather, they catch love, like the flu, by being exposed to it. When children see disrespect, verbal or physical abuse at home, they're hurt more than in any other way. Jesus warns us in Luke 17:2 about giving bad example to others, especially to children.

201. HIGH ROAD   *Forgiveness*

Some years ago James received a bike for Christmas. He rode the bike every day until it disappeared from its usual place. Running to his front yard, James saw a man loading it into his car. He shouted, but the man drove off. Later that evening, the boy's mother told her husband that their young son had already forgiven the thief. What's more, he wanted the thief to know he was forgiven. The child dictated a message that his mother wrote on a large poster board. He signed it, stapled it to a sawhorse, and put it in the front yard. The message read, "To the person who stole my bike: You really hurt my feelings when you took my bike. But I am a Christian and because Jesus forgave me, I forgive you!" When the boy's father left for work the next day, the sign was face down in the yard and the bike was back, complete with new handlebars, grips, and a new front fork assembly.

REFLECTION

Forgiveness is a disposition toward others that pardons real or imagined disappointments, deliberate or unintentional hurts, actual wrongs and injustices, sins of commission or omission. This Godlike quality, the ability to forgive others, is demanded of us all. In the Old Testament we hear Sirach counsel Israel: "Forgive your neighbor the wrong he has done, and then your sins will be pardoned when you pray" (28:2). In the New Testament, to Saint Peter's question, "Lord...how often must I forgive?" Jesus replies, "I say to you, not seven times but seventy times seven" (Matthew 18:21–22). In the Lord's Prayer (Matthew 6:9–13; Luke 11:2–4), Jesus teaches us to pray: "Forgive us our trespasses, as we forgive those who trespass against us." God forgives us if we are genuinely sorry and seek his forgiveness and be willing to forgive others who offend us.

202. HOW'S YOUR WIFE?   *Bereavement*

"How's your wife?" the man asked an old friend he hadn't seen for years. "She's in heaven," replied the friend. "Oh, I'm sorry." Then he realized that was not the thing to say, so he added, "I mean, I'm glad." And that was even worse. He finally came out with, "Gee, I'm surprised."

REFLECTION

When we meet someone who has recently lost a loved one, very often we can say what is clumsy, trite, or even offensive, none of which are really comforting, such as, "Well, that's good. He was suffering." Or "It's God's will, my dear." At such a time, a silent hug will say much more to the bereaved.

203. HOLES IN THE FENCE   *Anger*

There once was a little boy with a temper he didn't control very well. His father gave him a bag of nails and told him to hammer a nail in the back fence every time he lost control. The first day the boy drove thirty-seven nails into the fence. Over time, the number dwindled, until the boy discovered it was easier to hold his temper than to drive those nails into the fence. Finally the day came when the boy didn't lose his control at all. He told his father about it and the father suggested that the boy now pull out one nail for each day that held his temper. The days passed and the young boy was finally able to tell his father that all the nails were gone. The father then led him to the fence. He said, "You have done well, my son, but look at the holes in the fence. The fence will never be the same. When you say or do hurtful things out of anger, they leave a scar just like this. It doesn't matter how many times you say 'I'm sorry,' the wound will still be there."

REFLECTION

Some words or actions may deserve an angry response, as we see when Jesus looked at the people in the synagogue with anger (John 2:13–17). We so easily recall the wounds others inflict on us. Do we as easily recall the wounds we inflict on others? By our words, our acts, our attitudes, our preoccupations, our selfishness, and our pride we have the capability of hurting another very deeply.

204. ELDERLY AFFAIRS   *Aging*

Three sisters, ages 92, 94, and 96, lived in a house together. One night the ninety-six year old drew a bath. She put her foot in and paused. She yelled downstairs, "Was I getting in or out of the bath?" The ninety-four year old yelled back, "I don't know. I'll come up and see." She started up the stairs and paused. "Was I going up the stairs or down?" The ninety-two year old was sitting at the kitchen table having tea, listening to her sisters. She shook her head and said, "I sure hope I never get that forgetful." She knocked on wood for good measure. She then yelled, "I'll come up and help you both as soon as I see who's at the door."

REFLECTION

This anecdote illustrates in a humorous way that as we grow older our lives change. What we are able to do at twenty, we ordinarily are not able to do at forty or fifty.

What we might be able to do at forty, we may not be able to do at sixty. What we can do at sixty, we may not be able to do at eighty. As well, it is not unusual for us to slow down in other ways. For example, as we get older we are not as energetic or mobile as we once were. In all of this, our focus must always remain fixed on the dignity of human life, no matter how young or old, no matter if the person is fully functional or totally disabled. The value of life is measured by who a person is and not by what a person can or cannot do.

205. DENTS   *Anger, parenting, patience*

A man came out of his home to admire his new truck. To his dismay, his three-year-old son was happily hammering dents into the shiny paint with his toy. The man ran to his son, knocked him away, and as the boy fell his head hit the curb. The child lay there motionless, but still breathing. The father called out to tell his wife where he was going and asked her to follow. He put the boy in the truck and drove as fast as he could to the hospital, where the child was diagnosed with a severe concussion, and where he stayed for a few days for observation.

REFLECTION

Think about the possible consequences of your response the next time you see a child spill milk at table, or leave a bike out in the rain, or even dent the car. Think first before you lose your patience with someone you love. Trucks and bikes can be repaired. Spilled milk can be wiped up. Too often we fail to recognize the difference between the person and their actions. But how we respond while in a temper can haunt us forever.

206. CAN READ AND WRITE   *Human dignity, creation*

A young teenager asked his father, "Why did you sign my report card with an X instead of your name?" The father replied, "Because I didn't want your teacher to think that anyone with your grades has parents who can read and write."

REFLECTION

How good that our heavenly Father thinks differently than this father. God said that all of his creation is good. We have been marked by the Creator's signature, created in God's holy image (Genesis 1:27). God's sacred imprint is on every person, regardless of sin and failures. "You are mine," God says to each of us. "Before I formed you in the womb I knew you, and before you were born I consecrated you," God says to Jeremiah (1:5). Also, our lives are sustained now and forever through the action of the Spirit of God, who is "the Lord and Giver of life."

207. GOLDEN BOX   *Love*

Some time ago a father became annoyed when his three-year-old daughter wasted a whole roll of gold wrapping paper, decorating a box to put under the Christmas tree. The little girl brought the gift to her father the next morning and said, "This is for you, Daddy." He was embarrassed by his overreaction, but his annoyance rose again when he found that the box was empty. He scolded her, "Don't you know that when you give someone a present, there's supposed to be something inside of it?" The little girl looked up at him with tears in her eyes. "Oh Daddy, it's not empty. I blew kisses into the box. All for you, Daddy." The father was crushed. He put his arms around his little girl, and begged her forgiveness. The father kept that gold box by his bed for years. Whenever he was discouraged, he would take out an imaginary kiss and remember the love of his daughter who had put it there.

REFLECTION
The most precious gifts a child gives to a parent are often intangible. A child's imagination itself is, in a very real sense, a valuable gift that most parents have experienced. Unconditional love and kisses are also valuable gifts from their children. What could be more precious?

208. HAVE A HOME   *Family*

A family had difficulty finding a house to rent in a new city. They were living in a motel until they could find a permanent residence. In the lobby one day, another guest said to the little girl of the family, "It's too bad you haven't a home." The alert child answered, "Oh, we do have a home. All we need is a house to put it in!"

REFLECTION
Victor Hugo, best known for his works The Hunchback of Notre Dame *and* Les

Misérables, said it well: "A house is built of logs and stone, of tiles and posts and piers. A home is built of loving deeds that stand a thousand years."

209. SPEAKING IN RHYME   *Stewardship*

There was a boy who had the skill and inclination to speak a good deal in rhyme. Many people admired his clever ability, but his family heard too much of it. His father asked him, quite pointedly, to stop speaking so much in rhymes, and even threatened punishment if he persisted. One day, when he was about to put his threat into action, the child on his knees begged, "Pray, Father, do some pity take….And I will no more verses make."

REFLECTION

The child's parents face a double challenge. The main one is to encourage the child to develop his talent so that others might benefit from it, if only by way of entertainment. The other challenge is to make clear to the boy that he control his use of rhyming so that he doesn't overdo it and annoy people.

210. CHALLENGES   *Parenting, family life*

The young father was speaking about some challenges confronting parents today. He gave an example: "I was opening a box of cereal this morning for my little girl. The box featured a special prize that was placed in the bottom of the cereal box. Since my child wanted the special gift immediately, I found myself up to my elbow in corn flakes trying to find it. Next time I'll open the box upside down."

REFLECTION

If only this was the greatest challenge that parents face today! Unfortunately, the concerns and challenges are much more significant. Never in the history of our culture has a parent's job been more challenging. The dominant, secular norms that pervade every avenue of our society make it difficult to maintain a moral, religious, or even an ethical approach to child-rearing. Difficult, but not impossible. With Christ as its head and the church as its guide, every family should take solace in the divine assistance offered to parents to fulfill their responsibility as "the first and most important teachers of their children in the faith."

211. MEDIA GUARDIANS   *Parenting, media*

President Ronald Reagan, who complained that pornographers have more rights than parents, said, "Music and the media flood their children's world with glorifications of drugs and violence and perversity...."

REFLECTION

Cicero once asked, "What gift had Providence bestowed on [humans] that is so dear [to them] as children?" When the primary teachers of our children are not their parents, but popular music and video games and other media, there is a grave renouncement of parental responsibility. This means that parents should see to it that the joy of innocent living is not quickly stolen from their precious children. Children have a right to be shielded from themes and preoccupations that pollute their minds, hearts, and souls.

212. WHAT'S IN A GIFT?   *Eucharist*

An only son decided that he wanted to do something special for his mother on her eightieth birthday, so he went to a pet shop and asked for the most expensive pet available. The owner showed him a rare parrot that could recite the Ten Commandments and the Lord's Prayer in English, Latin, and ancient Aramaic. It cost $10,000. "Nothing's too good for my dear mother," said the man. So he bought the bird and had it delivered to her. The following weekend her son called. "Did you get the bird I sent?" he asked. "I surely did, son," she replied. "Thank you. It was a delicious meal. It tasted just like chicken."

REFLECTION

Like the mother who received a gift she did not understand, we too have been given a precious treasure we don't always understand and appreciate, the Eucharist. In the accounts of the Last Supper (Mark 14:22–24; Matthew 26:26–28; Luke 22:19–20), Jesus gave us the gift of himself, really present in the consecrated bread and wine: "This is my body...my blood." But he gave us, too, the sacred rite by which he offers himself sacrificially day after day, at every Mass, to the Father, a continuation of the sacrifice on Calvary. We who participate in the Eucharist offer ourselves to the Father in union with Jesus.

213. SEIZING THE MOMENT — *Repentance, regret*

A mother was recently asked, "If you had your life to live over, would you change anything?" At first she thought not, but then reconsidered. Here are some of her comments: "I would have sat on the lawn with my children and not worried about grass stains. Instead of wishing away nine months of pregnancy, I'd have cherished every moment. I would have realized that the wonder growing inside me was my only chance in life to assist God in a miracle. When my child kissed me impetuously, I would never have said, 'Later; now go get washed for dinner.' There would have been more instances of saying 'I love you,' more 'I'm sorry.'" I would seize every minute, live it, and never give it back."

REFLECTION

How beneficial regret often is. When we realize the sins committed, the mistakes of the past, the opportunities missed, the people we might have hurt, we are motivated to be more watchful and sensitive in the future. But the past, of course, is past, and we must move on, not letting past errors and sins distract us from the loving work of the present.

214. GLORIOUS MOTHERHOOD? *Mother's Day, witness*

Cardinal Mindszenty said the following: "The most important person on earth is a mother. She cannot claim the honor of having built Notre Dame Cathedral. She need not. She has built something more significant than any cathedral, a dwelling for an immortal soul, the tiny perfection of her baby's body. The angels have not been blessed with such a grace. They cannot share in God's creative miracle to bring new saints to heaven. Only a human mother can. Mothers are closer to God the Creator than any other creature. God joins forces with mothers in performing this act of creation. What on God's good earth is more glorious than this: to be a mother?"

REFLECTION

A mother has the unique privilege of sheltering God's unique creation from the first moment this new child comes into being. Later, it will be the mother who will likely be the first one to introduce the new child of God to a life of love and to our precious faith.

215. MOMMY CAME TO WORK   *Marriage preparation*

The little girl was a typical four year old: cute, inquisitive, bright, and very curious. When she expressed difficulty in understanding the idea of marriage, her
father decided to pull out the wedding photos, thinking visual images would
help. Page after page he pointed out the bride preparing herself, arriving at the
church, during the marriage liturgy, leaving the church, as well as numerous
photos taken at the reception. "Now do you understand?" he asked. "I think so,"
she said. "Is that when mommy came to work for us?"

REFLECTION

*Who doesn't know the work and expense that goes into preparing for a wedding
and reception? The more important preparation, of course, involves the engaged
couple taking part in marriage preparation counseling, praying together, discussing
topics such as finances and employment, sex, communication, children, housing,
including God in all their plans.*

216. HONOR THY MOTHER   *Love, commitment*

There was a mother who was a very difficult person and, as she aged, her negative behavior became even more intense toward her children. Two of her three
children broke off all contact. Their anger at her made it impossible for them
even to visit her. Eventually, she became disabled and the task of caring for her
fell on the daughter who had been able to come to some understanding of why
her mother was the way she was. Still, until the day the mother died, she continued to lash out at this daughter for not doing enough for her. When the mother
died, the two absent children experienced great guilt. The caretaker daughter, on
the other hand, experienced a sense of peace she had not anticipated.

REFLECTION

*Should we stop doing for others just because we are repaid with ingratitude? Our
motivation should not be the thanks we might receive, but the opportunity to love
another. Did Jesus, nailed to the cross, on hearing the many insults from the crowd,
give up the work of redemption? He calls us to be instruments of his peace, even in
difficult situations and even with those who are difficult to love. He challenges us
to let the Holy Spirit take hold of our lives and to join him in bringing justice and*

peace to the world, even if our sacrifice is ignored or ridiculed. Jesus warned us that if we make a big show of doing something for a person in need, we have already received our reward (Matthew 6:2).

217. MOTHER'S DAY   *Mother's Day*

Simplicity and understated dedication were the goals of Anna Jarvis when she first conceived of Mother's Day in 1907 in Grafton, West Virginia. She foresaw recognition of the day being a letter of appreciation to Mother, the wearing of a carnation, a visit, or simple gesture. Her profound devotion to her mother, Anna Reeves Jarvis, earned national recognition in 1912, when the U.S. Congress proclaimed the second Sunday of every May as Mother's Day.

REFLECTION

Mother's Day is not a holy day or a religious feast of any kind but a secular day of recognition of our mothers. Still, it is most fitting that we celebrate Mother's Day in May because May is the month dedicated to Mary, the Mother of God and our mother in heaven. Through Saint John, the beloved disciple, Jesus gave Mary to us as our heavenly Mother when he said on the cross, "'Woman, here is your son.' Then he said to the disciple, 'Here is your mother'" (John 19:26–27).

218. MOTHER'S SACRIFICE   *Sacrifice, stewardship*

Elizabeth of Bavaria, a member of a royal family, gave up her entire collection of precious jewels to her son, the Duke of Orleans, when he was Regent and in need of money not only for himself but for others he helped. In one of her letters she wrote: "Without this sacrifice, I should not have enough to keep my household, which is numerous and expensive. I thought it more rational and more humane not to deprive so many people of their daily necessary subsistence than to adorn my old and ugly figure with diamonds."

REFLECTION

Elizabeth of Bavaria would not have been swayed by the thought that diamonds are a girl's best friend. Her more precious concern was to sacrifice her diamonds for her son's more pressing needs, which included providing daily necessities for those in need.

219. SIGN IN THE DORM *Personal responsibility*

A sign in a college dormitory reads: "Your Mother Does Not Work Here. You will have to pick up after yourself."

REFLECTION

An adage has it that when we drop a burden from our shoulders, another person has to pick it up and carry it. The work that is ours to do, our responsibility, should not selfishly be shunted over to another. To turn around Saint Matthew's general judgment scene (25:31–46), "When you leave a burden for one of my brothers or sisters to carry, you leave it for me." Another adage sums the matter up: "You made the mess; you clean it up."

220. MOTHERS' INFLUENCE *Vocation, witness*

During the papacy of Pope Pius XII, an unusually high number of priestly vocations were coming from the Piedmont region of Italy. The pope sent a representative to investigate, who reported back to the pope with one simple sentence, "They looked to their mothers."

REFLECTION

Jesus gives us the perfect example of the dignity and respect we should have for mothers. His love and devotion to his mother became abundantly clear on Calvary when she became our mother as well. From the cross Jesus says, "'Woman, here is your son.' Then he said to the disciple, 'Here is your mother'" (John 19:26–27), thus allowing us to share the love of his mother. Another famous example of maternal influence is that of Saint Monica, the mother of Saint Augustine, who prayed for thirty-three years that her son would be converted to Christ. Over the centuries countless men and women have come to a lively and fervent faith because of their mothers' patient example and prayerful devotion. Mothers continue to be God's special stewards in supporting their children in discovering their vocation, especially in terms of the priestly vocation.

221. CALL FOR BACKUP *Prayer*

A police recruit was asked during the final exam, "What would you do if you had to arrest your own mother?" He responded, "Call for backup."

Mothers are not easily discouraged or put off, especially when they are faced with protecting their children. In fulfilling their demanding vocation, mothers have their hidden source of backup as well: prayer. Finding strength through communion with God, even when matters seem impossible, they don't give up.

222. ABORTION — *Abortion, moral demands*

Gianna Beretta Molla in Milan, Italy, the tenth of thirteen children: With simplicity she harmonized the demands of being a wife, mother, and physician. What sets this mother apart is that she died in 1962, a martyr of maternal love. In September 1961, when she was thirty-nine years old and pregnant with her fourth child, her physician discovered a large ovarian cyst that required surgery. To save her life, it was recommended that she undergo an abortion. Her decision was prompt and decisive: "I will accept whatever they will do to me, provided they save the child." She underwent the surgery but her fate was sealed. The following Good Friday, she gave birth to a healthy daughter, Gianna Emanuela, but she herself died seven days later. A few days before the delivery she told her husband, "If you must decide between me and the baby, have no hesitation: Choose—and I demand it—the baby. Save him." In the last week of her pregnancy she repeated, "Whatever God wants." Pope John Paul II later canonized her.

REFLECTION

There are many heroic mothers in the history of the church who exemplify Jesus' command to love. Saint Gianna teaches us most dramatically that, although very demanding at times, it is possible to live Jesus' radical command of love. What she teaches is that we must profess our faith not only in a formula of words, but also in the sometimes stark realities of life. In this case, forgoing abortion and surrendering one's own life for another's. Long before science made clear that each individual is genetically new and unique from conception, the church taught it and has insisted on protecting that life.

223. FAMOUS SLOGANS — *Obedience, discipleship*

In a marketing course, a professor was conducting a class on company slogans. "John," he asked, "which company has the slogan, 'Come fly the friendly skies'?"

"United," John answered. "Louise, can you tell me which company has the slogan, 'Don't leave home without it'?" Brenda answered with the correct credit card company without difficulty. "Now Thomas, tell me who uses the slogan, 'Just do it'?" Thomas was quiet for a moment before answering, "Mom?"

REFLECTION

Perhaps one of the first mothers to have offered a variation of this slogan was Mary, the mother of Jesus. We read in St. John's Gospel that when Jesus and his mother attended a wedding at Cana in Galilee, it happened that the wine ran out. Mary pointed to her son and instructed the waiters, "Do whatever he tells you" (John 2:5). Mary continues to offer us the same advice, to do God's will, to "do whatever he tells you." As we wrestle with the daily challenges of Christian discipleship, we just might listen to the gentle whisper of Mary, the first and most perfect disciple, to "just do it!"

224. WHO WAS THAT? *Moral behavior, forgiveness*

After putting her children to bed, a mother changed into old slacks and blouse she would never wear in public or around her family, and later decided to wash her hair. As she heard the children getting more and more rambunctious, her patience grew thin. At last she threw a towel around her head and stormed into their room, putting them back to bed with stern warnings. As she left the room, she heard her four-year-old say with a trembling voice, "Who was that?"

REFLECTION

There are times when we reflect on our own words or activities and ask the same question, "Who was that?" We don't recognize ourselves, our uncharacteristic behavior. There are times when we are a mystery, even to ourselves. Perhaps we overreact to an unexpected comment or experience. Maybe someone just comes across our path at the most inopportune time and they become the object of misdirected anger or frustration. Perhaps we become preoccupied by an unexpected illness or disappointment. These are the occasions, of course, when we might ask for God's forgiveness, perhaps in the sacrament of penance, but also be spiritually mature enough to ask forgiveness of the person we have offended. But also it is the occasion to remind ourselves that the word or act was exceptional, uncharacteristic of our usual attitude and behavior.

225. CAN'T GET NEAR ME   *Stewardship*

A young mother of three small children received a playpen as a gift from her in-laws. They soon received a thank you note from her that read: "Thank you so much for the playpen. It is a perfect God-send. I sit in it every afternoon and read, and the children can't get near me."

REFLECTION

The vocation of every disciple of Jesus is to be a good steward. If we are to answer for every possession we have, it becomes imperative to use it in a way that benefits oneself or another. The responsible use of a gift becomes paramount.

226. EXISTENCE OF HELL   *Hell*

Returning from a date with her boyfriend of two years, a young woman was distraught. She told her mother, "Anthony proposed to me an hour ago." "Then why are you so sad?" her mother asked. "Because he also confessed that he is an atheist. He doesn't even believe there's a hell." Her mother replied, "Marry him anyway. Between the two of us, we'll show him how wrong he is about the existence of hell."

REFLECTION

There are many people who often feel they are living their hell on earth due to lengthy sickness, suffering, disappointment, or heartache. Others may be given a special glimpse by family members, as in the promise the mother made in the story. We believe hell exists as an unending separation from God, not a fixed location in space, because we believe what Jesus told us in the gospels. In fact, Jesus makes more references to "hell" than to "heaven." He clearly indicates that the body, as well as the soul, will be subjected to the agonies of hell (Gehenna) (Matthew 5:29–30, 10:28; Mark 9:43–48).

227. A SISTER'S DEATH   *Compassion, bereavement*

At the 1988 Olympics in Calgary, Canada, after learning of his sister Jane's death, the American speed ice skater, Dan Jansen, took a couple of spills during a race and ultimately lost the gold medal. Many said that he was anxious and distraught over his sister's death. Through televisions across the world millions witnessed his great anguish. After his defeat, Dan went home and visited his sister's husband and their three young children and gave them his Olympic participant's medal and his love. An article in a national magazine commented, "At home the postman keeps bringing carts of mail full of sympathy and admiration. Dan Jansen may have fallen on the ice, but the world would reach out, if it could, to lift him up."

REFLECTION

Dan experienced something we will never experience, great humiliation in front of the whole world. On the other hand, grief is universal. No wonder so many were sympathetic to his double loss and expressed their compassion and were instrumental in his healing.

228. THIS FAVOR   *Commitment, service*

A cardinal asked Pope Paul III for a special favor, but the pope judged what he requested to be unfair and was unable to fulfill the cardinal's request. The cardinal protested, "Your Holiness knows very well how hard I worked to help make you pope, and therefore you should not deny me this favor." Pope Paul III responded, "Since you helped make me the pope, let me be one."

REFLECTION

There is never any room for favoritism, especially in the chief shepherd of the church, representing Christ on earth. To be the pope is to be Christ and to have the best interests of the church and the world always at heart, and to recognize that a position of power is not license for corruption, but a commission for service to all humanity.

229. "ONLY A JEW"   *Compassion*

In the summer of 1847 Blessed Pope Pius IX was going down one of the streets in Rome when he saw an old man lying unconscious in the street. The pope ordered that his carriage stop immediately and inquired who the man was. "He is only a Jew," came the uncharitable response. The Supreme Pontiff was very upset that such an unkind, racial comment had been made. He immediately got out of his carriage, helped the man up, and took him to the papal apartments where the pope's personal doctor was summoned to care for him.

REFLECTION

Unwilling to be like the Levite or the priest in the story of the Good Samaritan (Luke 10:25–37), who ignored the wounded man lying by the roadside, Pope Pius IX acted with compassion. Like the Good Samaritan, he took the wounded man home and saw to his care.

230. OFFER STILL STANDS — *Prejudice, ecumenism*

While walking about the Vatican one day, Blessed Pope Pius IX met a young man who was mesmerized by a painting by Raphael. When he saw the pope, he bowed politely. The pope inquired who he was and he replied that he was a painter who was unable to attend art school due to the cost. When the pope offered to pay his expenses, the man explained, "Your Holiness, I am a Protestant." The pope smiled and responded, "That makes no difference. My offer still stands."

REFLECTION

We sometimes place the successor of Saint Peter on such a high pedestal that it is difficult for us to imagine him going about his routines at the Vatican without fanfare. More than this, it would seem inconceivable to many that any pope prior to Vatican II would have reason to be in such close proximity to ordinary people. What is especially important in this anecdote is that the pope saw the painter as a human being, not as someone of another faith tradition. Christian love must not discriminate who is loved and served, as we see in Matthew 25:31–46.

231. BEAUTIFUL RING — *Marriage*

Before Pope Pius X became Bishop of Mantua, Italy, he was known as Monsignor Giuseppe Sarto. Upon his appointment as bishop, he went to visit his mother to tell her the news. During the visit the future pope showed his mother the bishop's ring, a sign of his episcopal authority. She admired the ring, then smiled and said, "Your ring is very beautiful, Giuseppe." Calling attention to her wedding band, she continued, "But you would not have it if I didn't have this one."

REFLECTION

Marriage is an extraordinary gateway through which our loving Father blesses us. Giovanni Sarto and Margarita Sanson cooperated with God in giving the world eight children, though they were very poor. The eldest, Giuseppe, became a priest, then a bishop, later a cardinal, then a pope, and finally a canonized saint. It would be very beneficial for men and women of all faiths to examine the lives of Giovanni and Margarita Sarto to discover how spiritually productive and valuable individual lives can be when lived according to God's will.

232. ULTIMATE IRONY　　　　　　　*Spirituality*

At the end of World War II, President Roosevelt suggested that Pope Pius XII should be among those consulted on the fate of postwar Europe. Soviet dictator Josef Stalin disagreed. He contemptuously asked, "How many divisions does the pope have?"

REFLECTION

Stalin's question was the ultimate expression of worldly arrogance. Mao's obscene observation that "Power grows out of the barrel of a gun" showed the naivité of communism. Communists understood the language of power, and nothing more. Now the Soviet Union is gone, but the Catholic Church remains. There is a force, a lasting presence in spirituality that people fail to appreciate. It seems the pope had many, many divisions, and some of them were inside the Soviet Union. Power does not grow out of the barrel of a gun, but out of hearts aglow with the love of God and is found most especially in the power of prayer.

233. HARLEM GLOBETROTTERS　　　　　　　*Papacy*

At his summer residence in Castelgandolfo, Italy, Pope Pius XII once received the Harlem Globetrotters, a touring basketball team. They gave him a present of a basketball with all their signatures on it. The Holy Father said to them, "We have heard about your prowess, but have never had the opportunity to watch you play." Five members of the team then gave the pope a demonstration of their razzle-dazzle style of play.

REFLECTION

Pope Pius XII received a basketball. Years later Pope John Paul II was given a hockey stick when he visited St. Louis, Missouri. Do you ever wonder where these countless gifts to the popes ultimately end up? Perhaps they are stored in some huge warehouse at the Vatican. Perhaps they are donated to charity or to the next child who visits the Holy Father. What is more significant is the significance of gift-giving. It has become a custom for those who visit the Holy Father to come bearing gifts. The gesture is rooted in the Scripture story of the wise men (Matthew 2:11). The symbol suggests presenting a gift to Christ, since the pope is the Vicar of Christ, his representative on earth.

234. TO VISIT YOU   *Pastoral visits*

Soon after being elected, Pope John XXIII went to visit a prison in Rome. He told the inmates, "You couldn't come to visit me so I came to visit you."

REFLECTION

How fitting the pope's visit was, in light of Saint Matthew's Last Judgment narrative (25:31–46). Jesus might have said to the pope, "I was in prison and you visited me." When we visit those who are sick or homebound, it is more than a matter of showing up; it entails making ourselves present to the other, giving ourselves to the other, in specific circumstances. A pastoral visit is all the more significant, especially when it entails bringing Holy Communion, reconciliation, or anointing. How vital it is that such a visit is one of presence and not pressure. How important that we become "another Christ" as we visit the Christ in need!

235. LOOKING RESPECTABLE   *Meals*

Time and time again Pope John XXIII loved being in the company of others. He expressed a desire to walk around the Vatican garden each day. Some time later, he learned of a plan by Vatican officials to build a fence around the path so that he would not be observed by passing visitors. "What's the matter?" he inquired, "Don't I look respectable?" He also found it very strange that the pope was expected to eat alone. He observed, "When I eat alone I feel like a seminarian being punished. I tried it for one week and I was not comfortable. Then I searched through Sacred Scripture for something saying I had to eat alone. I found nothing, so I gave it up and it's much better now."

REFLECTION

The pope knew not only how human it is to eat with others, but also how sacred a time such companionship can be. Doesn't "companionship" imply eating with others? He also knew that Jesus enjoyed being at meals with others, and was in fact criticized often for dining with outcasts and sinners (see Luke 5:27–32, 15:1–2, 19:1–10).

236. JUST THE VICAR OF CHRIST   *Holy Spirit*

Having arrived at the hospital run by the Sisters of the Holy Spirit unannounced, Pope John XXIII walked through the hospital rooms visiting the patients. Informed that the pope was there, the Mother Superior rushed to him and introduced herself, "Your Holiness, I'm the Superior of the Holy Spirit." The pope responded, "Oh, and I'm just the Vicar of Christ."

REFLECTION

In the Acts of the Apostles we read that in Ephesus Saint Paul found a group of converts and asked, "Did you receive the Holy Spirit when you became believers?" They replied, "No. We have not even heard that there is a Holy Spirit" (Acts 19:2). We've certainly heard of the Holy Spirit, but maybe we do not think enough about the Spirit or what the church teaches about him. We cannot visualize the Holy Spirit in the same way we visualize Jesus, but we should not confuse vividness with reality. The Spirit is as real and divine as the Son of God. This is our faith, and we profess this every Sunday when we recite the creed at Mass: "We believe in the Holy Spirit, the Lord and Giver of life, who proceeds from the Father and the Son. With the Father and the Son he is worshiped and glorified."

237. RING OF ENGAGEMENT   *Ecumenism*

When Pope Paul VI met Arthur Michael Ramsey, the Anglican Archbishop of Canterbury, in Rome in December 1966, he gave his guest a papal ring and reportedly remarked, "This is not yet a ring of marriage, but it is a ring of engagement."

REFLECTION

This engagement, which will emphasize how much the churches hold in common, just might be the longest one in history but if and when the wedding occurs, we can be sure that it will be centered not on compromise, but on Christ.

238. HOW TO BE A PATRIARCH
Positive criticism, baptism

Cardinal Albino Luciani, who later became Pope John Paul I, loved his priests. He welcomed them, listened to them, and helped them. Although he often excused them and defended them, he also knew how to be firm, but it happened rarely. Once a priest wrote a letter to the Vatican, accusing the then Cardinal-Patriarch: 1) of not visiting the parishes frequently; 2) giving too much importance to people; and 3) not knowing how to be a Patriarch. A letter arrived from Rome without delay, asking the Patriarch for an explanation. He responded: "1) I think I have always gone regularly to the parishes and also have returned gladly when I was invited; 2) I have the habit of treating everyone as a brother; 3) You are right that I do not know how to be a Patriarch."

REFLECTION

False accusation, not fraternal correction, was the motivation behind the priest's letter concerning his bishop. False accusation is always wrong. Fraternal correction (Matthew 18:15–17), positive criticism, on the other hand, offered in the right spirit, is good. It is not always easy to offer correction to a spouse, a child, a neighbor, or a friend. When we do, however, our motivation must be one of love for that person, intent on that person's welfare and the welfare of the community. This is the work of the prophets, and by baptism we are all to be prophets.

239. IN MY APARTMENT
Jesus

Having had the privilege of meeting Pope John Paul II on four separate occasions within three days, two priests later described the pope as humble, prayerful, and humorous. During the fourth and final meeting, the pope jokingly stated, "Dear Fathers, you can't stay here indefinitely. You must leave and return to your priestly duties in the United States." One of the priests responded, "Yes,

Holy Father…and in fact, the next time you visit the United States, I would like you to stay in my apartment at the cathedral." The pope quickly replied with a smile, "Does that mean you want me to let you stay in my apartment while you're visiting the Vatican?"

REFLECTION

The pope's focus on the person he was speaking or listening to made it seem as if that person was the most important person in the world. His humor and accessibility to so many people reinforces the fact that he genuinely loved people. Does this not remind us of Jesus' encounters with individuals and groups? Nothing mattered so much at the time as when Jesus spoke to Bartimaeus, the Centurion, the Pharisees, Judas, Nicodemus, and Mary.

240. LONGER IN PURGATORY — *Speech*

While he was assisting at the Second Vatican Council, Karol Wojtyla, the future Pope John Paul II began to write his book, *The Acting Person*. In Poland, it was a fiasco. He asked the opinion of his favorite student, Tadeusz Styczen, who responded, "First of all, I would have it translated from Polish into Polish." A while later, teaching at the University of Lublin, the future pope was illustrating the concepts in his book and noticed a priest who was chatting with a classmate. He called out to him, "Hey, if you do that, you'll stay longer in purgatory." The student responded, "Yes, to read your book as penance." A year later, the priest died. Wojtyla commented, "Now he's finally reading my book."

REFLECTION

Lengthy lectures and speeches are often forgotten with the passage of time but it is not unusual to recall a unique one-liner or circumstance that becomes all the more meaningful when the unexpected happens. The humorous comment uttered by the young priest who linked his teacher's book with purgatory gave the teacher reason to do likewise a year later. Our simple words and comments today may become the most important memories that another will have of us tomorrow.

241. HABEMUS PAPAM — *Vocation, creation*

On July 4, 1958, Father Karol Wojtyla was on a canoe trip with his friends in

Masuria, Poland. He received word from Warsaw to return for an urgent meeting with Cardinal Stefan Wyszynski. In Warsaw the cardinal told an anxious Father Wojtyla, who had then been a priest for only twelve years, that he had been named auxiliary bishop of Krakow. After lunch with the cardinal, he had hoped to rejoin his friends on the canoe trip. First, however, he had to go to Krakow to see the acting archbishop, Archbishop Eugeniusz Baziak, who introduced his new auxiliary bishop to the priests of the diocese with a prophetic greeting, *Habemus papam.*

REFLECTION

Karol Wojtyla's "yes" to Christ's invitation to the priesthood set him on the road to later becoming auxiliary bishop of Krakow and ultimately the pope. From Poland to Rome, Pope John Paul II never lost his love for the ordinary enjoyable experiences of the outdoors and the wonders of God's creation. It was important to meet the bishops, and it was also important to return to his friends and the canoeing.

242. THE ATTITUDE OF THE POPE   *Courage*

CNN reported a story about a visit that some bishops made to see Pope John Paul II just before his death in 2005. All the bishops of the world are required to make a visit to Rome to meet with the pope every five years, their *ad limina* visit. A group from Spain was making their visit, and among them was a very young bishop making his first visit. Upon seeing the pope, the young bishop was shocked by the frailness and obvious aging of the pope. Tears welled up in his eyes. He said, "Holy Father, I fear this is the last time I will see you." The pope responded, "Why? Are you sick?"

REFLECTION

Humor can serve as great medicine for a difficult encounter. Even those who suffer greatly can have the emotional courage to be a source of genuine comfort and affection for those facing unavoidable suffering.

243. PASSION OF THE CHRIST   *Humanity of Jesus*

Pope John Paul II, even with the challenges of advanced age and illness, knew of the controversy surrounding Mel Gibson's film *The Passion of the Christ*, and wanted to see it. As it turned out, producer Steve McEveety went to Rome uninvited to show the film to as many Vatican officials as he could, including the pope's secretary, Archbishop Stanislas Dziwisz. The bishop and the pope watched the movie together in the papal apartments. Afterward, Archbishop Dziwisz told Mr. McEveety that the pope found it very powerful, and approved of it, adding that the pope summarized his remarks in five words as the film neared its end: "It is as it was." A week later Mr. McEveety continued to marvel at what he felt was the oracular quality of the statement. "Five words. Eleven letters."

REFLECTION

The Holy Father thought the film told the story the way it happened: "It is as it was." The long hours of the passion began amidst the olive trees of Gethsemane (Matthew 26:36–50). Though scarcely on the threshold of that protracted martyrdom, Jesus' heart was already "deeply grieved, even to death" (Mark 14:34). Into the deepest shadows he withdrew to pray, but twice he came back to the apostles to seek their comfort (Mark 14:37–40). What an amazing sight! Jesus the Christ, divine and thoroughly human, sought support from ordinary people, even though they were soon to run away and abandon him. Why did Jesus do this? What else would a human being do when faced with such suffering? Perhaps he also wanted to encourage us to seek the help of others when we are troubled.

244. EVENING SNACK   *Humanity of Jesus*

In an interview following the death of Pope John Paul II, Cardinal Roger Mahoney of Los Angeles reminisced about an incident during the pope's visit to the Archdiocese of Los Angeles in 1987. Cardinal Mahoney didn't know where the Holy Father was during a visit one evening. He later found the pope and his secretary in the kitchen heating soup they found in the refrigerator. The cardinal wanted to call a staff member to assist him, but the Holy Father declined, saying that they just wanted to have some leftovers without disturbing the staff.

REFLECTION

We often think of the pope sitting in his office or apartment, with his staff standing in the shadows waiting to be of service. Yet, like other people, there are moments in the day when the pope simply wants to do something ordinary and spontaneous, such as preparing a snack without pressing others into service. This "hidden life" of the pope may resemble Jesus in his hidden life. How often did Jesus prepare a snack, fix a broken chair, or want to help someone without pressing his disciples into service?

245. RUNNING THE CHURCH — *Fear*

Pope John Paul II was once asked whether he planned to retire because of the difficulty he was having getting around. "No," he replied. "I don't run the church with my feet."

REFLECTION

Pope John Paul's physical difficulties progressed as he grew older, but he didn't stop working, letting fear immobilize him. Until his final breath, he lived the signature statement with which he counseled us from the beginning of his pontificate in 1978, "Be not afraid." (Deuteronomy 3:22; 2 Maccabees 7:29; Proverbs 3:25; Matthew 5:28; Mark 5:36; Luke 1:13; Luke 1:30; Luke 12:4; John 6:20; Acts 18:9; Acts 27:24; 1 Peter 3:14; Hebrews 13:6; Revelation 1:17). The reason for not being afraid? Jesus, who is eternally faithful, promised he would be with us.

246. A FIT POPE — *Physical fitness, stewardship*

On a visit to the Dominican Republic, Pope John Paul II kissed its soil. When he stood up, the Archbishop of Santo Domingo leaned over to brush the dirt from the pope's robe where he knelt to prostrate himself for the ceremonial kiss. But there was no dirt. Aside from a little dust, the pope's white robe was without a smudge. A miracle? Not at all, unless physical fitness is a miracle. The vigorous Pontiff explained that he did pushups every day. When he dropped to the ground, he had supported himself pushup-style, on toes and hands as he kissed the earth.

REFLECTION

Many have seen pictures of Pope John Paul II in the early days when he was physically fit, skiing and hiking, and later kissing the ground upon visiting a country. His spontaneity and zest gave us all a reminder that we are morally bound to take care of our bodies, to maintain our health, if only for this simple reason: The more fit and healthy we are, the more we will be able to accomplish in building God's kingdom of justice, love, and peace.

247. INFLUENCE AND INFLUENZA *Church, papacy*

When Pope John Paul II came down with the flu, he made a joke of it. But the next day there was no papal meeting or address to visitors. People wondered whether the pontiff was seriously ill. "Perhaps you will be surprised that the pope, even though a few steps away from children, did not hug or kiss them," Pope John Paul told the people of Sts. Fabian and Venantius Parish in Rome. "I was about to, but then I thought that the pope has a virus, and since he has had so much influence on you, it would not be right to add another kind." In Italian, influenza means both influence and influenza, or flu.

REFLECTION

Pope John Paul had a special way of allowing us to recall his message of Christ. To this day, there would be very few who were in the audience that day who would not recall the pope's play on words and by extension, the content of the message he delivered. Our Lord uttered a similar play on words when he called Simon Peter to be the chief shepherd of his church. This is not at all obvious in English when we read, "You are Peter, and on this rock I will build my church" (Matthew 16:18). In other languages, Jesus' pun is obvious. In Latin, the name for Peter is Petrus, *and the word for rock is* petra. *In Greek, the name for Peter is* Petros, *and the word for rock is* petram. *In Aramaic, the name for Peter is* Ke'pha', *and the word for rock is* ke'pha'. *The same is true of Italian, Spanish, and French. In French, then, we read Matthew 16:18 as: "Tu es Pierre, et sur cette pierre j'édifierai mon eglise." Jesus' intent would be more clearly understood in English if the English translation read: "You are Rocky, and upon this rock I will build my church."*

248. BRING THE SUN OUT *Witness*

At the National Catholic Prayer Breakfast in Washington, D.C. on May 20, 2005, President George W. Bush made this observation about the funeral of Pope John Paul II: "When the men were carrying [the wooden casket] up the stairs, they turned to show the casket to the millions that were there, and just as the casket reached the top, the sun shown for all to see it." The president's observation was reminiscent of the experience former Mayor Ed Koch of New York City relates about when he first met Pope John Paul II in 1979 at Kennedy Airport in a torrential rainstorm. "As he stepped out of the plane…the rain stopped." A police officer standing nearby yelled out, "That's the kind of guy you want to make a golf date with."

REFLECTION

In the Sacred Scriptures we see that the sun is an expression of the Lord's blessing on humanity. It is likewise a symbol of endurance and strength. In Psalm 84:11 we read, "For the Lord God is a sun and shield; he bestows favor and honor. No good thing does the Lord withhold from those who walk uprightly." We shouldn't be surprised, then, that the presence of Pope John Paul II, who was a blessing for us in his life and teaching, brought the sun out. We, whom Jesus calls to walk in the light, are to bring the sunshine of Jesus' presence to others by our example, our compassionate words, our acts of selfless love.

249. WATCH AND LEARN   *Witness*

On January 27, 1988, Cardinal Joseph Ratzinger (later Pope Benedict XVI) was delivering the Erasmus Lecture titled "Biblical Interpretation in Crisis" at St. Peter's Lutheran Church in New York City. About a quarter of the way through his lecture, a group of dissident Catholics disguised as priests rose from their seats, cursed the cardinal, and chanted, "Rats, rats, rats." One of the elder priests in the audience, a Jewish convert named Msgr. John Oesterreicher, whispered to the younger priests nearby, "Watch and learn." Surrounded by boisterous and aggressive critics, the cardinal remained serene. He simply stopped his lecture and led the audience in reciting the Lord's Prayer. Meanwhile, those causing the disturbance were led to the exit. Before resuming his speech, Cardinal Ratzinger remarked, "I would have been very happy to answer their questions if they had simply asked me in an orderly fashion."

REFLECTION

This incident reveals the ease and humility with which this very intelligent man presented himself, even under difficult, embarrassing, and potentially dangerous circumstances. The experience was reminiscent of Jesus in many gospel passages when he was criticized and even ridiculed by the scribes and Pharisees. What the lecture audience was able to "watch and learn" was a German Cardinal visiting from Rome reflecting the attitude of Jesus under similar circumstances. How would Jesus have acted on that podium? How would we have acted?

250. MEETING A FUTURE POPE *Witness, discipleship*

Two priests were visiting Rome in 1993 and had the privilege of celebrating Mass at St. Peter's, meeting the pope, and visiting the usual attractions, including the Vatican Museum, the Sistine Chapel, the Coliseum. One afternoon the priests decided to leave their hotel room to make a quick visit to a souvenir shop. Near the store entrance they suddenly came eye to eye with Cardinal Joseph Ratzinger (later Pope Benedict XVI). Those who did not know the cardinal would have assumed that he was an ordinary parish priest, because he was wearing a simple black cassock. Unfortunately the visiting priests were not wearing their proper priestly garb, since they intended to make a quick stop at the store and return to their hotel. They apologized to the cardinal for their appearance. The cardinal remarked, "No problem. Everyone deserves a day off." Then the cardinal blessed the two priests, consented to have a few photographs taken with them, and then continued on his way.

REFLECTION

The chance encounter with the future Pope Benedict XVI left a positive impression on the two priests. The prelate they met that fall day was a humble servant of God who radiated a prayerful presence and virtuous, understanding demeanor, appealing qualities that are the hallmark of a true disciple of Jesus Christ.

251. ACT OF CHARITY *Eucharist*

Bishop Fulton J. Sheen was once invited to address an interfaith audience in Baltimore. As he approached the podium, he was greeted by applause. He raised his hand for silence and then said, "When you applaud me at the start, that's faith; midway through, that's hope. But, ah, my dear friends, if you applaud me at the end, that will be charity!"

REFLECTION

Bishop Sheen was a great preacher because he realized what was at the heart of the human struggle. He understood that Jesus had the power to touch hearts. On the day of his ordination, Father Sheen resolved to spend one hour in the presence of the Blessed Sacrament every day of his life, and this he did faithfully. This spiritu-

al nourishment served as the very root of his prayer life and vocation and was the foundation of his successful ministry of preaching and television evangelizing.

252. HELP ME   *Prayer*

In the days before automobiles, the old-time priest was on his horse rushing to get to church on time. Suddenly his horse stumbled and pitched him to the ground. In the dirt with a broken leg, the priest called out, "All you saints and angels in heaven, help me get up on my horse!" Then, with superhuman effort, he leaped onto the horse's back and fell off the other side. Once again on the ground, he called to heaven, "All right, just half of you this time!"

REFLECTION

Our prayer has to be an act of faith. We pray for something, and then place the outcome in God's hands, trusting God to care for us, believing that God may answer our prayer in ways unimagined. Faith-filled prayer also tells us that our prayer may not seem to be answered at all, but we leave that matter, too, with God.

253. STATUE   *Faith*

While visiting the home of his sister, a priest noticed the beautiful statue of Jesus on the mantle. He thought to himself, "Wonderful! They still have this figure of Jesus, a symbol of God's great love for this family." He walked to the dinner table and sat down for the meal. A little boy, his nephew, age four, looked at him and said, "I always know when you're coming, Father Donald, because Mom puts that statue out."

REFLECTION

The statue in the house, as any statue, evokes our faith. The statue of Jesus can speak to our belief in the divinity of Jesus, in the love for us manifested in his life, in his challenge to live as he did. It is a gift from God. Faith, of course, is not just having the statue, but demands of us something much more deeply rooted. Faith is even more than accepting as true what God has revealed in Scripture, in our tradition, in the church's authoritative teaching. It goes beyond intellect; it engages the whole person. It means being open to God in the everyday events of life, trusting God to care for us. It informs everything we do.

254. CUT THE HOMILY   *Preaching*

A parishioner noticed that the priest had a small bandage on his face and, in a motherly tone, she asked, "What happened, Father?" He told her, "While I was shaving this morning I was thinking about the homily and I cut my face." With that she responded, "Next time you shave, think about your face and cut the homily."

REFLECTION

Whatever the length of a homily, it is important that we acknowledge its significance at Mass. When the word of God is proclaimed, Jesus is present to the assembly, and the preacher, who need not be polished and learned, breaks open God's word for us in a well-prepared homily, giving us an opportunity to hear God speaking to us, inviting us, challenging us, comforting us. We should have the frame of mind that something important is taking place, a word of inspiration tailored for us as long as we are receptive to it. It's a matter of who we are, not what we have, what God asks of us, through reading (including and especially Scripture), praying, reflection, seeking the advice of others. God reaches out to us and waits to hear Jesus' words echo in our hearts: "I have come to do your will" (Hebrews 10:7, 9). When we can sincerely utter those words, we, too, will have opened ourselves to God; we, too, will have become vulnerable, and then God will be able to do with us as he wills.

255. A GOOD HOMILY   *Preaching, character*

A priest, known for his lengthy homilies, noticed a man get up and leave during the middle of his message. The man returned just before the Great Amen and Our Father. After the weekday Mass the priest asked the man where he had gone. "I went to get a haircut," was the reply. "But," asked the priest, "why didn't you do that before Mass?" "Because," the gentleman replied, "I didn't need one then."

REFLECTION

The quality of a homily is determined not by it length or brevity, but by the content of its message. Similarly, the quality of a person should not be judged by his or her lifestyle, profession, residence, or possessions, but by content of character.

256. TELEVISION MASS   *Speech*

A priest regularly celebrated daily Mass on television. One Sunday morning following the parish Mass, a parishioner approached him and commented, "Father, your homilies on the TV Mass mean so much to my mother since she lost her mind."

REFLECTION

Too often we speak without thinking. Our best intention to compliment another, as in this incident, can quickly become an unintended insult. In more significant matters, though, this principle of speech is very important to bear in mind: A harmful, mean-spirited word once said cannot be unsaid; like a bell once rung, it cannot be unrung.

257. WASH AWAY INIQUITIES   *Stewardship*

When the priest washes his hands at Mass, he says a short prayer in a low voice, "Lord, wash away my iniquities; cleanse me from my sin." In a small parish in upstate New York, there was a shortage of altar servers; one by one they were leaving on summer vacation until only one young boy remained. When the time came for him to go away on vacation with his family, the priest was resigned to celebrating Mass without a server. But the boy showed up unexpected one morning. The priest asked, "I thought you were going away on vacation?" The boy responded, "But, Father, who would wash away your iniquities?"

REFLECTION

We all need to rest from the busyness of our lives, "to get away from it all." A vacation is a matter of being a good steward, using our time well, periodically doing nothing or at least doing something different from our usual routine, so that we may be more productive when we return to our ordinary fare. Pope John Paul II echoed this sentiment in a speech to pilgrims on Sunday, July 6, 1997, when he stated, "We all need an occasional period of extended physical, psychological and spiritual rest....For a vacation to be truly such and bring genuine well-being, in it a person must recover a good balance with self, others and the environment. It is this interior and exterior harmony which revitalizes the mind and reinvigorates body and spirit....Escape can be beneficial, as long as one does not escape from sound moral criteria."

258. WALKING LIKE FRANKENSTEIN
Tolerance, prudence

Having recently undergone leg surgery, a priest wrestled his way out of bed to attend to a parishioner dying in a nursing home. He made his way to the second floor with the help of a cane but when he was ready to leave, his difficulty walking, coupled with the pain, was quite noticeable. As he made his way to the elevator, he overheard an elderly woman say to another, "Oh look, there's a priest." The other responded, "That's not a priest…he walks like Frankenstein." The priest hesitated and then said to them, "Good morning, ladies. That comment wasn't very nice." Whereupon one of the women said, "I didn't say it, she did." And the other protested, "No, I didn't say it, she did." Needing a quick exit, the priest simply extended his hand and blessed them and stumbled on his way. As he was getting on the elevator, he overheard them: "He blessed me because I'm a Catholic," the first woman said. Her friend responded, "He didn't bless you, he blessed me." As the elevator door closed, their argument continued. "He did." "He didn't." "He did." "He didn't."

REFLECTION

Even the priest's mild rebuke may have been better left unsaid. No harm done to ignore the women's negative comment and their bickering. Perhaps it might have been better to say something positive, on another subject, setting an example of kindness in response to a small insult. Sometimes it may be advisable to tolerate a relatively minor slur, rather than risk turning up the volume.

259. THE LIFE OF ONE PRIEST   *Eucharist, baptism*

A priest who died at a very young age displayed this plaque in his office, which captures the distinctive intimacy with which he viewed his life as a priest of Jesus Christ: "My life must be Christ's broken bread; / my love his outpoured wine; a cup overfilled, a table spread / beneath his name and sign, that other souls, refreshed and fed / may share his life through mine."

REFLECTION

The plaque expresses what is expected not just of a priest, but of every baptized person: a life nourished by the Eucharist and spent for others, becoming, like Jesus, "a man for others." This one priest, perhaps little remembered, made some mark in life by his example, leaving the world more Christ-like.

260. PRIEST   *Vocations, priesthood*

If a priest preaches more than ten minutes, he is long-winded. If his homily is short, he didn't prepare it. If the parish funds are in the black, he has business savvy. If he mentions money, he's money-mad. If he visits parishioners, he is nosy; if he doesn't, he's a snob. If he has fairs and bazaars, he is bleeding the people. If he doesn't, there isn't any life in the parish. If he takes time in the reconciliation room to advise sinners, he takes too long. If he doesn't, he doesn't care. If he celebrates the Mass in a quiet voice, he is boring; if he puts emphasis in his words, he's an actor. If he starts Mass on time, his watch is fast. If he starts late, he's holding up the people. If he's young, he's inexperienced. It he's old, he ought to retire. But…when he dies, there may be no one to replace him!

REFLECTION

In addition to the large number of parishes across the country who have no resident priest, there are also a large numbers of foreign-born priests on parish staffs. "A shortage of priests" is a cliché. But beyond praying for an increase of vocations to the priesthood, we should also pray for the priests who minister to us day after day. The lives of these dedicated men are difficult. Many demands are placed on them and much is expected of them.

261. POOREST PREACHER   *Holy Spirit*

Having finished his last Mass on Sunday, the pastor greeted the parishioners as they left church. After shaking several hands he came upon Anthony, seven years old. "Good morning, Anthony," the priest said. As he shook the child's hand, he felt something in the palm of Anthony's hand. "What's this?" the priest asked. With a big smile the child responded, "It's a dollar and it's for you!" "I don't want to take your money," the priest objected. "I want you to have it," said Anthony. After a short pause the boy continued, "My daddy says you're the poorest preacher we ever had and I want to help you."

Good preaching is always better than poor preaching, but even "poor" preaching will have more value than most people realize. The fact is that no matter how inadequate a preacher may be, due to poor preparation or none, or his personality or lack of training, there is always something in each homily to inform or inspire us. After all, it takes place during the Liturgy of the Word, after God's word is proclaimed, and the Spirit of God is present to touch any heart that is open to it.

262. UNTIL THE LAST MINUTE   *Death*

A priest waited on the gas line to have his car filled just before a long holiday weekend. The attendant worked quickly, but there were many cars in front of the priest at the service station. Finally, the attendant motioned him toward a vacant pump. "Father," said the young man, "I'm sorry about the delay. It seems everyone waits until the last minute to get ready for a long trip." The priest chuckled, "I know what you mean. It's the same in my business."

REFLECTION

Our faith teaches us, to use the words of the Eucharistic Liturgy, to wait always "in joyful hope for the coming of our Savior, Jesus Christ." Unfortunately, some put off genuine conversion, turning a deaf ear to God, the "Hound of Heaven," who pursues us relentlessly, seeking final intimacy with us. Jesus warns us in the gospels about such procrastination. Death may come like a thief in the night, and we know not the day or the hour (Luke 12:40).

263. SALES, NOT MANAGEMENT   *Trust, providence*

The airplane flew into a violent storm and was being tossed about alarmingly. One nervous woman happened to be sitting next to a nervous priest, so she turned to him for comfort. "Can't you do something?" she asked. "I'm sorry, ma'am," replied the priest gently, "I'm in sales, not management."

REFLECTION

Most storms in our lives are not in airplanes or highways, of course, but in the all too ordinary circumstances of life. It is precisely when we face such squalls that we must trust God to take us through the difficult period. When we are storm-tossed in life, we must work to survive as if all depends on us and pray and trust God as if all depends on God, which it does. We must choose to believe that God is at work in ways that are not apparent to us.

264. APPLYING IT   *Gospel living*

A priest was sitting next to a soap sales rep on a flight from New York to Boston. Noticing his Roman collar, the sales person said, "There is so much evil in the world and so many wicked people. The message you preach hasn't done much good, has it?" Minutes later they were walking through Logan Airport and the priest noticed a man who had obviously not washed in days. He turned to the sales rep and observed, "Obviously, soap hasn't done much good in the world either." "Oh," replied the salesman, "soap is only useful when it is applied." "Exactly," added the priest, "the Christian message only works when we use it."

REFLECTION

The story goes that when someone asked Mohandas Gandhi what he thought of Christianity, he replied that he thought it would be a good idea. In other words, the theory seemed good to him, but he implied that it was not practiced. Jesus' teaching and example is always good but, like soap, it must be applied, lived, day in and day out, to the hilt. God's invitation always stands, but it comes with a R.S.V.P.

265. WHAT THEY ALWAYS TELL US
Welcoming the stranger

A tearful parishioner saying farewell to the priest who was being reassigned to another parish said, "I don't know what we will do when you are gone, Father." The outgoing pastor replied, "Oh, the church will soon get a better man than I am." To this the parishioner replied, "That's what they always tell us when a new priest comes, but they keep getting worse and worse."

REFLECTION

A new pastor assigned to the parish, a new supervisor at work, a new neighbor who has just moved in—such occasions may incline us to be judgmental, and even intol-

erant, especially if they are "different." Their personalities, the changes they bring, their mannerisms may prove irksome. That's going to happen and it may be understandable that it affects us the way it does. But governing the whole situation should be the overriding awareness that this person is beloved of God, presumably trying to do a good job. Do we see the face of Jesus in that man or woman? Do we welcome him or her as we would Jesus? Are we open to the possibilities of cooperation, of having an open mind?

266. PASTOR AND ASSOCIATE · *Visiting the dying*

Father O'Toole, pastor of St. Augustine Parish, was in the hospital, near death. The young associate pastor was called to anoint his brother priest. As the priest stood next to the bed, Father O'Toole's condition appeared to deteriorate and he motioned frantically for something to write on. The young priest lovingly handed him a pen and a piece of paper, and Father O'Toole used his last bit of energy to scribble a note. Then he died. The young priest thought it best not to look at the note at that time, so he placed it in his pocket. At the funeral, as he was finishing the homily, he suddenly remembered the note so he announced, "You know, our beloved pastor handed me a note just before he died. I haven't looked at it, but knowing Father O'Toole, I'm sure there's a word of inspiration there for us all." He opened the note that read, "Please, dearest Father, you're standing on my oxygen tube!"

REFLECTION

Sooner or later we may find ourselves at the bedside of a dying person: a friend, a spouse, a son or daughter; it might even be more formal, such as bringing Holy Communion to a parishioner. It is a sacred time, a privileged moment that we may have only once with that person. What will we say or do? How will we act? How will we pray with the person? There is much to learn about being with or ministering to a dying person, and there are many books, articles, as well as audio and video resources available offering a great deal of practical advice derived from experience. We owe it to these people and to ourselves not to leave the occasion to pure impulse and chance, but should learn how to be with the dying, how best to spend those precious moments.

267. A FEW WORDS *Preaching*

Three boys were in the schoolyard bragging about their fathers. The first boy said, "My dad scribbles a few words on a piece of paper, he calls it a poem, and they give him $50." The second boy said, "That's nothing. My dad scribbles a few words on a piece of paper, he calls it a song, and they give him $100." The third boy said, "I got you both beat. My dad who's a deacon scribbles a few words on a piece of paper, calls it a homily, and it takes eight people to collect all the money!"

REFLECTION

Whether a deacon, priest, or bishop, the preacher is never able to simply scribble a few words and turn it into a homily any more than a poet or a song writer can scribble a few words and turn it into art. The homily is a sacred tool used in a sacred setting to accomplish a sacred purpose: to open the word of God to the assembly in a stimulating and inspiring manner. To be inspirational, informational, and formational takes much effort. Only clear thinking and research, coupled with prayerful reflection, produce a homily worthy of the Sacred Liturgy.

268. LETTER FROM A FOOL *Preaching, charity*

A pastor was opening his mail one morning. Removing a single sheet of paper from the envelope, he found written on it only one word: "Fool." The next Sunday the pastor announced, "I have known many people who have written letters and forgot to sign their names. But this week I received a letter from someone who signed his name and forgot to write a letter."

REFLECTION

It is not an exaggeration to state that if a priest, deacon, or bishop is faithful in preaching authentic Catholic teaching, he just might receive "hate mail" from someone who wishes to water down the gospel of Christ. It may happen as well that a preacher may receive a letter from someone who believes the preaching has been overly lax or erroneous. In either case, those in the assembly should feel free to express an opinion about the preaching, but it must be done with clarity and charity. If it is, there should be no need to do it anonymously. All should be guided by the ancient rule: In matters essential, unity; in matters non-essential, liberty; in all matters, charity.

269. CONSCIENCE AS YOUR GUIDE
Conscience, prudence

After the heaviest snowstorm of the season, a thirteen-year-old boy decided to pick up some extra money shoveling driveways. His first stop was the rectory. "How much is it worth for me to shovel your driveway?" he asked the priest. The priest replied, "This is the church, God's House, and it's your house too. I leave it to your own judgment and sense of honor how much you ought to charge or whether you ought to charge anything at all. Let your conscience be your guide." Two hours later the boy knocked on the rectory door and told the priest, "The job is finished, Father, and I have decided I'm going to charge you absolutely nothing. Now, let your conscience be your guide."

REFLECTION

Following our conscience is not always an easy matter. It is often difficult to discern what is the right thing to do. In difficult, complicated matters, there is much to consider: the teaching of the church, of Tradition; the perceptive counsel of another; prayerful reflection; one's experience. All of these factors go into the mix to discover the will of God, to make a prudential judgment in a particular, concrete matter. In the final analysis, conscience is "a man's secret core and his sanctuary. There he is alone with God whose voice echoes in his depths" (Pastoral Constitution on the Church, Second Vatican Council).

270. THE WINNER
Lying, truth

Father Murphy encountered several young boys with a dog sitting on the front lawn of the church. He inquired as to what they were doing. One of them responded, "We're telling lies, and the one who tells the best lie gets to keep the dog." The shocked priest replied: "I never even thought of telling a lie when I was your age." One of the children in the group shouted: "Give Father the dog, guys. He's the winner!"

REFLECTION

The suggestion that a person has never told a lie is, more often than not, a lie itself. Sometimes severe and harmful, and at other times much less so, lying is an attempt to deceive another; it is a violation of one's word, an offense against the truth, delib-

erately harming one's relationship to another. The fact that lying is one of the Ten Commandments should give us reason to take its prohibition very seriously (Exodus 20:16; Deuteronomy 5:20). The Catholic Catechism (2465) reminds us, "the Old Testament attests that God is the source of all truth. His Word is truth. His Law is truth. His 'faithfulness endures to all generations' (Psalm 119:90; Proverbs 8:7; 2 Samuel 7:28; Psalm 119:142; Luke 1:50). Since God is 'true,' the members of his people are called to live in the truth" (Romans 3:4; Psalm 119:30).

271. SAYING YES TO THE CALL *Holy Orders, dying*

A newly ordained priest was assigned to a parish where the local hospital routinely called in the middle of the night to request a priest to visit the sick and dying. One such night the telephone rang on three separate occasions. The first call came about 1 AM. The second came at 2:20. During the second visit the hospital staff assured him that there was no other patient in need of a priest and assured him that there would be no additional calls during the night. He had no sooner returned home and fallen asleep, when the telephone rang at 3:30. Driving back to the hospital, he felt that the hospital personnel were really passing the envelope. Feeling very tired, he entered the sick room with some reluctance. To his surprise there was an elderly woman overflowing with faith and hope. She immediately thanked him for coming to bring her the sacraments of the dying. "Father, I want to receive Jesus now as my last act, trusting that he will welcome me when I die." During the visit the woman explained her incredible life of faith. Before administering the sacrament of the sick, he asked if she wanted him to call her family. She explained that her son and daughter, who lived out of state, were no longer in contact with her. To the priest's astonishment, she explained that she had made all necessary arrangements for her death prior to being admitted to the hospital. She even left a suitcase at the funeral home with the clothing they would need. Her final wish was to receive the sacraments. During the anointing, the woman responded to the prayers with firm conviction, but then she suddenly took her last breath. The priest completed the sacrament and sat with her in prayer, vividly aware how fortunate he was for God's call to be a priest and for saying yes to it.

REFLECTION

Being present with a dying person, administering the sacraments, touching and comforting the person, can be reward enough for a life lived in service to others. The priest, acting in the person of Jesus, spends himself for others, as Jesus did. The entire spiritual and academic preparation for the sacrament of holy orders is an insignificant price to pay for this privilege. Even a priest can sometimes take for granted the profound gift of the priesthood of Jesus Christ in which he so intimately shares.

272. GETTING MORE MILEAGE
Responsibility, preaching

A visiting priest had only one homily prepared, which he delivered at Sunday Mass. The pastor was overjoyed with his preaching, so he asked him to preach again at the Monday morning liturgy. The problem was that the visiting priest was not up to preparing another homily. He worried the whole night on what to do to rescue himself from the predicament. The dreaded hour arrived. When he stood at the pulpit, he announced with great solemnity: "My dear brothers and sisters, some have accused me of advancing propositions to you yesterday, contrary to the faith, and of having misrepresented church teaching as well as several passages from Sacred Scripture. Now, to convince you how much I have been wronged, and to make known to you the authenticity of doctrine, I will repeat yesterday's homily this morning with the hope that you will now be more attentive."

REFLECTION

The priest's very poor, self-centered attitude aside, this is probably one of the more creative ways a preacher has used to avoid composing a new homily. Preparing a homily well for the celebration of the Eucharist is the obligation of any preacher. If this priest had put as much energy into composing a new text as he did trying to solve his quandary, he may have come up with a very effective homily. In similar ways, many of us are sometimes occupied with how we can escape, postpone, or downplay our responsibilities, what we rightly owe to family, employer, friends, and strangers.

273. CALL A PRIEST   *Catholic Church*

Some decades ago, a man was struck by a bus on a New York City street. He lay dying on the street as a crowd of spectators gathered around. "A priest. Somebody please get me a priest!" the man gasped. A policeman surveyed the crowd but there was no priest, no minister, no cleric of any kind. "A priest, please!" the dying man insisted. Then out of the crowd stepped a little Jewish man about eighty years old. "Officer," said the man, "I'm not a priest, not even a Catholic. But for fifty years now I have lived behind St. Elizabeth's Catholic Church and every night I've listened to the Catholic litany. Maybe I can be of some comfort to this man." The policeman agreed and brought the octogenarian over to where the dying man lay. He knelt down, leaned over the injured man and said in a solemn voice: "B-4, I-51, N…"

REFLECTION

We would today consider this image of the Catholic Church a caricature, to be so closely linked with running Bingo nights. What was true years ago to varying degrees no longer is. This is also true of the image that some people who used to be active Catholics have of the church today. They carry with them a view of the church, an understanding of what the church is like, that is no longer true. The church, like any institution, changes over time. A church of saints and sinners, it is always in the process of modification. We might say to them, "Since you've been gone, this is what has happened…."

274. TO DIE AS JESUS DIED   *Dying*

An old priest lay dying. He had already received the last sacraments and now he had one final request. He asked that his banker and his lawyer, both parishioners, come to his bedside. When they entered the room, the priest motioned for them to sit on each side of the bed. He grasped their hands, sighed contentedly, smiled, and stared at the ceiling. Both the banker and lawyer were touched and flattered that the elderly priest would ask them to be with him during his final moments. They were also puzzled because he had never given them any indication that he particularly liked either of them. They both remembered his many long, uncomfortable homilies about greed, covetousness, and avaricious behavior that often made them squirm in their seats. Finally, the banker said,

"Father, why did you ask us to come here?" The old priest mustered up his strength and then said weakly, "I want to die as Jesus died, between two thieves."

REFLECTION

The sacred time of dying is not a time for holding grudges, a time for not forgiving. It is a final opportunity to make right all the relationships one has ever had: with spouse and family, with friends and enemies. It is a time for finding the ultimate peace of mind, knowing that all is right with God, with others, and with oneself.

275. COST OF CONVERSION   *Discipleship*

The priest-chaplain at a Catholic hospital was called to the room of a dying man who had once professed himself godless. "Father," said the man, "I am dying. I know all about the Catholic faith and its obligations. I want to make sure about getting my eternal reward so I want you to admit me into the church before I die. But before you baptize me, I want to know how much it is going to cost." "Well," said the priest, "it won't cost you a cent to become a Catholic, but, if you live, it will cost you plenty of blood, and sweat, and tears to follow Jesus."

REFLECTION

Does this man know what he is asking for? If he takes the gospel to heart, a great deal will be asked of him. The authentic disciple of Jesus will not be content with what someone has called "soft Christianity," and another "Christianity Lite," which is a minimalist approach to discipleship. Just pondering Matthew, chapters five to seven, will make this very clear.

276. FIFTY MILLION DOLLARS   *Stewardship*

A couple who belonged to a local parish purchased a lottery ticket and unexpectedly won fifty million dollars. The husband, though, was getting along in years and was suffering from heart trouble. The wife was afraid that if she told her husband that they had won such a large sum of money that he would really die of a heart attack. So she went to the pastor and said, "Father, please break the news to my husband in such a way that it will not kill him." So the pastor spoke to him about many things and finally said to the man, "Suppose you won fifty million dollars, what would you do with it?" "Oh," he said, "I'd give it to you, Father." And the priest dropped dead.

REFLECTION

To have so much money would really test our vision of our Christian life; it would force us to reevaluate our priorities. As stewards of all that we have received, what would we do with that money? It's been noted that a parish budget is a theological statement because it reveals what its priorities are. So, too, our new budget with that money would reveal what we really think is important, what place God's reign holds in our hearts. Read Matthew 25:14–30 and decide which servant you will be.

277. MASS IN PRIVATE HOMES   *Episcopal authority*

A woman came to the rectory door and asked if she could have the Eucharist celebrated in her home for her and her husband's silver wedding anniversary. "No, I'm sorry," replied the priest, "the bishop has forbidden Masses in private homes." "But just last week one of my neighbors had one in hers," she protested. "I know. Some priests don't obey the bishop's directives, but here we do." "Then," asked the woman, "can you give me the names of a couple of pastors who don't?"

REFLECTION

We accept the teaching and direction of legitimate church authority not as a matter of blind, unthinking obedience, but as a matter of faithful discipleship. Have you noticed the crosier, or staff, that the bishop carries in formal liturgical celebrations? It is like a shepherd's crook, a symbol of his authority as the chief shepherd of the diocese. Read Matthew 7:24–27.

278. GOD TELLS ME   *Inspiration, ministry*

Among the most important priorities in the weekly schedule of a priest is the preparation of a homily for the weekend Masses. Recently, a parish secretary happened to go into the pastor's office and, noticing that he was working on his Sunday homily, she asked, "Father, how do you always know what to say in your homily?" The priest replied, "Well, I guess God tells me." Then with some hesitancy she asked, "Then why do you keep crossing things out?"

REFLECTION

Like the priest preparing his homily, we, too, often look to the Holy Spirit for guidance in our decision making. But God has only human, fallible instruments to work with in building the kingdom of God. Thus, mistakes will be made, sins will be committed, good works will be left undone. But, inspired by God, we move along as individuals and as a church, on our pilgrimage toward the kingdom of God, ready to refine, reevaluate, rethink, and repent. "Come, Holy Spirit, Creator blest, and in our hearts take up Thy rest."

279. WATERMELONS FOR SALE   *Stealing*

A parish priest grew watermelons behind the rectory to supplement his meager income. He was doing pretty well, but some kids would sneak into his watermelon patch at night and steal the watermelons. After some thought, he came up with a clever idea that he was sure would scare the kids away. He posted a sign in the field: "Warning! One of the watermelons in this field has been injected with cyanide." The kids ran off and made up their own sign and posted it next to the priest's. When the priest surveyed the field the next day, he noticed that no watermelons were missing, but the sign next to his read, "Now there are two!"

REFLECTION

People can be quite clever and inventive in stealing, whether a thief by night or an accountant juggling a corporation's financial books. And as clever as we might be in taking reasonable steps to protect our property, stealing goes on, in spite of God's command, "You shall not steal" (Exodus 20:15). But are we creative in taking what is not ours, depriving another of what is his or hers? Our guide has to be that if something is not rightfully mine, I don't want it. Or, as one ancient writer expressed it, "Every thing cries out for its owner!"

280. CHANGE, PLEASE   *Judging*

The regular collector for the 9 AM Sunday Mass didn't show up one morning. The pastor asked another member of the parish to substitute for him. When the substitute collector started passing the basket from the back of the church, he first put a 100 dollar bill in the basket. By the time he had collected from pew to pew and moved to the front of the church there was enough money to get change for his $100. Unaware of his intention, the congregation watched as he helped himself to two twenties and one ten.

REFLECTION

The substitute collector's simple act of donating to the parish might have turned into a serious misunderstanding. As imprudent as his act was, not foreseeing how it would appear to the assembly, they should not have been hasty in judging the man or his deed, but should have reflected on his character and the circumstances of such an act, and also reflected on Jesus' words in Matthew (7:1–2), "Do not judge, so that you may not be judged. For with the judgment you make you will be judged, and the measure you give will be the measure you get."

281. PRAYING TO ICONS   *Stewardship, time*

The elderly monsignor observed the young priest kneeling on the floor to check his e-mail on his laptop computer. The monsignor remarked, "Is this what it has come to, praying to your computer now?" The young priest replied, "Sure, Monsignor, I'm praying before the icons."

REFLECTION

The monsignor's humorous comment led to the equally humorous response by the other priest, a result of fraternal friendship and affection. The computer, like other electronic gadgets, can become an obsession with surfing, blogging, games, and e-mail, rather than a tool to help us fulfill our obligations more efficiently. It can evolve very stealthily into our "personal chapel." When we use too much of our time gazing at a monitor, we might ask, "Where do I find time for prayer, for interaction with my spouse and husband, friends, and business colleagues?"

282. PALM SUNDAY   *Family*

On Palm Sunday, the priest announced that following Mass he would pass out miniature crosses made of palm branches. "Put a cross in the room where your family argues the most," the priest advised. "When you look at the cross, it will remind you of the extent of God's love and the love we are to have for one another." As she was leaving the church, a woman walked up to the priest, shook his hand, and said, "I'll take five."

REFLECTION

This poor woman, as any family member, knew about household disagreements, but she had experienced many of them, and more intensive. There was no place for her to escape them. But she can strive to change the character of the disagreements, taking her cue from the palm reminders and persuading herself that love is to reign in her home, that she is to see the face of Jesus in all the members, as hard as that may be sometimes. Perhaps her example of careful listening, a lowered voice, and loving patience might rub off on others. Her goal? That Saint Paul would not say to her family as he did to the Corinthians, "I fear that when I come, I may not find you as I wish…I fear that there may perhaps be quarreling, jealousy, anger, selfishness…" (2 Corinthians 12:20).

283. AVOIDING EMBARRASSMENT *Charity*

There lived in England two young women from a respectable family who were reduced to poverty and had to do needlework to secure some income. A priest became aware of the situation and wanted to help them without embarrassing them. He paid them a visit and said, "I see, Ladies, that you have in your possession a most valuable picture. I see it is by the hand of a great master; and if it is not too great a favor, I ask you to let me have it for one hundred pounds." The offer was immediately accepted.

REFLECTION

There are times when we can perform great acts of charity while allowing the recipients to maintain their God-given human dignity. In addition to disguising our attempts to help another, such as the priest did in this story, we should also try to remain anonymous when we contribute to the welfare of another, lest it appear that we want to "help" another but really only want the notice it may engender. "So when you give alms, do not sound a trumpet before you, as the hypocrites do…so that they may be praised by others. Truly I tell you they have received their reward" (Matthew 6:2).

284. CLOTHE THE CHILDREN   *The poor, charity*

In eighteenth-century France, a parishioner paid a visit to a priest at a Parisian parish in the middle of the winter. Noticing that the priest was living in a house with naked walls, the man inquired why he did not have wall hangings to protect him from the severe cold. The good pastor showed him two little children that he was taking care of, and replied, "I had rather clothe these poor children than my walls."

REFLECTION

Caring for the poor is one of the noblest acts a person can undertake. Sometimes it is very easy; at other times it involves felt sacrifice. At all times it includes a decision for Christ, because when we do it for one of his brothers or sisters, we do it for (or, to) Jesus, as Matthew makes graphically clear (25:31–46). The prophet Zechariah reminds us, "Do not oppress the widow, the orphan, the alien, or the poor" (7:10). Throughout the gospels we see time and again that Jesus had a special affection for the poor (Matthew 11:5; Luke 4:18; Luke 14:13; Luke 18:22; Luke 21:3).

285. WANT TO GO TO HEAVEN?   *Heaven*

Father Murphy walked into a pub in Ireland and said to the first man he met, "Do you want to go to heaven?" The man replied, "I do, Father." The priest said, "Then stand over there against the wall." Then the priest asked a second man, "Do you want to go to heaven?" "Certainly, Father," was the reply. The priest said, "Then stand over there against the wall." Then Father Murphy walked up to Shamus O'Toole and said, "Do you want to go to heaven?" O'Toole said, "No, I don't Father." The priest said, "I don't believe this. You mean to tell me that when you die you don't want to go to heaven?" O'Toole said, "Oh, when I die, yes. I thought you were getting a group together to go right away."

REFLECTION

When we speak about matters of eternal salvation, our message ought to be clear, lest we be misunderstood. But how clear can we be about heaven, other than it is to be with God forever? Outside of conjecture, we can't be more specific than that. But what else matters? There may be as many descriptions about heaven as there are people, but in the end we must for now settle on this: God " will wipe every tear from their eyes. Death will be no more; mourning and crying and pain will be no more" (Revelation 21:4).

286. ON YOUR TOMBSTONE   *Stewardship, afterlife*

A priest recently gave his friend an envelope containing the funeral arrangements he wanted. About to get into his car, the friend opened the envelope and began to read the instructions as a truck went by. He glanced up and read the following on the side of the truck: "What Do You Want on Your Tombstone?" The truck was carrying frozen pizza!

REFLECTION

More important than, "What do you want on your tombstone?" are significant questions about life, about what is important and what really counts. In the book of Ecclesiastes, written in the third century before Jesus, and at a time in Jewish history when there was no great belief in the afterlife, the priest Qoheleth asks, "What do people gain?" (Ecclesiastes 1:3) "All is vanity," he also comments (1:2). "Vanity" could better be understood as "useless." So, is everything "useless"? No. All the things of this world are good and are to be used for the glory and praise of God. But they must not lead us away from loving God and others and all of creation. When they do, they become worse than useless. What would you want engraved on your tombstone? Something like, "I used everything for the greater glory of God"!

287. GOOD NEWS, BAD NEWS
Stewardship, Christian living, money

The pastor stood before his parishioners and announced, "I have some bad news, some good news, and more bad news." Everyone listened attentively. "The bad news is that the church needs a new roof." The parishioners groaned. "The good news is that we have enough money for this major project." The parishioners made a sigh of relief. Finally, the pastor said, "The bad news is that the money is still in your pockets."

REFLECTION

The challenge for parishioners is to respond with respect and obedience to all of the precepts of Scripture and church teaching. This inevitably includes temporal affairs. Christian stewardship includes the proper maintenance of the parish facilities, where the community of faith may thrive, and be vigorously enfleshed in daily life.

288. GOD'S TOOLS   *Providence*

On a Saturday night, a deacon was working late in his office at Christ the Good Shepherd Parish, and decided to call his wife before he left for home. It was about 10:00 p.m. but his wife didn't answer the phone. He wondered why she didn't, but he decided to continue working and try later. When he called again, she answered right away. He asked her why she hadn't answered before, and she said that the telephone didn't ring. The following Monday morning, the deacon received a call at the church office. The man calling asked why the parish had called on Saturday night. The deacon couldn't figure out what the caller was talking about. Then the caller said, "It rang and rang, but I didn't answer." The deacon remembered the incident and apologized for disturbing him, explaining that he had intended to call his wife. The man said, "That's okay. You see, I was thinking about committing suicide, but before I did, I prayed, 'Lord, help me if you don't want me to do this; give me a sign now.' At that point my phone rang. I looked at the caller ID, and it said, 'Christ the Good Shepherd' and I was afraid to answer."

REFLECTION

God uses the most ordinary circumstances of life to accomplish extraordinary things, and we may never know how or when God will use us as his instruments for good, even when, as most often happens, we may not be aware of it. In the prayer attributed to Saint Francis, we pray that God will use us as instruments of his peace. We must trust that our prayers may be answered, but in ways we might never expect.

289. CAN'T REMEMBER   *Humor, preaching, teaching*

A permanent deacon who felt that he was "humor impaired" attended a conference to better equip deacons for their ministry, which includes preaching. One of the conference speakers boldly approached the pulpit and, securing the audience's attention, said, "The best years of my life were spent in the arms of a woman who wasn't my wife!" The listeners were shocked! After several seconds he continued, "And that woman was my mother!" The crowd burst into laughter and he delivered the rest of his engaging talk. The next week, the deacon decided he would give this humor thing a try, and use that joke in his homily. As he approached the pulpit that Sunday morning, he rehearsed the joke in his head but it seemed a little foggy to him. In any event, he spoke loudly into the microphone, "The greatest years of my life were spent in the arms of another woman who was not my wife!" The people in the congregation were stunned. After standing there for almost several seconds in the dismayed silence, trying to recall the second half of the joke, he finally blurted out, "And I can't remember who she was!"

REFLECTION

It can be very effective for preachers and teachers to use humor, and it can for all of us as well. The humor, though, not only has to be properly executed, but in the case of preachers and teachers it must not be used for its own sake. Although a joke may be appropriate and useful to make a point, it is not wise if the content of the homily is ordered around the joke instead of the joke being used to reinforce the central message. The best homilies and teaching, after all, are the examples we set by how we live from day to day, more than by what we preach or teach. As the adage states, "We cannot preach what we practice unless we practice what we preach."

290. FEEDING THE HUNGRY   *Witness*

In the Archdiocese of St. Louis there was a man named Tony who was the head chef at a large hospital in the city. It bothered him to see so much food that had never been touched being thrown away daily. So he decided to gather the surplus food and take it down along the Mississippi River and distribute it to those living in caves and sewer openings along the river. Over the years this single act of kindness grew as more people got involved in the work. Later, Tony was ordained a deacon and continued his ministry to the homeless. By the time of his death, his ministry was feeding hundreds every night and involved people from all over the St. Louis metropolitan area, with many hospitals and restaurants contributing their surplus food each night. All of this happened without one word of publicity, without one appeal for funds or help. It happened because one person, interested in helping human beings in need, saw how to go about it. Others saw the need and joined in.

REFLECTION

We often ask, "What can one person do?" But that's exactly the point. Change has to start with one person, with one act, with one idea. Deacon Tony spent little or no money in his ministry. Rather, it was initially his sensitivity, and then his time and commitment that counted. Like this one man, we have to become personally involved in our world to make it a better place. To be true disciples of Jesus, we have to pick up and do what Jesus would do. We have to be his hands and feet in the present. Like Jesus, we have to be like a light to the world. "For once you were darkness, but now in the Lord you are light. Live as children of light (Ephesians 5:8). What is Jesus asking us to do?

291. SUNDAY MORNING HAPPENINGS   *Compassion*

It was a chilly Sunday morning when the parish deacon noticed a woman crouched beneath the church steps to absorb the warmth of the boiler room door. Upon seeing him, she attempted to leave but the deacon encouraged her to stay as long as she wanted. Another Sunday the deacon saw a limousine in front of the church. A nicely dressed man with an anxious expression jumped out of the car and hurried into Mass, which had already begun. He told his chauffeur to meet him in the last pew so their tardiness would not be noticed. After Mass, the deacon encountered the same man and asked him what he thought about the homily. The visitor replied that he felt desperate and had too many worries to listen to the homily and as his car pulled away the license plate read: I B RICH.

REFLECTION

Which desperate person would you help? The two come from very different economic backgrounds but each has serious problems. Both are desperate in different ways and both need help. We might think first of the woman's physical poverty. What about the man's spiritual poverty? The fact is that wealth can have a nega-

160

tive effect on our lives. We read in Proverbs 30:8–9 and Hosea 13:6 that wealth can tempt us to turn our backs on God.

292. ONE WOMAN'S RELIGION　　　　　*Church*

A once-faithful woman became dissatisfied with her Catholic faith and with all existing religions, so she decided to begin one of her own. One day a reporter who genuinely wanted to understand her point of view asked her, "Do you really believe, as people say you do, that no one will go to heaven except you and those who become members of your church?" The woman pondered the question and then answered, "Absolutely, no exceptions, not even Mary."

REFLECTION
The church, founded upon the apostles by Jesus Christ, with apostolic authority, the custodian of God's revelation, cannot be reduced to personal opinions or personal agendas or the tenets of a feel-good religion. In every age the church has been invaded by champions of objective heresy and disparaged by anti-Catholic ideologies. This is true in the present as well. But this should not frighten us. Rather it should encourage us to be ever more attentive, more vigilant, more faithful to our Catholic identity.

293. GLUTTONY IN THE PARISH HALL
Gratitude, stewardship, compassion

Parish potluck suppers have become popular in recent years, an occasion of fellowship and pleasant camaraderie. At one supper a few years ago, parishioners had prepared a simple but delicious meal of rice, vegetables, choice cuts of meat, with a generous assortment of desserts. One fellow stepped to the front of the line and, desiring the wide array of food, piled the many meat cuts on his plate, leaving the other food behind. Before anyone even noticed, he sat down with his plate heaped with these choice cuts and began to eat. Everybody else got the rice and vegetables. The kingdom of God went out the door that evening and the sin of gluttony took a seat in the church hall.

Gluttony is overindulgence in food or drink, and may involve being uninterested in and uncaring of those around us who do not have enough. God wants us to avoid this deadly sin and come to a place in our lives where we can recognize that he has so blessed us in every way that we praise him for all the blessings we have received, and then share those blessings with others. There is also a matter of taking reasonably good care of our body and spirit, for each of which we are responsible.

294. NOURISHMENT   *Gratitude, Eucharist*

An old man recently wrote a letter to the editor of a local newspaper: "I've gone to church for thirty years now and in that time I have heard about 3000 homilies. But for the life of me, I can't remember a single one of them. So, I think I'm wasting my time and the priests are wasting their time by giving homilies at all." This started a spirited exchange of letters to the editor, much to his delight. It went on for weeks until someone wrote this clincher: "I've been married for thirty years now. In that time my wife has cooked some 32,000 meals. But for the life of me, I cannot recall the entire menu for a single one of those meals. But I do know that they all nourished me and gave me the strength I needed to do my work. If my wife had not given me these meals, I would be physically dead today. Likewise, if I had not gone to Mass for the nourishment of the fellowship, homily, and Eucharist, I would be spiritually dead today."

REFLECTION

We should thank God every day for our physical and spiritual nourishment, which can come in so many ways, often without our being aware of it! Beyond the food for our bodies, we are nourished by prayer, the sacraments, the good witness of others, by spiritual reading and reflection. In the spirit of stewardship, we know that whatever we have is a gift to be shared with those who have less. We do all for the glory of God. As the psalmist urges us: "O give thanks to the Lord, for he is good; for his steadfast love endures for ever" (Psalm 106:1).

295. STOPPED AT THE INTERSECTION   *Faith*

It happened at an intersection. The light turned green but the driver didn't

notice it and remained stopped. A woman in the car behind him began to
pound on her steering wheel and yell in her loudest voice. The man's car still
didn't move and the woman was just beside herself. She continued to rant and
rave. Finally the light turned yellow and she began to blow the horn again, while
making obscene gestures and continuing to scream. The man finally looked up
and made his way through the intersection just as the light turned red again.
The woman continued screaming in frustration because again she missed her
chance to get through the intersection. Suddenly she heard a tap on her car window and looked up into the face of a policeman. The policeman told her to shut
off her car while keeping both hands in sight. After she shut off the engine, he
ordered her out of the car, placed her in handcuffs and took her to the police
station. Several hours later she was finally released. The arresting officer
explained, "I'm really sorry for this mistake. But, you see, I pulled up behind your
car while you were screaming, blowing your horn, and making obscene gestures.
Meanwhile, I glanced at the bumper stickers on your car: Choose Life, What
Would Jesus Do?, Follow Me to Church, as well as the chrome-plated Christian
fish emblem on the trunk. Naturally I assumed you had stolen the car."

REFLECTION

*Faith is reflected not in clever slogans alone. By faith we mean firmly accepting the
truths revealed to us by God, even though we may imperfectly understand them.
Faith also implies trust, relying on God who is ever present and faithful. Faith
enables us to see the world differently, taking God's viewpoint of the world as God
has revealed it, and living according to God's teaching. Believing is seeing! It is a
commitment to a way to life modeled on the teachings of Christ. This is what we
mean when we say that our faith must be living. This is what Saint James meant
when he said, "Faith without works is barren" (James 2:20). A living faith is seeing
eye to eye with God. Saint Augustine said, "Faith has its own eyes."*

296. RETURNING A GIFT   *Honesty, stealing*

Walking through a large department store shopping for a twenty-fifth wedding
anniversary gift for her husband, Rebecca noticed an expensive vase identical to
the one she had received as a wedding gift twenty-five years before. She went
home and carefully wrapped the vase she had been given long ago and returned

it to the store. She told the salesperson that she wanted her money back and, knowing that a receipt was necessary, passed another receipt from a purchase she had recently made. When the salesperson pointed out that it was the wrong receipt, Rebecca apologized and said that she would go home to get the correct receipt. Recognizing Rebecca's innocent mistake and sincerity, and not wanting to cause her any inconvenience, the salesperson gave Rebecca a full refund for the twenty-five-year-old vase.

REFLECTION

Deceit can take many forms; human imagination can see to that. Deceit, especially when wrapped in plausible sincerity, is still deceit. The momentary gain can never outweigh the huge personal cost of becoming a liar and a thief, manipulating the good will of another, and causing a company financial loss. What has this woman gained? What has she lost? She was actually engaged in an act of self-deceit. Read Micah 6:10–11 and other prophets who long ago condemned the woman's behavior.

297. NO EXCUSE SUNDAY   *Mass*

A notice in a parish bulletin read as follows: Next week we will have a "No Excuse Sunday" in order to enable everyone to attend church. A cot will be placed in the center aisle for those who say "Sunday is my only day to sleep." Steel helmets will be provided for those who say "The roof would cave in if I ever went to church." Blankets will be furnished for those who think the church is too cold, and fans for those who think it's too hot. We will have hearing aids for those who say "The priest speaks too soft." And cotton will be given to those who say "He speaks too loud." Score cards will be provided for those who wish to count all the hypocrites present. One hundred take-out dinners will go to those who say they cannot go to Mass and also cook their Sunday dinner. Relatives will be invited for those who like to go visiting them on Sunday. A section of the sanctuary will be devoted to grass and trees for the benefit of those who like to find God in nature. And a putting green will be set up in the vestibule for those who say "Sunday is my only day to play golf." Last, but not least, the sanctuary will be decorated with both Easter lilies and Christmas poinsettias for those who have never seen the church without them.

REFLECTION

We constantly meet people who are skillful in citing excuses for not regularly joining the assembly of believers on Sunday to celebrate the Eucharist. It is not that God's word—proclaimed at Mass or read privately—is too hard to believe; it's too good to be true. The God of infinite power and majesty has reached out to hold us in his arms, to claim us as his children, making us co-heirs with Christ. Yet, how many of us remain indifferent to God and bypass the unique act of thanksgiving, the Mass? Ironically, the often boycotted Eucharist is the source and summit of our very spirituality, as the document on the liturgy from Vatican Council II pointed out.

298. NATIONAL PRAYER BREAKFAST   *Sin, forgiveness*

In January 1979, Bishop Fulton J. Sheen was the guest speaker at the National Prayer Breakfast in Washington, DC. Turning to the chief executive and his wife, Bishop Sheen began, "Mr. President," he said, referring to President Jimmy Carter, "you are a sinner." Having everyone's undivided attention, he then pointed to himself and said, "I am a sinner." He looked around the huge ballroom filled with sophisticated and influential spectators, and continued, "We are all sinners, and we all need to turn to God."

REFLECTION

Bishop Sheen pointed out the obvious, but the audience's first response was one of surprise. But, of course, every president, as well as every human being—Mary excluded—is a sinner in need of God's mercy. We are a church of saints and sinners and a country of saints and sinners, each person a mix. Sacred Scripture reminds us again and again that we are all sinners. "There is no one who is righteous, not even one" (Romans 3:10) and to Titus Saint Paul says that we have been given the gift of faith "not because of any works of righteousness that we had done, but according to his mercy" (Titus 3:5). We all have need of God's merciful forgiveness because without it we deserve to "go away into eternal punishment" (Matthew 25:46).

299. SHINE YOUR LIGHT   *Witness, light*

A man stopped at a garage just at dusk one evening because something about the engine needed attention. A mechanic examined the trouble while a helper stood holding a light under the hood. The helper turned away and turned off the flashlight by accident. The mechanic looked up and exclaimed, "Shine your light! What are you here for?"

REFLECTION

When Jesus sent out the seventy-two disciples to proclaim the Good News, he didn't tell them that they would be exempt from suffering and difficulties because they were doing God's work. He even told them they would be like "lambs into the midst of wolves" (Luke 10:3). But when he sent them out two by two, he showed them and us how much we need one another as we walk through life. Each of us has to be a light to others, being Christ for one another, seeing Christ in one another, escorting one another along the sometimes dark and dangerous path mapped out for us by Christ. "Shine your light! What are you here for?"

300. DECISION FOR CHRIST · Eucharist

With Christ there is peace even in war; without Christ there is war even in peace. With Christ the poor are rich; without Christ the rich are poor. With Christ adversity is sweet; without Christ prosperity is bitter. With Christ the ignorant are wise; without Christ the wise are fools. With Christ life is a journey to heaven.

REFLECTION

It is difficult to always make a decision for Christ, to have the mindset of Jesus. It is often difficult to know what we should do, and even more difficult to do it. That is why the Lord Jesus gives us himself in the Eucharist as the nourishment we need for the journey, as the light to see our way. "I am the light of the world" (John 9:5). "I am the bread of life" (John 6:35). Jesus sends us, enlightened and nourished, back to our everyday lives. It is there, outside the church walls, that the option we have made for Jesus Christ is put to the test in our everyday lives, where we live out our faith and work out our eternal liberation and salvation.

301. AUTHENTIC RELIGION · Nonviolence

The Duke of Guise, François, who commanded the Catholic armies in France, narrowly escaped being assassinated at Rouen, by a soldier. The young soldier was placed under arrest and taken before the duke. The soldier confessed his crime, and when asked what had influenced him in his desperate attempt, he replied, "I had determined to kill you, that I might deliver religion from one of its most powerful adversaries." The duke replied, "If your religion teaches you to assassinate one who never injured you, my religion, which holds to the principles of the gospel, commands me to pardon you. Go, therefore, and judge which of the two religions is the more like God."

REFLECTION

When we use religion as a means to promote hatred, violence, or murder, we can be assured that either the religion we subscribe to is false or hollow or we have misinterpreted its principles. Those who follow the God of Abraham, Isaac, Jacob, and Jesus will be disciples of peace and nonviolence, intent on loving even enemies and praying for those who persecute them, as Jesus instructed us (Matthew 5:42–45).

302. SIGNS OF INSPIRATION — *Discipleship*

If you ever visited Disney World in Florida, you would be inspired and moved by the many signs that accompany the various attractions at the theme park and at Epcot Center. Some of the signs read as follows: "A link with the past and appreciation for the present is our promise and hope for the future." "Energy brings our lives new graces." "If we can dream it, we can do it." "This way to the kingdom" (referring to Disney's Magic Kingdom).

REFLECTION

If we change these a little, every disciple of Jesus could proudly hang them from their heartstrings: "In Christ we find a link with the past and an appreciation for the present. He is our promise and hope for the future." "In Christ we find the energy to bring our lives new graces." "In Christ we find the fulfillment of our deepest dreams." "In Christ we find the way to the kingdom." This is how we can make Saint Paul's exhortation operative: "Let the same mind be in you that was in Christ Jesus" (Philippians 2:5).

303. SIGN — *Mission*

The following was posted on the bulletin board in an office building: "We, the willing, led by the unknowing, are doing the impossible for the ungrateful. We have done so much for so long with so little that we are now qualified to do anything with nothing."

REFLECTION

One might interpret this as meaning the following: We, disciples of Jesus, are compelled by our belief in him to invite others to join us as we "wait in joyful hope for the coming of Our Savior Jesus Christ." But we do not wait idly, merely passing time in our secure hope. Instead, as members of the church, driven by the love of God, we labor to bring peace and justice, faith and hope, to the ends of the earth. "I am grateful to Christ Jesus our Lord, who has strengthened me, because he judged me faithful and appointed me to his service" (1 Timothy 1:12).

304. THE TELL-TALE HEART   *Abortion*

James J. Stahllnecker editorialized in *Catholic New York* on January 12, 1995: In Edgar Allan Poe's classic horror tale, "The Tell-Tale Heart," a murderer dismembers his victim and hides the pieces under the floorboards. When the police call to investigate, he prides himself on his cleverness, but gradually becomes unhinged, at last screaming out the location of the corpse. He was undone by the sound of his victim's heartbeat, drumming in his ears. Why, after so many years of legalization, does the abortion debate continue in America? Why haven't we accepted it as a matter of fact as we do any other "surgical procedure"? I believe that it has something to do with a tell-tale heart. Deep inside we know that someone dies in every abortion, a tiny growing child with hands and eyes and a face and a beating heart. Four thousand times a day that beating heart is stopped, but in our conscience it seems to go on.

REFLECTION

For someone to say "I choose to have an abortion" makes no sense, because to have an abortion is contrary to the nature of pregnancy. The infusion of the soul takes place at the moment of conception. God's creative act now puts the new person in place and we cannot interfere with it, deciding whether that life should continue or not. The right to life now exists in the new person. There exists only one legitimate choice, which is to respect the child created by God and to allow nature to take its proper course. Christ is Life, and to stand with him is to stand with life, and against whatever destroys life. Under no circumstances can followers of Christ ever pro-

---

mote, defend, or participate in abortion or any other kind of abuse toward children. The words of Our Lord come to mind, "'Occasions for stumbling are bound to come, but woe to anyone by whom they come! It would be better for you if a millstone were hung around your neck and you were thrown into the sea than for you to cause one of these little ones to stumble" (Luke 17:1–2).

305. YOUR OWN DIRT   *Creation*

One day a group of scientists decided that humans had developed so well that they no longer needed God. So they picked one scientist to tell God. The scientist walked up to God and said, "God, we've decided that we no longer need you. We are to the point that we can clone people and do many miraculous things, so we don't need you any more." God listened very patiently to the man. After the scientist was done talking, God said, "Very well, how about this? Let's say we have a human-making contest." To which the scientist replied, "Okay, great!" "But," God added, "we're going to do this just as I did back in the days of Adam." The scientist said, "Sure, no problem" and bent down and grabbed himself a handful of dirt. God looked at him and said, "No, no, no. You get your own dirt."

REFLECTION

We should never be intimidated by science. In the pursuit of truth we should always be mindful that there is only one truth. There isn't one truth in the realm of science and another in the realm of faith. If the scientist is sincere in the pursuit of truth, his or her findings will always be in continuity with, and never contrary to, the One Truth who is God. In terms of this story, we are also reminded of the present fascination by some scientists to aggressively pursue "life" matters such as embryonic stem cell research and human cloning. The problem arises when scientists seek to remove from God his unique role as creator. They seek to remove from God's control that which is God's alone. As the story illustrates, humans can only go so far in this aggressive pursuit. The basic component or raw material used by the scientist is God's creation, not ours. "The heavens are yours, the earth also is yours; the world and all that is in it—you have founded them" (Psalm 89:11).

306. FOR LENT   *Lent*

Pray. Mend a quarrel. Seek out a forgotten friend. Trust God. Write a letter of love. Share some treasure. Give a soft answer. Visit Jesus in the Blessed Sacrament. Encourage youth. Keep a promise. Find the time. Read Scripture. Forgive an enemy. Listen. Laugh. Go to Mass every day. Appreciate what you have received. Be loyal to your calling. Be nonviolent in your thoughts, words, and actions. Pray.

REFLECTION

Lent is the opportunity to examine and rededicate our lives, to fine tune our relationship with God and others, to turn our backs on what diminishes our relationships, to live as faith-filled disciples of Jesus, to live up to our baptismal calling, to return to the Father's will, and so find that glory for which we were created. Lent, in other words, is another opportunity to "put on the Lord Jesus Christ" (Romans 13:14).

307. NO PLACE TO GO   *Communion of saints*

A man was visiting a funeral home to pay his respects to the family of the deceased. He entered the room and went right up to the casket to view his long-time friend. He stood there for a minute and then began to laugh. All the mourners looked at him but said nothing. He spent time talking with the relatives of the deceased and then he went to the casket again for a last look at his friend. Again, he began laughing. A man came over to him and said, "Sir, this is no place for laughing." The man responded, "Why? My friend here didn't believe in heaven or hell, and here he is all dressed up with no place to go."

REFLECTION

The incident at the funeral home is a sad commentary on one unbelieving man who passed from this life through death to eternal life. There are people who do not share the widespread human belief in life after death, and, even less, do not believe in the communion of saints, as we know it in our Catholic tradition. We pray for the dead as we would want others to pray for us after we die. We can be sure that our prayers, our sacrifices, and especially the Masses offered on behalf of the deceased will be fundamentally beneficial for them and for us. "[Judas] made atonement for the dead, so that they might be delivered from their sin" (2 Maccabees 12:45).

308. HEAVEN'S PAVEMENT   *Heaven*

There once was a rich man who was near death. He was very grieved because he had worked so hard for his money and he wanted to be able to take it with him to heaven. The man implored an angel to ask whether God might bend the rules. The angel informed the man that God had decided to allow him to take one suitcase with him. Overjoyed, the man got his suitcase and filled it with pure gold bars. Soon afterward he died and showed up at the gates of heaven. Saint Peter greeted him and, seeing the suitcase, said, "Hold on, you can't bring that in here!" The man explained to Saint Peter that he had permission, and asked him to verify his story with God. Sure enough, Saint Peter checked and came back. "You're right. You are allowed one bag, but I have to check its contents before letting you in." Peter opened the suitcase to inspect the items that the man found too precious to leave behind and exclaimed, "Oh, you brought pavement?"

REFLECTION

The most precious things in the world are less than insignificant when compared to what awaits us in heaven. Saint Paul can only say, "No eye has seen, nor ear heard, nor the human heart conceived, what God has prepared for those who love him" (1 Corinthians 2:9).

309. LIFE AFTER DEATH   *Lying*

"Do you believe in life after death?" the boss asked one of his employees. "Yes, sir," the new employee replied. "I do too," said the boss, "especially since yesterday." "What do you mean?" asked the puzzled employee. "Because after you left early yesterday to go to your grandmother's funeral, she stopped in to see you!"

REFLECTION

Did the grandmother know that her grandchild had lied to the employer in order to leave work early? Did the employee appreciate the harm he did to his position at the company, damaging his credibility? (Would the employer give him time off at some future time when his grandmother or other relative really died?) Did he consider the consequences of his sin? Did he appreciate the immorality of his act, the violation of God's (Exodus 20:16) and the natural law's command not to lie?

310. AT YOUR FUNERAL   *Judging*

In the first hours of his new parish assignment, the pastor went to a funeral home to attend the wake of a parishioner. He knew nothing about the man whose body lay in the casket. So he asked those present to offer some thoughts. "Is there anyone here who can say something good about this man?" Silence. He went on, "Is there someone here who can say something worthwhile about this man?" More silence. For a third time he asked, "Is there someone who can say anything at all about this man?" Finally an elderly gentleman stood up and said, "We are glad that he is finally dead. He was an absolutely terrible person."

REFLECTION

One would hope that the same would never be said of us. It's one thing to pray for a loved one who has died, or even to rejoice at the death of a loved one who lived a long and faithful life. It is something much different to pray, hope, rejoice or be glad at the demise of another human being who may have been less than faithful. Whatever we may think of the person and the life he or she led, that person was the object of God's love. Our task is to be instruments of God's love and mercy, and not of God's judgment. We leave that to the Creator. "There is one lawgiver and judge who is able to save and to destroy. So who, then, are you to judge your neighbor?" (James 4:12).

311. HEAVEN ON EARTH   *Creation, environment*

There was a man who was obsessed with the idea of going to heaven to escape this cruel world. Finally he died, and an angel walked him around to see the beautiful sights, including the sandy seashore, the majestic mountains, the beautiful flowers, and the lovely sunsets. The man exclaimed, "Isn't heaven wonderful!" The angel replied, "This isn't heaven. It's the world you lived in but you never really saw."

REFLECTION

For generations busy people have been advised to "stop and smell the roses." The poet Gerard Manley Hopkins has reminded us that the world is "charged with the grandeur of God." Joseph Mary Plunkett says the same in his poem "I See His Blood Upon the Rose." We live in a world that is obsessed with busyness. Ironically, the more inventions and discoveries that come our way promising to help lighten our workload invade our precious time even more. Like those who lose their hearing or eyesight, many of us go from place to place and from task to task with such intensiveness that we often miss the good things that God places in our path along the way. Isn't it sad that we take for granted, or perhaps don't even notice, the little bit of heaven that God has already blessed us with?

312. DIDN'T RECOGNIZE YOU   *Stewardship*

A middle-aged woman had a heart attack and was taken to the hospital. While in surgery, she had a near-death experience. She saw God and asked if this was the end of her life on earth. God said "No" and explained that she had another thirty to forty years to live. Since she had that much time, she figured that she might as well make the most of it, so, after her recovery, she decided to stay in the hospital and have a face lift and a tummy tuck. She even had someone come in to change her hair color. When she walked out of the hospital, she was struck and killed by a speeding ambulance. She arrived in front of God again and said, "I thought you said I had another thirty to forty years." God replied, "Sorry. I didn't recognize you."

REFLECTION

It is one thing to keep ourselves in good shape, to take reasonable care of our body, which is a temple of the Holy Spirit and the instrument with which we work for God's kingdom. It is another thing, out of vanity or envy, to take drastic measures to change the way God made us. As with other areas of faith, our approach in these matters should be marked with modesty and moderation.

313. SOMEONE ELSE'S TALENT   *Creation, stewardship*

Do you ever wish you had someone else's talent or ability? Can we all be actors? Athletes? Poets? Astronauts? Professors? Carpenters? Admirals? The created world reveals unimaginable diversity, and that includes humans and their talents.

REFLECTION

Saint Paul tells the Corinthians that we are all meant to be united as one human family, as the one body of Christ, baptized into one Spirit. Each of us is given dif-

ferent talents and abilities. "Now you are the body of Christ and individually members of it. And God has appointed in the church first apostles, second prophets, third teachers; then deeds of power, then gifts of healing, forms of assistance, forms of leadership, various kinds of tongues. Are all apostles? Are all prophets? Are all teachers? Do all work miracles? Do all possess gifts of healing? Do all speak in tongues? Do all interpret?" (1 Corinthians 12:27–30). We each have different talents. If we had the same talent, we would be in sad shape, lacking diversity. We must, in God's name, discover our talents and develop them for God's kingdom. The church and the world need our unique contributions. Let someone else play the guitar or fly to the moon. We have been created by God to be who we are. Without applying our abilities, the world would be less blessed.

314. DAILY OFFERING   *Spirituality, witness*

O Jesus, through the Immaculate Heart of Mary, I offer you my prayers, works, joys, and sufferings of this day in union with the Holy Sacrifice of the Mass throughout the world. I offer them for all of the intentions of your Sacred Heart: the salvation of souls, reparation for sin, the reunion of all Christians. I offer them for the intentions of our bishops and of all Apostles of Prayer, and in particular for those recommended by our Holy Father this month.

REFLECTION

More important than a particular formula is the spirit behind it. The one who prays, "Lord Jesus, with you I offer myself to the Father this day," and really means it, is a genuine apostle of prayer. The formula we call the daily offering, however, has these advantages: 1) It unites us with Jesus in his Eucharistic offering. 2) It is inspired by God's love for us revealed in the Sacred Heart of Jesus. 3) It invokes the intercession of Mary. 4) It shows loyal concern for the church and her apostolic goals. 5) It puts into practice the spirit of prayer. The daily offering is more than a prayer; it is a way life. Those who recite this prayer are pledging themselves to live their lives in union with Christ and as witnesses to Christ. You cannot say this prayer with sincerity unless you are determined that every action of your day is going to be done in conformity with the will of God. The fullest of your daily offering comes only when you live your life in such a way that you are making Christ present to the world.

315. BEST POSITIONS FOR PRAYER *Prayer*

A priest, a minister, and a guru sat discussing the best posture for prayer while a telephone repairman worked nearby. "Kneeling is definitely the best way to pray," the priest said. "No," said the minister. "I get the best results standing with my hands outstretched to heaven." "You're both wrong," the guru said. "The most effective prayer position is lying on the floor." The repairman could contain himself no longer. "Hey, fellas," he interrupted. "The best praying I ever did was when I was hanging upside down from a telephone pole."

REFLECTION

More important than a prayerful position is prayerful disposition. When things are going well, it is easy to forget about God. At least it is easy for those who really don't love God preeminently as they should. Some people just use God as they would use a 24/7 ATM. Just slide in the card, press the right numbers, and out comes the money. Then just walk away without even a thank you and without giving the money machine another thought until next time you need it. Do we ever approach prayer that way? The disposition that lies behind this narrow concept of prayer is that prayer is only for asking. Is that all we have to say to God? Where is the prayer in our life that praises God, thanks God, adores God, acknowledges God's presence, expresses sorrow for sin? Read the Our Father as Jesus presents it to us in Matthew 6:9–13.

316. PRAYING FOR GRANDMA *Prayer*

A mother encouraged her five-year-old daughter to pray for her grandmother on the occasion of her birthday. Her mother said to her, "Dear, you must pray to God to bless your grandma, that she may live to be very old." The child looked with some surprise at her mother. The mother continued, "Well, will you not pray to God to bless your grandma, that she may become very old?" "Oh, Mommy!" said the child, "She is very old already, I would rather pray that she may become young."

REFLECTION

Children have a way of seeing things in a different, perhaps even in a better or more optimistic light. If only we could see through the eyes of a child, especially in our prayer, we just might acquire an attitude of prayer allowing us to seek not only the difficult but maybe even the impossible. Could it be that this is why Jesus insisted, "Let the little children come to me; do not stop them; for it is to such as these that the kingdom of God belongs. Truly I tell you, whoever does not receive the kingdom of God as a little child will never enter it" (Mark 10:14–15).

317. A PRIME DUTY   *Prayer*

A young man was recently sitting at the same desk beside which his mother had spent the last five years of her life in a recliner. Due to her illness, she found it difficult to lie down. As he stared at the desk, the young man's eyes were drawn to a wall hanging. Hanging on the wall behind the desk were these framed, hand-lettered words in gold: "Prayer is our first duty in life and to plead a lack of time for it is an insult to God."

REFLECTION

The words on the wall hanging say it all. Indeed, our prime duty in everyday life is prayer. We may recognize the need to pray but our busy lives have a way of interfering with the daily prayer that should mark our lives. We know we need to pray, that prayer is valuable, but we are masters of putting prayer off to another time. Because of our lack of disciplined habits of prayer—having definite times to pray, even if briefly—each day may well end without prayer. But we should also think of prayer moments throughout the day. Saint Paul implores us to "pray without ceasing" (1 Thessalonians 5:17), which we do when we are momentarily aware of God's presence during the day, when we briefly thank God, when we utter a word of regret to God for an unkind word.

318. PRAISE THE LORD   *Speech, truth*

A man's horse expired when he was far from civilization. He finally came upon a farm that had plenty of horses and asked the farmer if he could borrow one. "Well, son," the farmer said, "There is only one I can lend you, because all the others are working on the farm. It is a special horse, so you must take special care to follow the instructions to the letter. If you want to make it go forward, say, 'Praise the Lord', and if you want it to stop, you must say, 'Amen.'" So the man consented, climbed on, and shouted, "Praise the Lord." The horse galloped along, picked up speed after a time and didn't stop. By this time the man could not remember what to say to make it stop. He saw a cliff directly in front of him. Then he started to pray intently, concluding with the word, "Amen." The faithful horse stopped right at the edge of the cliff. The man breathed a sigh of relief and shouted joyfully, "Praise the Lord."

REFLECTION

What we say, how we speak can be very important. How we use or misuse words can have lasting consequences, both good and bad. The words we use—to console, to build a relationship, to bear witness to the truth—can be misunderstood or misinterpreted, even when they are meant to be kind. How important it is, then, to be careful in what we say, for once the words have passed our lips, they are hard to take back. Because we possess, through baptism, "the Spirit of truth who comes from the Father" (John 15:26), all the words from our mouths must build up the kingdom of God.

319. PRAY FOR ME   *Prayer, Communion of Saints*

One Sunday morning at the parish, a young child was "acting up" during Mass, squirming and fidgeting. The parents did their best to maintain order in the pew but were losing the battle, so the father finally picked the little fellow up and walked down the aisle toward the exist. Just before reaching the safety of the narthex, the little one called loudly to the congregation, "Pray for me! Pray for me!"

REFLECTION

Three simple words, "Pray for me," are a request made often among those who anticipate trouble and seek the prayer of others on their behalf, such as the young child at the Sunday liturgy. We use the familiar terminology at every Mass in the penitential rite: "I ask…you, my brothers and sisters, to pray for me to the Lord Our God." Asking for the prayer of others is the Communion of saints in practice and the continuation of the ancient Christian practice we read about in the epistles. In 1 Thessalonians 5:25, Saint Paul, writes, "Beloved, pray for us."

320. NOW I LAY ME DOWN TO SLEEP *Prayer, witness*

On Mother's Day, a mother was reminiscing about things her children did many years ago. She recalled what happened one night when one of her four children was saying his nighttime prayers: "Now I lay me down to sleep, I pray the Lord my soul to keep. When he hollers let him go, eenie, meanie, miny, mo."

REFLECTION

Although a child might confuse the words of a memorized prayer with a memorized nursery rhyme, a nursery rhyme is no more a prayer than the pledge of allegiance. The lesson for the young boy is not only the prayer itself, but the habit of prayer. Parents must never give up teaching their children simple prayers from a young age, but in doing so they should also be gradually helping them to understand what prayer is and how important it is. Children may become confused or uninterested, but the parents' persistence—and example—will succeed.

321. MORNING PRAYER   *Prayer*

Dear God, so far today, I've done very well. I haven't gossiped. I haven't lost my temper. I haven't been greedy, grumpy, nasty, selfish, or overindulgent. But Lord, in a few minutes I'm going to get out of bed, and from then on I'm probably going to need a lot more help. Thank you. In Jesus' name. Amen.

REFLECTION

God wants us to pray that we do his will, live according to Jesus' example, as we begin our daily routine and face the challenges of the day. That is why in the Lord's Prayer (Matthew 6:9–13; Luke 11:2–4), Jesus told us to pray, "Thy will be done on earth as it is in heaven." Saint Matthew tells us in his gospel that on one occasion Jesus spoke intimately of those who strive to live as God wants us to: "For whoever does the will of my Father in heaven is my brother and sister and mother" (Matthew 12:50).

322. GOD'S ANSWERING MACHINE
Prayer, divine love

Imagine if God decided to install an automated answering machine. Imagine praying and hearing this: "Thank you for calling my Father's house. Please select one of the following options: Press 1 for requests. Press 2 for thanksgiving. Press 3 for complaints. For all other inquiries, press 4." What if God responded with the familiar excuse, "All the angels are helping other customers right now. Please stay on the line and your call will be answered in the order it was received. For answers to nagging questions about the dinosaurs, the age of the earth, and where Noah's ark is located, wait until you get here. We are closed for the weekend. Please call again on Monday."

REFLECTION

There is no such thing as calling on God too often. We only need to call once, and God hears us, God is always listening. There is never a busy signal. God takes each call and knows each caller personally. And yet, some of us pray as if we needed to persuade an unjust God to somehow change and become merciful. When we doubt our heavenly Father's concern and attention toward us, we need only recall the words of Jesus: "Is there anyone among you who, if your child asks for a fish, will give a snake instead of a fish? Or if the child asks for an egg, will give a scorpion? If you then, who are evil, know how to give good gifts to your children, how much more will the heavenly Father give the Holy Spirit to those who ask him!" (Luke 11:11–13).

323. PRAYING AT ANY TIME   *Prayer*

There was an elderly woman who found herself homebound and no longer as active as she once was. She continued to knit afghans for her friends, however, and as she did she would meditate on the joyful, sorrowful, glorious, and luminous mysteries of Jesus' life. In that way, she explained, "I can pray, work, and enjoy myself, all at the same time."

REFLECTION

Prayer is an essential element of our spiritual life. It is not something to be engaged in just when we are worried or when we have reached the end of our resources. Prayer is making contact with God, which we can do at length or fleetingly. That is why Saint Paul could say, "Pray without ceasing" (1 Thessalonians 5:17). The story of praying while knitting afghans reminds us that, while prayer is very necessary, it can also be very easy. We can pray to God in any language. In fact, we don't have to use any language at all; no words are necessary. For prayer can be simply the raising of the mind and heart to God, being aware of the divine presence, being silent before God, listening. We can pray to God at any time, have a hearing at any time—while waiting for a traffic light, walking down the street, waiting for the toast. God is ever ready to converse with us.

324. HAROLD BE THY NAME   *Our Father*

A father was listening to his little daughter Judy praying. "Dear Harold," Judy prayed, "please bless Mommy and Daddy and…" At this point, the father interrupted, "Wait a minute, Sweetie. Why are you calling God 'Harold'?" The little girl looked up and said, "That's what they call God at Mass. You know, Daddy, the prayer we all say, 'Our Father who art in heaven, Harold be thy name.…'"

REFLECTION

In the Lord's Prayer we pray "hallowed be thy name," easily misunderstood by the child as "Harold be thy name." We are all familiar with the prayer (Matthew 6:9–13; Luke 11:2–4), and, in fact, so used to saying it that we may not always realize that it is the perfect prayer. It contains seven petitions that spiritual writers have noted include the core of what we should ask of God: awareness that we are children of God, reverence for the person of God, desire for the establishment of the kingdom and living according to God's will, the food and clothing and shelter we require, forgiveness, protection. That is why the church has us recite it at every celebration of the Eucharist. If we ever wonder how to pray, we can do nothing better than to recite the Lord's Prayer sincerely and fervently.

325. READING OUR HEARTS   *Prayer*

A grandfather overheard his granddaughter repeating the alphabet in reverent, hushed tones. "What are you doing?" he asked. "I'm praying, Grandpa," she said. "I can't think of the right words, so I just say all the letters. God will put them together for me; God knows what's in my heart."

REFLECTION

The girl has it right, knowing instinctively that God knows our minds and hearts. But she is wrong to think that our prayer needs the "right words." Jesus has told us that when we pray, "do not heap up empty phrases.…Your Father knows what you need before you ask him" (Matthew 6:7–8).

326. PRAYING FOR PATIENCE   *Repentance, prayer*

Jimmy had been misbehaving and was sent to his room and told to pray. After a while he emerged and told his mother that he had thought it over and then prayed. Impressed, the mother said, "I'm glad. Good job. As I said, praying for God's help will help you to behave." "Oh, I didn't ask God to help me not misbehave," said Jimmy. "I prayed that you become more patient in putting up with me when I do misbehave."

REFLECTION

The boy's prayer may have been misdirected but beneficial nonetheless. What parent would not want to be more understanding and patient? What is missing in Jimmy's prayer is his willingness to surrender himself to God, trusting that God will touch his heart and enable him to turn his behavior around. Even his desire to change begins with God. Isaiah (6:5–8) understood this, as did Saint Peter (Luke 5:8–10) and Saint Paul (1 Corinthians 15:8–10).

327. GOD ISN'T DEAF   *Prayer, ministry*

A little boy was kneeling beside his bed with his mother and grandmother and softly praying, "Dear God, please bless Mommy and Daddy and all the family and please give me a good night's sleep." Suddenly he looked up and shouted, "And, Lord, don't forget to give me a bicycle for my birthday!" "There is no need to shout like that," said his mother. "God isn't deaf." "No," said the little boy, "but Grandma is."

REFLECTION

The little boy understood implicitly what many of us only learn later in life, that God may use others to ensure that a prayer does not go unanswered. We may all be instruments of God for building the kingdom of God, even when we are not aware of it: in heroic acts of love and small ones, daily prayer, concern for the poor and oppressed, loving speech, and so on.

328. THANKS FOR THE FOOD   *Prayer*

A four-year-old boy was asked to offer grace before Christmas dinner. The family members bowed their heads in expectation. The boy thanked God for all his friends, naming them one by one. Then he thanked God for Mommy, Daddy, his brother and sister, Grandma and Grandpa, and all his aunts and uncles. Then he began to thank God for the food. He gave thanks for the turkey, the stuffing, the fruit salad, the cranberry sauce, the pies, the cakes, the bread. Then he paused, and everyone waited and waited. After a long silence, the young child looked up at his mother and asked, "If I thank God for the broccoli, won't he know I'm lying?"

REFLECTION

In addition to his example that there already is the ability to distinguish right from wrong at an early age, the boy also teaches us something quite valuable about prayer: It is authentic when each word or each sentiment is intentionally offered, when it comes from a person's core and is not simply spoken as an empty, memorized formula. We might think of John Henry Newman's description of prayer, "Heart speaks to heart." Even more, consider these words of Jesus, "Come away to a deserted place all by yourselves and rest a while" (Mark 6:31).

329. THEY DON'T LISTEN   *Prayer, faith*

There is a story told of a poor boy who had no shoes. A neighbor saw him praying and immediately made fun of him, "You pray so much. If God really existed, he would tell someone to buy you a pair of shoes." "I'm sure God does," replied the boy, "but they don't listen."

REFLECTION

Of its very nature, prayer always "works," if by that word we mean that we are in touch with God, reaching out to God in some way, communing with God. Whether it works in a prayer of petition depends on several factors, especially our faith and persistence in praying—and God's idea of what is good for us. "Ask, and it will be given to you; search, and you will find; knock, and the door will be opened for you" (Matthew 7:7).

330. PRAISE THE LORD   *Instruments of God, ministry*

An elderly woman was well known for her faith and for her boldness in proclaiming it. She would stand on her front porch and shout, "Praise the Lord!" Next door to her lived an atheist who would get angry at her proclamations and shout, "There ain't no Lord!" Hard times set in on the elderly woman, and she prayed for God to send her some assistance. She stood on her porch and prayed out loud, "Praise the Lord. God, I need food! I'm having a hard time. Please, Lord, send me some groceries!" The next morning she went out on her porch and found a large bag of groceries and shouted, "Praise the Lord." The neighbor jumped from behind a bush and said, "Aha! I told you there was no Lord. I bought those groceries. God didn't." The woman started jumping up and down and clapping her hands. "Praise the Lord. God not only sent me groceries, but made the devil pay for them. Praise the Lord!"

REFLECTION

Prayer is often answered through the human intervention of others, knowingly or unknowingly. In an incarnational, sacramental world, it is part of God's ordinary dealings with us to use people and things as instruments to bring about his will. We are the hands and feet of God, and in the ordinary course of events, if we don't do something as agents of God, it doesn't get done. Even if we are not aware of our role—and very often we're not—we are instruments of carrying out the will of God, clay in the hands of the Potter. "Like clay in the hand of the potter, to be molded as he pleases, so all are in the hand of their Maker, to be given whatever he decides" (Sirach 33:13). Through the bold faith of the elderly woman, she becomes a catalyst enabling her atheist neighbor to perform an act of charity, even though the neighbor's motivation might be questionable. This is a beginning, however. It is an opportunity for the neighbor to make a new decision for God.

331. THE BIBLE   *Bible, apostles*

The following was found written on a scrap of paper in an old Bible: "This book contains the mind of God, the state of [humans], the way of salvation, the doom of sinners, and the happiness of believers. Its doctrines are holy, its precepts binding….Read it to be wise; believe it to be safe; and practice it to be holy. It contains light to direct you; food to support you; and comfort to cheer you. It is the traveler's map; the pilgrim's staff; the pilot's compass; the soldier's sword; and the Christian's charter. Here heaven is opened, and the gates of hell disclosed. Christ is its grand subject; our good its design; and the glory of God its end. It should fill the memory; rule the heart; and guide the feet. Read it slowly, frequently, prayerfully. It is given to you in life, will be opened at the judgment, and be remembered forever. 'Oh, the depth of the riches of the wisdom and of the knowledge of God!' (Romans 11:33)."

REFLECTION

Throughout the whole world, day after day, year after year, century after century, the same Holy Spirit who inspired the biblical writers and compilers awaits the faithful proclamation of the word of God to those who are on their earthly journey. Many men and women have, one after another, down to our day, proclaimed the Scriptures in order that you and I might receive the blessing of faith. We can thank the Lord Jesus whose prayer was effective: "I ask not only on behalf of these, but also on behalf of those who will believe in me through their word" (John 17:20). Whose word is Jesus referring to? The word of the apostles passed on from generation to generation through the successors of the apostles.

332. SPREADING THE WORD   *Inspiration, Bible*

There was a Christian woman who had to do a lot of traveling for her business. Flying made her nervous so she always brought her Bible along to read, and this gave her great comfort. On one trip she was sitting next to a nonbeliever, who gave a little chuckle when he noticed her devotional reading. After a while he turned to her and asked, "You don't really believe all that stuff, do you?" The woman replied, "Of course I do. It's the Bible." He said, "Well, what about that guy who was swallowed by that whale?" She replied "Oh, Jonah. Yes, I believe that; it's in the Bible." He asked, "Well, how do you suppose he survived all that time inside the whale?" The woman said, "Well, I don't really know. I guess when I get to heaven I'll ask him." "What if he isn't in heaven?" the man asked sarcastically. "Then you can ask him," replied the woman.

REFLECTION

The woman's perspective on the Bible is on the literalistic side (as is the skeptic's), but the larger picture is of a person who believes that the Bible is the word of God, that God had a clear hand in its creation and development. She approaches it with faith, confident that the living word of God has something to say to her. "All scripture is inspired by God and is useful for teaching, for reproof, for correction, and for training in righteousness" (2 Timothy 3:16).

333. WHO'D BELIEVE IT?   *Faith, trust*

One day when a mother had asked her ten-year-old son what he learned in religion class, the boy replied, "Well, the teacher told us about the Israelites crossing the Red Sea. They were being held captive by the Egyptians, so God sent Moses behind enemy lines to rescue them. When the Israelites got to the Red Sea, Moses ordered the Marines to build a pontoon bridge. Then, after they crossed over, they looked back and saw the Egyptian tanks coming. Quick as a flash, Moses picked up his radio and asked the Air Force to send F-16s to blow up the bridge so the Egyptians couldn't catch up." At this point the mother exclaimed, "But Bobby, is that really the way the teacher told you the story?" "Well, not exactly," Bobby admitted. "But if I told it her way, no one would ever believe it."

REFLECTION

Moses encountered God at the burning bush. At God's command he led the people of Israel "out of Egypt" (Exodus 13:16), the land of bondage. He led them in the desert for forty years, pleading with them, chiding them, praying for them (Exodus 16:35). He went to the top of Mount Sinai to receive the ten commandments (Exodus 19:20). After all he had done—and this may be harder to believe than his great accomplishments—he went to the top of Mount Nebo, saw the promised land, but never entered it (Deuteronomy 34:1–5). He was to die "there in the land of Moab." Why was he not to enter it? "You shall not cross over," God told him. Can we face a disappointment like that and be at peace?

334. YOU NEVER KNOW   *Providence*

A little girl sat on her grandmother's lap to listen to the creation account from the book of Genesis. As the creation story unfolded, the kind woman, noticing that the child was unusually attentive, asked, "What do you think of it, dear?" "Oh, I think it's great," replied the child, "You never know what God is going to do next."

REFLECTION

Like the child in the story, or like any childlike person, if we place ourselves total-ly in the arms of divine providence, we will always have as the overriding goal of life to "magnify the Lord" (Luke 1:46) and God alone. We can never imagine what God might do next, but when we submit ourselves to God's holy will in complete trust, we can be certain of this, that God will be faithful and take care of us.

335. DEVIL'S BEATITUDES   *Devil*

"The Devil's Beatitudes" has made the rounds on the Internet. It reads as follows:

Blessed are those who are too tired, too busy, too distracted to spend an hour once a week with their fellow Christians in church—for they are my best workers.

Blessed are those who wait to be asked and expect to be thanked—for I can use them in my business.

Blessed are those who are touchy. Soon they will stop going to church—for they will be my missionaries.

Blessed are those who sow gossip and trouble—for they are my beloved children.

Blessed are those who have no time to pray—for they are my prey.

Blessed are those who when they see evil being done, do nothing—for they are my secret agents.

Blessed are you when you think these beatitudes have everything to do with other people and nothing to do with you. I've got room for you in my garden.

REFLECTION

The devil's beatitudes are certainly not blessings as are the beatitudes that mark the opening of the Sermon on the Mount in the Gospel of St. Matthew (5:3–10) or as they are found in Luke 6:17–26. Rather, they are character statements about those who are welcomed guests in the garden of evil. Children of God should never entertain these statements of godlessness. As well, we should never assume the devil has no interest in us or that we are out of the devil's grasp. Wherever a human person exists, the devil is close by, waiting to lure him or her away from God.

336. HEALING HER BROKEN HEART   *Mary, Gospel*

A Japanese woman who had lost her husband sought healing for her broken heart. One day a neighbor brought her a worn little pamphlet and said, "I found this in the street. Somebody must have dropped it. I read it. There is a wonderful story in it of a man who helps those who are unhappy. I thought of you. It might do you good." The pamphlet was a copy of St. Luke's gospel. The Japanese woman not only read it but found her life changed by Christ whom she discovered in its pages.

REFLECTION

It should come as no surprise that the Gospel of St. Luke was the source of Christian insight and inspiration for the Japanese widow. Saint Luke's gospel shows special sensitivity to evangelizing gentiles. Luke's is the gospel of the poor and of social justice. It is also referred to as the gospel of prayer and the gospel of women, with special attention paid especially to Mary. It is only in Luke's gospel that we hear the story of the Annunciation (1:26–56), the Magnificat, or Canticle of Mary (1:46–55), the Presentation (2:22–40), and the story of Jesus' disappearance in Jerusalem (2:41–52). It is Saint Luke that we have to thank for the "Hail Mary, full of grace" (Luke 1:28), spoken at the Annunciation and "Blessed are you among women, and blessed is the fruit of your womb" (Luke 1:42), spoken by her cousin Elizabeth.

337. DRIVING ADAM AND EVE   *Scripture*

The first-grade teacher carefully explained the Genesis story of Adam and Eve being expelled from the garden. Following the story, the children were asked to draw a picture that would illustrate what they heard. Little Bobby was most interested and drew a picture of a car with three people in it. In the front seat, behind the wheel was a man and in the back seat, a man and a woman. The catechist was at a loss to understand how this illustrated the lesson of Adam and Eve. But little Bobby was prompt with his explanation: "This is God driving Adam and Eve out of the garden," he pointed out (Genesis 3:24).

REFLECTION

Experience often helps us understand the meaning of well-known stories, especially those found in the scriptures. It helps us grasp the meaning in Scripture that God intended. Without such experience, it is possible to miss the entire meaning of the story, as did the young artist in the faith formation class. How true it is that words and phrases can mean different things to different people. How important it is, then, to correctly discern the meaning behind such words and phrases. Without this, we might travel down a path never intended and in the process miss the entire point of the story.

338. WEDDING AT CANA   *Matrimony*

The small town of Cana made famous in the Gospel of St. John still exists today. The famous wedding at Cana took place on the third day, which means that it took place on a Tuesday. According to Jewish tradition, Tuesday is considered more blessed because in the Genesis creation story God looks back each day and sees that what he created is good. The word "good" in Hebrew is *tov* and appears on Tuesday twice (Genesis 1:9–13) and every other day only once. For this reason, the Jews have seen Tuesday as a more privileged day, a day that was popular for the celebration of marriage in the time of Jesus. Even today, most Jews marry on Tuesday. In the Gospel of John (2:1–11) we read that Mary came down from Nazareth to Cana and Jesus came with her. There was no wine left. At such a wedding, a meal would not be provided because food was out of the question unless the family was very rich. Instead, all the guests would come to toast the newly married couple. Now there were so many people coming to this poor family wedding that there was no more wine left. Jesus asked the servants to fill jugs with water and, at Mary's suggestion, Jesus converts it into wine.

REFLECTION

What a great honor it was for this young couple in Cana to have Jesus present at their wedding. What tremendous blessings must have occurred following the presence of such a guest. All couples who receive the sacrament of matrimony have the same honor and receive the same tremendous blessings. If a marriage is to be a happy one, Jesus must be invited to the wedding, must be really present in it, and be the center of the couple's lives throughout their married life. It takes three to make a Christian marriage.

339. TEN COMMANDMENTS   *Marital fidelity*

A second-grade religious education class was studying the Ten Commandments (Exodus 20:2–17). Ready to discuss the last one, the teacher asked if anyone could remember what it was. Susie raised her hand, stood tall, and exclaimed, "You shall not take the covers off your neighbor's wife."

REFLECTION

This amusing response might be considered a legitimate variation of the tenth commandment, "You shall not covet your neighbor's wife" (Exodus 20:17). The same message that the commandment is meant to communicate is conveyed by the child's answer. In other words, the one who removes the covers from a neighbor's wife is probably already violating this commandment.

340. ACTS 2:38 *Scripture*

An elderly woman had just returned to her home from an evening church service when she was startled by an intruder. As she caught the man in the act of robbing her home of its valuables, she yelled, "Stop! Acts 2:38!" ("Repent and be baptized, in the name of Jesus Christ so that your sins may be forgiven.") The burglar stopped in his tracks. The woman calmly called the police and explained what she had done. As the officer placed the man in handcuffs, he asked the burglar, "Why did you just stand there? All the old lady did was yell Scripture at you." "Scripture?" replied the burglar. "She said she had an axe and two .38s!"

REFLECTION

"What you bring away from the Scriptures depends to some extent on what you carry to them." This point is well taken in this encounter. The man's behavior did not reflect a life susceptible to God's word and, as such, there was no appreciation for the sacred text, even when the elderly homeowner shouted it at him. Had she even quoted the entire verse, would it have landed on fertile soil, or on rocky soil, as described in the Parable of the Sower (Matthew 13:3–9, Mark 4:3–8, and Luke 8:5–8)?

341. MOSES AND JESUS *Name of Jesus*

A man broke into a house and was creeping across the pitch-black living room when he heard a voice whisper, "Watch out, Jesus is behind you!" Startled, he turned on his flashlight and breathed a sigh of relief to see a parrot in front of him. Again the parrot whispered, "Watch out, Jesus is behind you." The robber said to the parrot, "What's your name then?" and the parrot replied "Moses." The robber laughed and said, "Who on earth would call a parrot Moses?" and the parrot replied, "The same one who would call a rottweiler Jesus!"

REFLECTION

Names mean different things to different people. The names of Moses and Jesus are no exception. In the story, we notice that they are names given to two family pets. The Scriptures give their names far greater prestige and respect. And for the centuries since they have been known among us, their names have been held in the highest esteem and revered as sacred, especially Jesus', of course, the "name that is above every name" (Philippians 2:9).

342. CAN GOD USE YOU?   *Ministry*

The next time you feel that you're unworthy, unfit to be a disciple, that God can't use you, just remember: Noah was a drunk…Abraham was too old…Isaac was a daydreamer…Jacob was a liar…Leah was ugly…Joseph was abused…Moses was a murderer…Gideon was afraid…Sampson was a womanizer…Rahab was a prostitute…Jeremiah and Timothy were too young…David had an affair and was a murderer…Elijah was suicidal…Isaiah preached naked…Jonah ran from God…Naomi was a widow…Job went bankrupt…John the Baptist ate bugs…Peter denied Jesus…the disciples fell asleep while praying…Martha worried about everything…Mary Magdalene was demon-possessed…the Samaritan Woman was divorced several times…Zacchaeus was too short…Paul was too religious…Timothy had an ulcer…and Lazarus was dead.

REFLECTION

God knows us more than we know ourselves. Like those well-known people in Scripture, God uses us, not because we are perfect, but despite the fact that we are not. We need only surrender our misgivings and feelings of inadequacy to the One who is, and God will lead us where he wants us to go. "In Christ we have also obtained an inheritance, having been destined according to the purpose of him who accomplishes all things according to his counsel and will" (Ephesians 1:11). We cannot try to plead, as Jeremiah did, that we don't know how to speak, that we are too young. The God who knew us before we were formed in the womb calls us to be instruments for the kingdom (Jeremiah 1:5–6).

343. IMPOSSIBLE DREAM   *Dreams, idealism, kingdom*

Miguel de Cervantes is to Spain what William Shakespeare, who died in the same year, is to England. Writing of victory, defeat, success, love, and tragedy, his stories always portray lives that possess self-confidence, as well as self-defiance. In his book *Don Quixote*, Cervantes sparks a love for the hero's idealism, his love for self and others. When the book became a Broadway show, *Man of La Mancha*, the song "Impossible Dream" depicted the idealism and self-confidence of Don Quixote. Only those who are self-confident find no dream impossible to dream, since the appreciation of self and recognition of the potential in self is already known.

190

The subject of dreams is a familiar biblical theme. Many of us recall the more famous dreams in Scripture, including the dream of Joseph, the dearest son of Jacob, in Genesis 37:5–36 and the dream of Joseph, the foster father of Jesus, in Matthew 1:20–22. As children, we may have been reprimanded for entering into "useless" daydreaming, but, as adults, we know that to "dream dreams" (Acts 2:17) may be counted among the precious gifts from a loving Father in heaven. What one might see as an impossible "pipe dream" can be transformed into one that is quite possible if we commit ourselves to dreaming with Christ to establish a kingdom of justice, love, and peace.

344. FATTED CALF   *Forgiveness, compassion*

The fourth-grade faith formation class was discussing the story of the prodigal son (Luke 15:11–32). Wishing to emphasize the resentful attitude of the elder brother, emphasis was placed on this part of the parable. After describing the rejoicing of the household over the return of the wayward son, the catechist spoke of one who, in the midst of the festivities, failed to share in the jubilant spirit of the occasion. "Can anybody in the class," he asked, "tell me who this was?" Nine-year-old Hanna had been listening sympathetically to the story. She waved her hand in the air. "I know!" she said. "It was the fatted calf."

REFLECTION

The story of the prodigal son is said to be the best-known story in the whole of literature. It is a masterpiece of literary art and skillfully conveys its message(s). Some suggest that the story has been misnamed the story of the prodigal son when, in fact, it is the story of two prodigal sons, as the opening passage of the story suggests, "A man had two sons" (Luke 15:11). There is much in this parable that can easily go unnoticed, such as the fact that no task could be more degrading for a Jew than to feed the pigs (pork) of a Gentile employer, or that the father ran out with open heart to greet his returning son and forgive him. In the end, Jesus is teaching us about the intimate relationship that must exist between the disciple and God, our Father. Anything that disturbs this relationship, whether it is open rebellion (as in the case with the younger son) or prideful independence (as in the case with the older son), causes a rift between the Creator and the creature and diminishes the relationship. Of course, as little Hanna pointed out in our story, the fatted calf also had little reason to celebrate that day.

345. TEETH PROVIDED   *Hell*

An evangelist was preaching a hell, fire, and brimstone sermon and shouted, "I warn you, as the gospel says, there will be weeping and wailing and gnashing of teeth" (Matthew 24:51). At this point an elderly woman in the congregation stood up and shouted, "But, Reverend, I have no teeth." "Madam," replied the evangelist, "teeth will be provided."

REFLECTION

The word of God, both in Sacred Scripture and in the Sacred Tradition of the church, warns us of the eternal destiny prepared for those who reject God's love and walk with the evil one. Hell is not an invention by man but a truth that we discover through God's revelation. Jesus is never timid when warning about the destiny of those who do not choose God. In fact, Jesus makes more references to "hell" in the gospels than to "heaven." Our Lord clearly indicates that the body, as well as the soul, will be subjected to the agonies of Gehenna *(hell) (Matthew 5:29–30, 10:28; Mark 9:43–48). The* Catechism of the Catholic Church *summarizes the teaching on hell: "The teaching of the Church affirms the existence of hell and its eternity. Immediately after death the souls of those who die in a state of mortal sin descend into hell, where they suffer the punishments of hell, 'eternal fire.' The chief punishment of hell is eternal separation from God, in whom alone people can possess the life and happiness for which they were created and for which they long" (no. 1033). Those who consider the existence of hell a matter of fiction would do well to remember that just as the righteous will be given everything needed to enjoy complete happiness in heaven, the unjust will be supplied with all that is needed to suffer the agony of complete and eternal alienation from God.*

346. POTLUCK SUPPER   *Scripture*

A young man was most excited after just getting his driver's permit. He asked his father, who was a permanent deacon, if they could discuss his use of the family car. His father said to him, "I'll make a deal with you. You bring your grades up, study the Bible a little, and get your hair cut and then we'll talk about it." A month later the boy came back and again asked his father if he could use the car. His father said, "Son, I'm very proud of you. You brought your grades up and studied the Bible well, but you still didn't get a hair cut." The young man waited a moment and then replied, "You know, Dad, I've been thinking about that. Samson had long hair. Moses had long hair, Noah had long hair, and even Jesus had long hair. So what's the big deal?" His father thought for a moment and then gave the perfect response, "You're absolutely right about those men who had long hair, but if you really want to go all the way and do what they did, then you can walk as well, since they walked almost everywhere they went."

REFLECTION

The young man was out of his league when he tried to manipulate the Scriptures for his own benefit. If we pick and choose the biblical texts that suit our agendas, we will always be left worse off than when we started. When we approach the inspired texts with the intention of applying God's word to our lives, we must accept the entire text and look for the meaning that the author intended, not just isolated bits and pieces, as if selecting from a table at a potluck supper. We can do this by reading Scripture often, praying and reflecting on the text, consulting church documents, reading commentaries, and participating in Bible study groups. What the inquirer walks away with from the Bible depends greatly on the motivation with which he or she approaches it. We ought to approach Scripture with an openness and acceptance born of the Spirit. "The Lord God has given me the tongue of a teacher, that I may know how to sustain the weary with a word. Morning by morning he wakens—wakens my ear to listen as those who are taught" (Isaiah 50:4).

347. CHOOSING WISELY   *Scripture*

In Paris four employees approached their Christian employer to receive their usual New Year's Eve gifts. "Well, my friends," said the man, "Here are your gifts. You may choose fifteen francs or the Bible." "I don't know how to read," said the first, "so I will take the fifteen francs." "I can read," said the second, "but I have pressing needs." He took the fifteen francs. The third also made the same decision. Next came the fourth, a young lad of fourteen. He observed, "Since you say the book is good, I will take it, and read from it to my mother." He took the

Bible, opened it, and found between the leaves a gold piece of forty francs. The others hung their heads, and the Christian employer told them he was sorry they had not made a better choice.

REFLECTION

It has been said that the Bible is the most popular book sold but the least read book. We choose to read the Bible, to make it our own, because within its pages we find the only inspired text in the history of the world. As Saint Paul advises Saint Timothy, "All scripture is inspired by God and is useful for teaching, for refutation, for correction, and for training in righteousness, so that one who belongs to God may be proficient, equipped for every good work" (2 Timothy 3:16–17). If we apply the teachings to our lives, we soon discover not only why God has given us the precious gift of life, but how we are to live this gift and ultimately find our pilgrim way to God, eternal in heaven. The added bonus for the young boy in the story is that he discovered a gold piece within its pages.

348. MONT BLANC   *Mountains, spirituality*

Located in Chamonix, France, is Mont Blanc, the highest point in the Alps, 15,781 feet. The visitor ascends to the summit in cable cars suspended thousands of feet in the air. The first stop is Terrasse Chamonix. The second (after traveling on a second cable car) is Terrasse Mont Blanc. The third (after an elevator ride) is Terrasse du sommet. Surprisingly, even the elderly go to the top with ease. The air on the top is very thin and almost all who make it this far walk with unsteady legs. The view from start to finish is magnificent. From the summit one can see the small village below and the snow-capped mountains are also most captivating.

REFLECTION

Like Mont Blanc, the mountains depicted in the Holy Scriptures are a sign of solidity and stability. They tower over us, touching the sky and conveying a sense of mystery. They hold a significant place in the history of divine-human relationship. Many have said that the mountain is the point where heaven and earth meet. It was also widely held in Old Testament times that the mountain was the place where God made his presence known to the people; for example, Mount Sinai, from which Moses descended with the Ten Commandments. The most famous moun-

tains in the New Testament include the mountain where the Sermon on the Mount took place (Luke 6:20), the "very high mountain" (Matthew 4:8) where Jesus was tempted by the devil, and Mount Tabor where Jesus' "clothes became dazzling white" during his transfiguration (Matthew 17:1–8).

349. ADAM AND EVE   *Matrimony*

When Adam began coming home late on several occasions, Eve became upset. "You're running around with other women," she charged. "Don't be ridiculous, honey," Adam responded. "You're the only woman on earth." The quarrel continued until Adam fell asleep, only to be awakened by Eve poking him in the chest. "What are you doing?" Adam inquired. "Counting your ribs," responded Eve.

REFLECTION

The most comprehensive and significant contribution to our understanding of marriage comes to us from Pope John Paul II's "theology of the body," consisting of a collection of 129 addresses delivered between September 1979 and November 1984. It provides the most extensive biblical theology of marriage in the history of the church. Among the many themes, we find the notion of trust as a key disposition in every marriage, a disposition that must come from deep within. Without it, one is susceptible to jealousy and rash judgment leading to behavior unbecoming a disciple of Jesus. It is only Christ who can help us restore God's original plan for marriage. We may see in the miracle of the wedding at Cana the story of marital redemption. The point is that when a couple "runs out of the wine" needed to live marriage according to God's original plan, Christ is present to "restore the wine" in abundance (John 2:1–11). As a symbol of divinity, wine symbolizes what God does for us in Christ: He divinizes us.

350. MARK CHAPTER 17   *Lying*

One of the announcements that Father O'Toole made before the end of Sunday Mass was the following: "Next week I plan to preach about the sin of lying. To help you understand my homily, I want you all to read Chapter 17 in St. Mark's Gospel." The next Sunday, as he prepared to deliver his homily, the priest asked for a show of hands. He wanted to know how many had read Mark 17. Several hands went up. The priest smiled and commented, "St. Mark's Gospel has only sixteen chapters. I will now proceed to preach on the sin of lying."

REFLECTION

We may be tested when we least expect it and often justify or excuse our poor behavior with little or no contrition. As Pope John Paul II once pointed out, "An excuse is worse and more terrible than a lie, for an excuse is a lie guarded." It is important for us to consider not only the wisdom of the pope's comment but also the Decalogue (the Ten Commandments). In three Old Testament accounts (Exodus 20:2–17, Exodus 34:12–26, Deuteronomy 5:6–21), Moses received the commandments from God on Mount Sinai and they became the framework of the Mosaic Law. Jesus resumed these commandments in the double precept of love of God and of neighbor and proclaimed them as binding under the New Law in Matthew 19 and in the Sermon on the Mount (Matthew 5). When we consider the commandment that reads "You shall not bear false witness against your neighbor" (Exodus 20:16; Deuteronomy 5:20), we correctly understand that the prohibition against lying is not a suggestion but a divine order. Who would be so bold as to ignore such an order that comes from God?

351. GENESIS TO REVELATION *Scripture*

The newly assigned pastor went out one Saturday to visit his parishioners. At one house, it was obvious that someone was home, but nobody came to the door even though the pastor knocked several times. Finally, the pastor took out his card, wrote out "Revelation 3:20" on the back of it, and stuck it in the door. (Revelation 3:20 reads, "Behold, I stand at the door and knock. If anyone hears my voice and opens the door, (then) I will enter his house and dine with him, and him with me.") The next day, the card turned up in the collection plate. Below the priest's message was written the following notation, "I heard you in the garden; but I was afraid, because I was naked, so I hid myself" (Genesis 3:10).

REFLECTION

God is revealed through the Sacred Scriptures and through the church's ongoing interpretation of Scripture. Yet, even scriptural passages can be manipulated, sometimes humorously, for purposes or meaning never intended by the divine Author, as our story illustrates.

352. SAINT PAUL'S RESUME — *Vocation, ministry*

I am more than fifty years of age. I have never preached in one place for more than three years. In some places, I have left town after my preaching caused riots and disturbances. I must admit that I have been in jail three or four times, but not because of any real wrongdoing. My health is not very good, though I still get a great deal done. The places I have preached in have been small, though located in several large cities. I have not gotten along well with religious leaders in towns where I have preached. In fact, some threatened me and even attacked me physically. I try to keep in touch by writing to the people in the places I have visited. I am not very good at keeping records. I have been known to forget whom I have baptized. However, if you can use me, I will do my best for you.

REFLECTION

Saint Paul can be fittingly spoken of as a one-time zealous Jew, an early convert to Christianity, an apostle, an early Catholic bishop, a prophetic preacher, and an inspired writer of Scripture. Ironically, however, in our present "sophisticated" world Saint Paul's resume would hardly make him eligible to even become a parish volunteer. Sacred Scripture itself echoes this sentiment. For example, in 2 Peter 3:16, Saint Peter comments on Paul's letters. He says, "There are some things in them hard to understand, which the ignorant and unstable twist to their own destruction, as they do the other scriptures." God has accomplished much through Saint Paul. We are most grateful that God is in control and not us.

353. TOUCHING THE POOR — *Ministry, compassion*

Sister Bonnie Steinlage spent twenty-two years as a nursing nun. Things changed on Ash Wednesday in 1986 when she was inspired to become a beautician for the poor after she heard the verse from Matthew 6:17 at Mass: "When you fast and pray, wash your face and groom your hair." Believing that the thing most sorely missed by the downtrodden is the feel of a human touch, Sr. Bonnie soon became a licensed cosmetologist and set up shop at a facility for the homeless in Cincinnati's poorest neighborhood. She calls it skin nourishment. "We all need it. Babies die if they don't get touched. We never outgrow our need to be touched. We never outgrow our need to be patted on the back, to be affirmed," she said. Recalling her first customer as having a tight, short skirt and admitting to taking drugs and being a prostitute, Sister Bonnie admitted, "I'm not used to dealing with people like that." Acknowledging that her particular ministry of hair styling gives her permission to touch another human being, she stated that "many poor people lack being touched in a gentle and kind way and being addressed respectfully with words such as 'How may I help you?'"

REFLECTION

Sister Bonnie saw that poverty has many faces. The poor are not necessarily those without money but those without dreams and without the most basic human need to be touched. Jesus himself seemed to recognize this most basic need to be touched when he allowed an unnamed woman to minister to him with a costly alabaster jar of perfumed oil. Saint Luke tells us, "A woman in the city...brought an alabaster jar of ointment. She stood behind him at his feet, weeping, and began to bathe his feet with her tears and to dry them with her hair. Then she continued kissing his feet and anointing them with the ointment" (Luke 7:37–38). Like the woman in the gospel who touched Jesus, Sr. Bonnie realized that she could touch Christ in the poor by becoming a beautician. She could bring Christ to them through her unusual ministry.

354. PAIN OF BAPTISM   *Liturgy, sacraments*

During the baptism of King Aengus in 450 AD, Saint Patrick leaned on his sharp-pointed crosier and inadvertently stabbed the king in the foot. When the baptism ceremony was over, Patrick, seeing a growing pool of blood, suddenly realized what he had done and begged the king's forgiveness. "Why did you suffer this pain in silence?" he asked. The king replied, "I thought it was part of the ritual."

REFLECTION

For the casual observer and those who are unfamiliar with them, the details of symbolism in church ceremonies and rituals can cause confusion, misunderstanding, and even boredom. The desire of the church, of course, is that the participants are transformed, informed, and inspired through the powerful symbols and language of the rituals. That is why the church calls us to "full, conscious, and active participation" in the liturgy (Vatican II: Constitution on the Sacred Liturgy). We are not to be mere spectators, but thoughtfully carry out our role in the common worship of God at the Eucharist and other sacraments.

355. A CHILD OF GOD   *Baptism*

King Louis IX of France, who died in 1270, was baptized in the castle chapel of Poissy. He was crowned king in the Cathedral at Rheims. However, he felt a greater affection and reverence for the chapel at Poissy than for the Cathedral at Rheims. When asked for the reason for this preference, he responded, "In the castle chapel I received the sacrament of baptism, thereby becoming a child of God. In the Cathedral of Rheims, I received the royal crown, whereby I became King of France. I deem divine sonship a greater dignity than earthly kingship. The dignity of kingship I will lose at the time of my death, whereas, as a child of God, I will obtain eternal happiness."

REFLECTION

King Louis IX of France was correct in recognizing the event of baptism as more meaningful an event than earthly kingship. Baptism is the first and most important of all seven sacraments because, as Jesus tells us, "No one can enter the kingdom of God without being born of water and Spirit" (John 3:5). Without baptism we cannot receive the other sacraments. Baptism takes away original sin and all actual sins, if there are any, and all the temporal punishment due to sin. If a person were to die immediately after being baptized, he or she would go straight to heaven. Baptism also unites us in a special way to Christ. That is why Saint Paul said, "As many of you as were baptized into Christ have clothed yourselves with Christ"(Galatians 3:27). A Christian is a person who has been baptized. For this reason, the outlook of the baptized should be very different from that of an unbaptized person. Because of our baptism, our thinking should always be centered on Christ and the church he founded.

356. FINE, BE AN ATHEIST   *Baptism*

The young son of a Baptist minister was in church one morning when he saw for the first time the rite of baptism by immersion. He was greatly intrigued and the next morning proceeded to baptize his three cats in the bathtub. The first kitten bore it very well, and so did the young cat, but the old family cat rebelled. It struggled, clawed, and tore at him until it finally got away. With considerable effort the boy caught the cat again and proceeded with the ceremony, but again the cat rebelled, clawing at him, spiting, and scratching the child's hands and face. Finally, he dropped the cat on the floor in disgust and said, "Fine, be an atheist."

REFLECTION

The method is questionable, but the point is well taken. We take seriously the command of Jesus when he said, "Very truly, I tell you, no one can see the kingdom of God without being born from above" (John 3:3). And a little later he again says, "Very truly, I tell you, no one can enter the kingdom of God without being born of water and Spirit" (John 3:5). Being conceived and born into the world puts us on the road to life. Being "born again" in baptism puts us on the road to eternal life with God. As with all the sacraments, no one is to be forced to receive baptism "kicking and screaming."

357. SKIPPING MASS   *Eucharist*

A man decided to skip Mass one Sunday and head to the mountains to do some bear hunting. As he rounded the corner on a perilous twist in the trail, he and a bear collided, sending him and his rifle tumbling down the mountainside. Before he knew it, his rifle went one way and he went the other, landing on a rock and breaking both his legs. That was the good news. The bad news was that the ferocious bear began charging at him from a distance, and he couldn't move. "Oh, Lord," the man prayed, "I'm so sorry for skipping Mass today. Please forgive me and grant me just one wish. Please make a Christian out of that bear that's coming at me. Please, Lord!" That very instant, the bear skidded to a halt, fell to its knees, clasped its paws together, and began to pray aloud right at the man's feet. "Dear God," the bear said, "Bless this food I am about to receive."

REFLECTION

Habitually skipping Mass can have devastating long-term effects. Worse than being eaten alive by a bear, our souls can wither from a lack of nourishment not only from not receiving the Body and Blood of Jesus at the Eucharist, but by not being fed with the food that is the word of God proclaimed and preached, and by not associating with the assembly united in faith. As Jesus reminds us, "Very truly, I tell you, unless you eat the flesh of the Son of Man and drink his blood, you have no life in you. Those who eat my flesh and drink my blood have eternal life, and I will raise them up on the last day" (John 6:53–54).

358. FIRST HOLY COMMUNION
Catechizing, Holy Communion, teaching

After he had prepared for several months in the 1960s to receive his First Holy Communion, the special day arrived and the young boy enthusiastically processed toward the priest. While approaching the altar rail he recalled his teacher's instruction, "Do not bite the host but let it melt on your tongue as a sign of reverence for the real presence of the Body and Blood of Jesus you are receiving." Upon receiving communion, the small boy accidentally bit his lip. Noticing the blood, he fainted on the spot assuming that he had inadvertently bit the host causing the body of Jesus to bleed. Many years later this child became a priest.

REFLECTION

In our efforts to catechize and to teach the faith in a complete and comprehensive way we should never assume anything. We sometimes forget to consider the age and imagination of our audience. Teaching the Eucharist in a complete way is important for children and adults. Conceptualizing all there is to understand about the Eucharist in an age-appropriate manner is equally important. This is what Jesus meant when he beckoned, "Let the little children come to me; do not stop them; for it is to such as these that the kingdom of God belongs" (Mark 10:14).

359. I ALREADY BELIEVE   *Real presence*

In the biography of King Louis IX of France we read the story that Mass was celebrated one day at his residence, but in the absence of the king. The words of the consecration had scarcely been pronounced when a wonderful phenomenon occurred. Jesus appeared on the altar in the form of a child. Word was sent immediately to the king that he might witness the miracle. But King Louis remained unmoved. "I firmly believe already," he stated, "that Christ is truly present in the Holy Eucharist. Christ has said it, and that is enough for me. I do not wish to lose the merit of my faith by going to see the miracle." The holy king remained in his room content in his belief, but directed those of his courtiers who had the least doubt in the presence of Christ in the Eucharist to go to the chapel and witness the wonderful power of God.

REFLECTION

In every age people report such phenomena. In our own day there have been reports of apparitions of the Blessed Virgin Mary in countries throughout the world. In recent years, her face is said to have appeared on a pane of glass in Perth Amboy, New Jersey, in a concrete formation under an overpass in Texas, and even on a cheese sandwich later sold on the Internet. Similar reports exist concerning the image of Jesus. Someone reported his image on a tree in East Hartford, Connecticut, on the wall of a carwash in Florida, and on a huge rock somewhere in Canada. As people flock to witness these curious events, it is wise for us to remember the counsel of King Louis IX. It is also more prudent and in our best interest to make our way to a church or chapel where we know the miracle of Christ present in the Eucharist has already taken place and remains present in the tabernacle for our adoration. The same guarantee cannot be said of any other place on earth. It is only at Mass where we know the words, "Do this in remembrance of me" (Luke 22:19), are spoken with authority by Jesus himself.

360. BALL OF WAX   *Identity of Jesus*

The young altar server was always very attentive to the details of the Mass. Once, just before the priest left the altar area to begin distributing Holy Communion, the boy noticed what looked like a host on the floor near the priest's feet. He informed the elderly priest who was celebrating the Mass. The priest immediately picked it up and reverently placed it in his mouth. It turned out to be a bit of wax dislodged from an altar candle.

REFLECTION

Although we should never be too casual in our reverence toward the Eucharist, we should also remember that a mistake in identity can be costly. Something similar happened once near Caesarea Philippi. Jesus asked those present, "Who do people say that the Son of Man is?" (Matthew 16:13). Several incorrect answers were offered until Peter correctly stated, "You are the Messiah, the Son of the living God" (Matthew 16:16). We should keep our eyes fixed on the real Christ lest we become distracted and reduce him to a ball of wax or something or someone other than who he really is, which is what the altar server in the story did, and the disciples who incorrectly answered the perennial question of who Jesus is.

361. MASS OFFERED FOR HIM   *Eucharist*

Saint Gregory the Great tells us the following in his thirty-fifth homily: "Not long ago it happened that a man was taken prisoner and carried far away. Now after he had been for a long time kept in prison without his wife knowing anything about it, she believed him to be dead, and she had Masses offered for him on certain days each week. After a long time had elapsed, this man returned home, and related to his astonished wife that on certain days of the week he was given more liberty than on others. In this way he succeeded in making his escape. Now when his wife inquired on which days of the week this favor was granted, she discovered that it was on those days when Mass was offered for him."

REFLECTION

The church has always held up the celebration of the Eucharist as the greatest and most perfect prayer, and the intercessory power of the Mass cannot be overstated. Echoing this sentiment, the Second Vatican Council speaks of the Eucharist as "the source and summit of the Christian life" (Lumen gentium, 11). Because of the role the Eucharist plays in the life of the faithful, the heart of each Christian must be in an attitude of communion with God through Jesus. The celebration of the Eucharist includes several forms of prayer: praise, thanksgiving, adoration, and intercessory prayer. When such prayer is sincere, we reap much, far beyond what we may have expected. As Jesus said at the Last Supper and repeats at every Mass, "Take, eat; this is my body.…Drink from it, all of you; for this is my blood of the covenant, which is poured out for many for the forgiveness of sins" (Matthew 26:26–28).

362. RED LIGHT   *Eucharist*

A young boy was sitting through a long and very tedious homily at Mass. Suddenly the flame from the red sanctuary lamp caught his eye. Tugging on his father's sleeve, he said, "Daddy, when the red light turns green, can we go?"

REFLECTION

We associate red and green lights with traffic signals. Like a red traffic light, a red sanctuary lamp should give us reason to stop and reflect on the awesome gift of the Eucharist. It is a great treasure Our Lord gave the church, the community of faithful disciples. Just as with our faith and the gift of life itself, if we take the Eucharist for granted, just going through the motions—ignoring it, not participating in its celebration, not seeking to learn more about it—we risk losing it. On the night he was betrayed Jesus took Peter, James, and John to the garden of Gethsemane and asked them to "remain here, and stay awake with me" (Matthew 26:38). Our eucharistic Lord invites us to do the same at Mass and outside of Mass.

363. FRONT PEW   *Compassion, Eucharist*

A woman recently wrote in her spiritual journal: "At Mass I enjoy sitting in the front pew. I have one problem with that location, though. My mind wanders after Communion when I should be giving thanks to God for the wonderful gift I have just received. Instead, I tend to watch the feet go by in front of me. Someone's shoes need a polish. Doesn't that man know he shouldn't wear brown shoes with black pants? Where could I find neat shoes like that? Then one day, after Communion thanksgiving, I opened my eyes. An older woman shuffled past, and I saw only that she walked with great effort, was overweight, and maybe needed someone to hug her. I wanted to put my arms around her and ask if there was anything I could do for her. Others walked by. One was struggling with a set of crutches. I wanted to ask how I could help. A small girl walked by, too young to receive Communion, she must have received a blessing. I wanted to bend down and hold out my arms to pick her up. And then I knew! This is how God feels toward us. God wants to comfort us, to give us whatever we might need. I was overwhelmed by a loving compassion I had never experienced before. God showed a little bit of himself to me, ordinary me, in the front pew that day."

REFLECTION

Every time we are engaged at Mass, the church wants us to recognize that we are continuing to witness the sacrifice of Jesus on Calvary (Matthew 27:35; Mark 15:24; Luke 23:33; John 19:23). On this occasion the church wants us to offer up our own sacrifices with that of Christ. This is the most important way we partici-pate at Mass. During the Liturgy of the Eucharist, the church invites us to pray that our sacrifice may be acceptable to God, the almighty Father "for our good, and the good of all his church." By extension we must pray that our sacrifice be acceptable for the good of the whole world and we must be willing to offer comfort, compas-sion, and support to all those in need.

364. COMMUNION, WITH CARE   *Communion*

Two students were having a serious discussion about dying and the afterlife. They agreed that if God would allow it, the one who died first would appear to the other, telling him how he fared in life beyond the grave. Shortly afterward, one of the two died and appeared soon after to his fellow student, shining bright with heavenly glory. In answer to his friend's inquiries, he said that by the mercy of God he was saved and in possession of the bliss of heaven. The other congratulated him and asked how he merited such unspeakable glory. "Chiefly," replied the happy soul, "by the care I took to receive communion with a pure heart." At these words he disappeared, leaving his surviving friend with feelings of great comfort and with a deep desire to imitate his friend's devotion to the Eucharist.

REFLECTION

Faith in the real presence of Our Lord in the Eucharist is one thing. Preparing ourselves to receive him worthily is quite another. The Catechism of the Catholic Church *reminds us that "the principal fruit of receiving the Eucharist in Holy Communion is an intimate union with Jesus Christ" (1391). This is the heart of what it means to be Catholic, as Vatican II reminds us when it comments that the Eucharist is the "source and summit of the Christian life" (Lumen gentium, 11). The church encourages us to receive Jesus not only on Sundays and holy days, but even daily if possible (Catechism, 1389). We are also encouraged to examine our consciences before we receive, bearing in mind that if we are aware of unrepented serious sin, we must first receive Christ's forgiveness in the sacrament of penance before receiving communion. The church also asks that we fast from food and drink for at least one hour before receiving, as a sign of respect. By being spiritually prepared to receive communion, we show our love for our eucharistic Lord and receive him with hearts and souls that have been cleansed and prepared for his sacramental presence.*

365. SUNDAY MORNING DRINKING   *Eucharist, faith*

An elderly Protestant woman was telling her friend about the awful shock of finding two empty whiskey bottles in her garbage can. "You can imagine my embarrassment," she said. "I got them out fast because I didn't want the trash collectors to think I drink." "What did you do with them?" asked the friend.

"Father Hanigan lives next door," came the reply, "so I put them in his garbage since everybody knows he drinks at the church service every morning."

REFLECTION

Even in the early days of the church, there were rumors that those involved in Christian worship drank alcohol and participated in cannibalism. Some people unfamiliar with the Catholic faith continue to embellish, exaggerate, or otherwise assume things that are simply false. Such is the case with the woman in the story. Having learned somewhere along the way that the priest uses alcohol during Catholic worship, she assumes that everyone knows that the priest drinks on a regular basis and therefore it would not be shocking to find empty whiskey bottles in his trash. What she doesn't know is that the priest uses a small amount of wine at Mass so as to follow the command given by Jesus, "Do this in remembrance of me" (Luke 22:19). What would she say if she knew that the priest regularly states at Mass, "Take, eat; this is my body" (Matthew 26:26). Like those in chapter 6 of St. John's Gospel, she might ask, "How can this man give us his flesh to eat?" Jesus said to them, "I tell you the truth, unless you eat the flesh of the Son of Man and drink his blood, you have no life in you....Whoever eats my flesh and drinks my blood remains in me, and I in him." Why do many Catholics not attend Mass every Sunday? Perhaps for the same reason that many of Jesus' disciples no longer followed him: "This teaching is difficult; who can accept it?" (John 6:60).

366. CHURCH FOOD — *Eucharist, transformation*

Small children often accompany their parents when they come forward at Mass to receive Holy Communion. The curious ones sometimes ask their parents, "What did you get?" or "What did he put in your mouth?" One little girl came out with this, "Why won't God let me have some church food too?"

REFLECTION

It is easy to make something simple complex. The challenge is to make something complex simple. The child's comment summarizes well, in simple language, the complex theology of the Eucharist. "Church food" is, of course, the wondrous gift Jesus gave us, the gift of himself to strengthen and sustain us on our journey to heaven. At every Mass we carry out his parting command to his disciples, "Do this in remembrance of me" (Luke 22:19). If our bodies can change ordinary food and drink into our flesh and blood, then why is it so hard to understand that God can change ordinary bread and wine into his flesh and blood? Or that the body and blood of Jesus that we receive can transform us into faithful disciples?

367. MASS IS ENDED   *Mission, discipleship*

Many years ago when the Mass was commonly celebrated in Latin, a class of young Catholic students was discussing the Holy Sacrifice of the Mass. Sister Margaret Mary asked them, "What is the most important part of the Mass?" Several responses were offered: "The *Pater Noster* (Lord's Prayer), because Jesus himself taught it." Another child said, "The *Agnus Dei* (Lamb of God), because this is what John the Baptist called Jesus." One child responded, "The consecration, when bread and wine are transformed into the body and blood of Jesus." The final comment was this: "The most important part of the Mass are the words, *Ite, missa est.*" (Go. The Mass is ended.) With the exception of the teacher, everyone giggled.

REFLECTION

The Mass is the continuing sacrifice of Jesus, but the ingredients that make up the Eucharist hold special, often multilayered meaning. The curious response by one child that the most important part of the Mass are the words, "Go. The Mass is ended," although humorous, is nonetheless quite significant. This final instruction is not simply a way to complete the liturgy but is a special charge given to those assembled to live the fruit of Jesus' sacrifice in their daily lives as Jesus requested: "Peace be with you. As the Father has sent me, so I send you" (John 20:21) to be my disciples, to transform the world and to hasten God's reign.

368. CONFESSION   *Penance, forgiveness of sin*

This conversation is said to have occurred during confession somewhere in a small town in Ireland.

Confessor: I stole a fat goose from a poultry yard!

Priest: That is very wrong.

Confessor: Would you like it, Father?

Priest: Certainly not. Return it to the one from whom you stole it.

Confessor: But I have offered it to him and he won't have it.

Priest: In that case you may keep it yourself.

Confessor: Thank you, Father.

The priest arrived home to find that one of his geese had been stolen.

REFLECTION

The sacrament of penance, also known as reconciliation, is meant for our sanctification, not our manipulation. As with all the sacraments, the most important person in this sacrament is Jesus Christ, who is eager to forgive sin when there is genuine repentance. Many people do not appreciate this sacrament and fail to take advantage of its benefits: not only forgiveness of sin, but spiritual guidance, regular examination of conscience, a call to conversion, and consolation as well. Those who have been away from confession for so long that they are afraid to return should realize that God awaits their return, as the father did the prodigal son's. The church encourages greater use of this remarkable sacrament of forgiveness: "This is my prayer, that your love may overflow more and more with knowledge and full insight to help you to determine what is best, so that on the day of Christ you may be pure and blameless" (Philippians 1:9–10).

369. SECRECY TEST   *Seal of confession*

A man went to confession and told the priest that he had several sticks of dynamite and was intending to blow up a nearby building later that evening. The priest tried desperately to dissuade him, but couldn't. That night the priest went to bed thinking that the building might be destroyed before morning. But it never happened. He thought the man had changed his mind. He met him again in the confessional some days later and the man told the priest that he just wanted to test the law that the priest could not break the seal of confession.

REFLECTION

People may approach the sacrament of reconciliation with the firm conviction that the priest may never—under any circumstances—reveal what was said in the confession. The seal of confession, which is a commitment to absolute secrecy, is never to be violated by a priest for any reason. Church law (Code of Canon Law) states: "The sacramental seal is inviolable; …it is a crime for a confessor in any way to betray a penitent by word or in any other manner or for any reason" (983 §1). And:

"A confessor who directly violates the sacramental seal incurs…excommunication reserved to the Apostolic See; one who does so only indirectly is to be punished according to the gravity of the [violation]" (1388 §1). This is how the church has understood and interpreted Jesus' words, "If you forgive the sins of any, they are forgiven them; if you retain the sins of any, they are retained" (John 20:23).

370. CONFESSIONAL SECRET — *Seal of confession*

Many years ago, *La Temps*, a Paris newspaper, reported an event that shook the world of jurisprudence. On her deathbed a woman known as Madame Jeanette, admitted that she was the one who, in 1924, had murdered a parish priest in Entrevaux, a crime for which Abbé Bruneau was convicted and sentenced to death. This priest, who heard Jeannette's confession and knew who the murderer was, had allowed himself to be executed so as not to break the silence imposed on him by the seal of confession.

REFLECTION

It cannot be overstated that keeping the seal of confession is a singular event this side of heaven that holds the highest sacred trust. The seal of confession must always be upheld. There are absolutely no exceptions. This is how the Church understands and interprets the words that Jesus spoke to the apostles in the locked room, "If you forgive the sins of any, they are forgiven them; if you retain the sins of any, they are retained" (John 20:23). As with the priest in the story, even with the possibility of severe personal consequences, a priest is never permitted to disclose the content of a penitent's confession.

371. TELL IT ALL — *Presence of Jesus, fruits of the Holy Spirit*

A Catholic boy and a Jewish boy were talking one day on the school playground. The Catholic boy blurted out, "My priest knows more than your rabbi." The Jewish boy quickly responded, "Of course he does; you and everyone else tell him everything in confession."

REFLECTION

Even non-Catholics have a certain awareness that there exists in the sacrament of reconciliation an exchange of information and counseling between the priest and penitent. Beyond this, we have to recognize that, as in all the sacraments, Jesus is also present. This changes everything. Without his presence, confession would be reduced to a counseling session or a simple human exchange. The priest acts in the person of Christ, his instrument to mediate God's authentic mercy and forgiveness of sins, engendering the fruits, or benefits, of the Spirit mentioned by Saint Paul in his letter to the Galatians: "The fruits of the Spirit are love, joy, peace, patience, kindness, generosity, faithfulness, gentleness, self-control" (5:22–23). These are likewise the fruits of the sacrament of penance.

372. HEAD OF THE HOUSE   *Matrimony*

It happened in the Dutch region of Pennsylvania. There was a newly ordained priest preparing to celebrate the sacrament of matrimony for the very first time. The night before the wedding the mother of the groom sat her son down and counseled him, "You are my son and I want what's best for you. Tomorrow, in a church, when the priest says join hands, make sure that your hand is on top of hers so that you'll be the head of the house." But down the road at the bride's house the mother was advising her daughter, "Nellie, you are my daughter and I want what's best for you. Tomorrow when the priest gets to the part where he asks you to join hands, make sure your hand is on top of his so that you'll be the head of the house." Well, the next day at the Nuptial Mass, it came to the point when the nervous priest said, "Join your right hands." Suddenly, the hands started going in and out and in and out. The priest knew exactly what was happening but wasn't sure what to do. He thought there was going to be an quarrel there and then. Suddenly, he remembered that he had a small wooden crucifix in his pocket. He removed it and placed it between the couple and pointing to it he said, "He'll be the head of your house." And it worked!

REFLECTION

Marriage is a covenant "by which a man and woman establish between themselves a partnership for the whole of life" (Catechism, 1601). There is no room for lording it over one's spouse. Sacred Scripture teaches that "the two become one flesh" (Genesis 2:24; Mark 10:8; Ephesians 5:31). And, as in every sacrament, the most important one present is Jesus Christ. In every Christian marriage, Jesus must always be the head and the heart of the home.

373. PASSWORD   *Mary*

Many years ago. when there was deep, mutual distrust between Catholics and Protestants, St. Patrick Church in Leicester, England, was holding a parish dance. It was for Catholics only. As a password to the dance hall the participants were required to recite the "Hail Mary" to ensure that they were Catholic. Those who sought admission that evening without knowing the password were turned away.

REFLECTION

Catholics cannot hold Mary captive, because Mary is the new Eve, the mother of all humanity, as the tender account from the cross communicates: "When Jesus saw his mother and the disciple whom he loved standing beside her, he said to his mother, 'Woman, here is your son.' Then he said to the disciple, 'Here is your mother'" (John 19:26–27). This recognition of Mary is becoming more apparent in recent years as we witness non-Catholics, and even Protestant ministers, in conversation, in sermons, and in articles acknowledging Mary at least as a most dedicated disciple of Jesus and even as the mother of God. Mary prayed in her Magnificat: "[God] has looked with favor on the lowliness of his servant. Surely, from now on all generations will call me blessed; for the Mighty One has done great things for me, and holy is his name" (Luke 1:48–49). Saint Bonaventure's observation is applicable, "God could have created another and more beautiful world but God could not have created a more beautiful mother."

374. I NEVER DREAMED   *Mary*

There is a story told about the stormy events of the French Revolution when a mob was surging through the corridors of the royal palace in Paris determined to kill Queen Marie Antoinette. In the forefront of the large crowd was a young girl. The milling crowd pushed her with such force against the door that it gave way and she was hurled forward and lay unconscious on the floor. Bruised and bleeding, she finally regained consciousness to see, bending over her, the beautiful, compassionate face of Marie Antoinette. With her handkerchief the queen was trying to stop the bleeding. The young girl burst into tears and thought, "Oh, I never dreamed she was like this…I never dreamed she was so beautiful."

REFLECTION

Like the young girl, some people have little idea of the beauty and kindness of one far more attractive and kindly than the French queen: Mary, the virgin mother of Jesus. Before they even learn about Mary, they harbor mistaken ideas about her. When we honor Jesus' mother, they think "idolatry." When we pay any attention to her, they say, "You are neglecting the son." And when we pray in the creed, "We believe in Jesus Christ...born of the Virgin Mary," they think, "Impossible!" Once people come to know Mary, study her in the gospel accounts, once they know what Catholics really believe about her and why, they may more readily agree with the young girl, "Oh, I never dreamed she was like this." Elizabeth's words to Mary in Luke's Gospel ring true: "Blessed are you among women, and blessed is the fruit of your womb" (1:42).

375. DUMB OX   *Ministry, Thomas Aquinas*

Young Thomas Aquinas was nicknamed "the dumb ox" by his fellow students. His teacher, though, was most impressed with him. He once announced in his lecture, "You call your brother Thomas a dumb ox. Let me tell you that one day the whole world will listen to his bellowings."

REFLECTION

Saint, philosopher, theologian, doctor of the church, patron of Catholic universities, colleges, and schools, the world continues to listen to Thomas Aquinas more than 700 years after his death. His massive writings continue to influence not only Catholic theology but several components of Western civilization, including politics and law. He wrote many commentaries on the works of the Greek philosopher Aristotle and many other philosophical and theological works. His unfinished Summa Theologica, *which includes his views on the nature of God, including his five proofs for the existence of God and his exposition of natural law, represents the most complete statement of his philosophical system. So much for being called "dumb." More than that, isn't it amazing how one individual has made such a positive influence on the world having lived fewer than fifty years in it. Near death he referred to his achievements, magnificent as they were, as so much straw. How much "straw" are we producing for God and God's reign?*

376. JEWISH-CATHOLIC SAINT   *Discipleship, sacrifice*

Unique among the saints of the twentieth century is Edith Stein. She was born into a German Jewish family in 1891, was assistant for two years to the famous philosopher Edmund Husserl. She converted to Catholicism in 1922, and took her vows as a Carmelite nun in 1934. She wrote philosophical works and taught at German universities. When the Nazis rounded up Jews for extermination, Edith Stein proudly identified herself as Christian and Jewish. On August 2, 1942, after offering herself as a sacrifice in an effort to save others, she went to her death in Auschwitz at the age of fifty-one, murdered in a gas chamber, wearing the star of David on her nun's habit. On May 1, 1987, Sister Teresa Benedicta of the Cross (the name she took as a Carmelite) was beatified by Pope John Paul II. Eleven years later she was canonized as "the first Jewish Catholic saint of our time."

REFLECTION

It would have been inconceivable that Edith Stein could ever reach the heights of sainthood. At an early age she rejected her Jewish mother's piety and in her teenage years was practically a professed atheist. Ultimately, however, she responded to God's grace and recognized the truth of divine revelation. This led her to the Carmelites where she used her intellectual gifts, coupled with her Catholic faith, to teach and write. Saint Teresa Benedicta teaches us that we must use our gifts for the greater honor and glory of God. She also teaches us that, in imitating Christ, we must be willing to embrace our crosses in life as she embraced her cross at Auschwitz. She understood the high demands set forth by the Lord and repeated throughout the gospels. To take up ones cross and follow Jesus is necessary to qualify of being "worthy" of Jesus (Matthew 10:38) and to be his "disciple" (Luke 14:27). This she did unto death.

377. EVENTUALLY PARDONED   *Forgiveness, penance*

In 1170, the four knights who martyred Saint Thomas Becket fled for refuge to Knaresborough Castle. Their names were Sir Richard Breton, Sir William Tracey, Sir Reginald Fitz-Urse, and Sir Hugh de Morville, whose descendants later settled in Cumberland, where the sword with which they killed Saint Thomas Becket was long kept, in memory of the event. They remained in hiding for a year but eventually submitted to the church and were pardoned on condition of performing a pilgrimage to Jerusalem.

REFLECTION

In every age, following Our Lord's command to "love your enemies, do good, and lend" (Luke 6:35), the church has responded to evil with good. This is especially true when we consider the formal way in which mercy and forgiveness are imparted through the administration of the sacrament of penance. As well, in response to violent acts, including murder, the church has often responded with mercy. Such is the case in the murder of Saint Thomas Becket. Other notorious crimes which fall into this category include the murder of Saint Maria Goretti, whose murderer later entered the monastery after a spiritual conversion, and the assassination attempt of Pope John Paul II. The pope later visited his would-be assassin in prison to forgive him.

378. CRUCIFIED WITH CHRIST · *Suffering*

When a seriously ill nun complained to Saint Francis de Sales that pain prevented her from praying and meditating, the saint said, "It is much better to be crucified with Christ than to pray before a crucifix."

REFLECTION

The one who undergoes pain and suffering patiently achieves much, having the privilege of sharing in Christ's redemptive suffering. Such suffering can be offered for oneself, for others, and for the intentions closest to the heart of Christ. Saint Paul, who experienced much suffering for the sake of the gospel, teaches us that "we suffer with him so that we may also be glorified with him" (Romans 8:17). He considered such suffering a privilege. In 1 Peter 3:13 we read, "But even if you do suffer for doing what is right, you are blessed." Similarly, "for he has graciously granted you the privilege not only of believing in Christ, but of suffering for him as well" (Philippians 1:29). What is our outlook on suffering that comes from living an authentic Christian life or from the illnesses that are part of the human condition?

379. KILLING THE SOUL · *Mortal sin, repentance*

Saint Louis IX, King of France, once asked a friend, "Tell me, what would you rather do, commit a mortal sin or become a leper?" The friend replied, "Your Majesty, I would sooner commit thirty mortal sins than be a leper." The king responded sadly, "My poor friend, that just goes to show that you really don't understand what a mortal sin really is."

REFLECTION

Mortal sin, lethal sin, is the leprosy that corrupts and kills the soul and ends up casting the one who dies without repentance into hell, separated from God forever. This is why the same theme remains consistent throughout the preaching and teaching of Jesus in the gospels: "Repent, for the kingdom of heaven has come near" (Matthew 4:17). No wonder it is the same message his cousin John preached: "John the Baptist appeared, preaching in the wilderness of Judea, proclaiming, 'Repent, for the kingdom of heaven has come near!'" (Matthew 3:1–2).

380. GIVE IT TO GOD   *Hell, witness, martyrdom*

Saint Thomas More was imprisoned by King Henry VIII and was going to be executed unless he swore to acknowledge the king as head of the church in England. His wife went to see him in prison with their children and tearfully appealed to her husband, "Have pity on your children and your wife. Take the oath and the king will set you free." Fifty-five-year-old Thomas replied, "How many more years could we live together?" His wife responded, "Maybe twenty years or more." Then her saintly husband said, "I will not do what you ask, even for a thousand years. He would be a poor businessman who for a thousand years would sell his soul for all eternity. To tell you the truth, had I two souls, I would give one to the king, but having only one I have to give it to God, my Creator."

REFLECTION

Our DNA can be traced to our parents' DNA. The creation of our souls, on the other hand, is totally God's work. If there were the equivalent of DNA of our souls and we could examine it under a microscope, we would discover, not the DNA of our parents, but of the Holy Spirit, "the Lord and Giver of life." This helps us to partly understand the perspective of Saint Thomas More in his final days. Thomas understood well his origin and his destiny. To turn his back on the church of Christ and turn away from Christ would have been tantamount to turning his soul away from its source and its destiny. Just perhaps Saint Thomas was recalling the words of Psalm 90 when his family visited him. "Our years come to an end like a sigh. The days of our life are seventy years, or perhaps eighty, if we are strong; even then their span is only toil and trouble; they are soon gone, and we fly away....So teach us to count our days that we may gain a wise heart" (Psalm 90:9–12).

381. SONG OF BERNADETTE   *Discipleship, perseverance*

In 1858 a teenage girl reported having seen the Blessed Virgin Mary in Lourdes, France. Many years later, her experience was captured in a movie called *The Song of Bernadette*. Among the many great scenes in the movie, a favorite to many, remains the rather harsh treatment from the mistress of novices toward the young Sister Bernadette Soubirous, who is bedridden. The older nun accuses the inexperienced novice of fabricating the story of Mary's appearance. If the Blessed Mother were to appear at all, in the older nun's estimation, it would probably be to someone like herself who was much more experienced and hard working. "My lips are parched from speaking God's Word and my eyes are burning like the fires of hell from lack of sleep," says the experienced novice mistress.

REFLECTION

A genuine disciple of Jesus is a stewardship person, giving one's talents, time, treasure to further the work of God. We learn this from the early Fathers of the Church, from spiritual writers through the ages, through the voice of the church and from the lips of the Master as recorded in the gospels. True discipleship is only gained by confronting the problems we face, admitting our sins and failures, and acknowledging the suffering to be borne in order to live with the mind of Jesus. The only way we can be truly alive is to walk through the difficulties, not back away from them. God will never ask us to take on something without giving us the strength necessary to bear it. God fed Elijah in the desert (1 Kings 17:4–6), and now God feeds us in the Eucharist with the Body and Blood of Jesus (John 6:50–51). Saint Bernadette understood this well. The mistress of novices did not. Whereas Bernadette looked inward to God for strength, the mistress of novices looked outward and was distracted by jealousy.

382. MY GOD   *Martyrdom, Eucharist, perseverance*

When Saint Polycarp, Bishop of Smyrna, was approaching his execution in the second century, he was told, "Renounce Christ and you will be set free immediately." Polycarp responded, "I have been serving Christ for the past eighty-six years. Why should I renounce him? What harm has he done to me? He is my God, my Savior, and my supreme benefactor." Praising God's most holy name, Polycarp died a brutal death, burned at the stake.

REFLECTION

Imagine the torment and terror that surrounded Saint Polycarp and all Christian martyrs in their final moments before death. They were men, women, and children. They were educated and wealthy, illiterate and poor. They were thrown into dark caves and dungeons, bound in chains and ropes, deprived of food and drink. They were burned at the stake, fed to wild animals, beaten to death, skinned alive, stabbed, whipped, crucified. Yet, they exemplified heroic courage and strength, even in their weakness. What was the secret to their persistent bravery? In a word, the Eucharist. Their courageous witness unto death would not have been possible without their faith and their dependence on Christ in the Eucharist, who strengthened them to the end. They arrived at that state where "every tear from their eyes" was wiped away and where "death will be no more; mourning and crying and pain will be no more" (Revelation 21:4).

383. REFUSING TO GUARD   *Pro-life, discipleship*

Toronto police officer David Packer received disciplinary action from his superiors for refusing to guard an abortion clinic from pro-life picketers. Two years earlier Officer Packer was commended and received a police decoration for risking his life to save a three-month-old child from a burning building. Mother Teresa of Calcutta made the following remarks about the incident: "I find it difficult to understand the logic by which you would punish a man who is obviously heroic in trying to save life. Why was he a hero two years ago, yet today he must be punished?"

REFLECTION

Wherever we are and whatever we do, we must always stand with Christ, our life, and with his Holy Spirit, "the Lord and giver of life." Living our Christian faith is not always easy but it is always possible. It calls for a consistent ethic of life, being truly pro-life. Seeking to protect and nurture human life whenever it is threatened. It is the way Jesus lived, concerned with doing God's will: "I do not seek my own will but the will of the one who sent me" (John 5:30). We too must be concerned only with doing God's will, even when it collides with human laws.

384. CRECHE   *Christmas, faith, holy family*

Just three years before his death, Saint Francis of Assisi, decided to celebrate the birth of Jesus in Bethlehem. At Greccio, he had a crib built, with hay and an ox and an ass. In addition to the friars, crowds came from all over to view the display of faith. The forest echoed with their voices and the night was lit up with hundreds of torches. Francis stood before the crib and his heart overflowed with tender compassion. Then he preached to the people about the birth of the poor King, whom he called the Babe of Bethlehem. A Knight named John of Greccio, a pious and truthful man who had abandoned his profession in the world and was a great friend of Francis's, claimed that he saw a beautiful child asleep in the crib, and that Francis took it in his arms and seemed to wake it up. The hay from the crib, which the people kept, was said to cure sick animals and drive off various diseases.

REFLECTION

The example that Francis of Assisi put before the world was intended to rouse the hearts of those weak in the faith. Thanks to him, we all know the familiar scene of the Christmas creche. The scene reminds us that when the shepherds went to the stable in Bethlehem, "they went with haste and found Mary and Joseph, and the child lying in the manger" (Luke 2:16). Notice that they found not only a baby, but an entire family. No wonder Christmas has been described as the season of the family; no wonder the feast of the Holy Family falls close to Christmas. In light of the humble love and genuine joy manifested at Bethlehem in the holy family, we should be moved to examine our own family life. In what ways does our family imitate or ignore the example of the holy family?

385. BROTHER ANDRÉ   *Holiness, discipleship*

Alfred Bessette, later known as Brother André of Montreal, knew hardship his entire life. His father died when he was only ten years old, and his mother when he was twelve. From the age of fourteen he worked menial jobs. In 1870, with the encouragement of Father André Provençal, he was sent to join the Congregation of Holy Cross. The priest had observed young Alfred spending whole nights in prayer and sent a note with him that read, "I am sending you a saint." Alfred's poor health, coupled with his illiteracy, made it doubtful that he would be permitted to take religious vows. Bishop Ignace Bourget, Archbishop of Montreal, intervened, with the assurance that Alfred could pray. Alfred was admitted to the Holy Cross Order as Brother André, spending the next sixty-seven years of his life as a lay brother serving in such menial positions as porter, gardener, baker of the altar bread, and janitor. In the meantime, he gained a reputation for working miraculous cures that drew many pilgrims to Montreal. His strong devotion to Saint Joseph led him to build Saint Joseph's Oratory in Montreal in 1904. The popularity of the oratory grew because of the many healings attributed to the intercession of Saint Joseph and Brother André. He was beatified by Pope John Paul II on May 23, 1982.

REFLECTION

Among priests and consecrated religious, through those who are educated or well versed in theology, we expect God to work most effectively. The life of Brother André reminds us, though, that God is very close to the ordinary circumstances of life— an incarnational God—and works through those who perform the most ordinary tasks, through the weak and uneducated, all of whom can be tools in the hands of God. What God wants most of all is our love. There are no academic requirements to live a life of holiness. The only requirement is to trust in God and allow God to do with us whatever he desires. With Brother André and the psalmist before him, we should shout from the rooftops, "I delight to do your will, O my God; your law is within my heart" (Psalm 40:8). That's the only condition for discipleship.

386. ONE-MINUTE FEAST — *Providence, patience*

Some years ago on the day before Thanksgiving, a cooking hotline service received a telephone call from a youthful woman asking how long it took to roast a twenty-pound turkey. The food specialist responded, "Just a minute," as she turned to consult a chart on the wall in her office. "Thanks a lot!" said the caller and she hung up. That young cook must have served a Thanksgiving feast fit for wild animals.

R E F L E C T I O N

To believe that a twenty-pound turkey could be cooked in one minute is a sign of our times. What once took hours or days, now takes only minutes, whether it is preparing food, calculating math problems, or communicating with someone at a great distance. But some things, some achievements still require time and are well worth the time. Friendship takes time. Education takes time. Character building takes time. Delicious and wholesome meals take time. The development of a solid Christian faith and mature spiritual life takes time as well. To live in faith means to live with the virtue of patience, confident that God is with us in the process. As such, one must enter into the mystery of time and God's providence. "For everything there is a season, and a time for every matter under heaven" (Ecclesiastes 3:1).

387. PERFECT EYESIGHT   *Trust*

A man went to his doctor, very upset about his health. "What's your problem?" asked the doctor. "It's terrible!" said the patient. "When I look in the mirror every morning, I see thinning hair, sagging jowls, crooked teeth, and bloodshot eyes. I'm a mess! What is it?" "I really don't know," said the doctor. "But the good news is, your eyesight is perfect."

R E F L E C T I O N

Reality doesn't always match our hopes and dreams. Consider Saint Joseph. He had a problem: Mary was pregnant, and he wasn't the father. But God led him through another door and, although what lay beyond it was still invisible, Joseph trusted God thoroughly and walked through that door. What lay beyond was Jesus. Imagine being a part of Jesus' life, even before he took his first breath. Imagine watching over him and being his guide as he developed into a young man. It was more than Joseph would ever have hoped for. But none of it would have happened if he had said no to God's invitation and refused to enter into the great unknown. Instead, Joseph trusted God's message. Matthew tells us that "when Joseph awoke from sleep, he did as the angel of the Lord commanded him, he took [Mary] as his wife" (Matthew 1:24).

388. DAD AND THE DEVIL   *Devil*

Two boys were walking home from faith formation class after hearing a lengthy and strongly worded lesson on the devil. One said to the other, "What do you think about all this Satan stuff?" The other boy replied, "Well, you know how Santa Claus turned out. It's probably just your dad."

REFLECTION

Sacred Scripture teaches us that the devil is not just a myth or a fantasy (Genesis 3:1; 1 Chronicles 21:1; John 8:44; Revelation 12:9). The devil really exists and will fight to the end to steal our souls away from God. But the church also gives us comfort by reminding us, through Scripture and Tradition, that no matter what happens in our lives, none of us have to face Satan alone. Even Jesus, the Son of God, was tested and tempted, but he had the Spirit of God leading and guiding him (Luke 4:1). We should take comfort in the fact that we have the same Spirit as our guide that Jesus had, who guides us on our pilgrimage to what can be a better way of living, and eventually to eternal joy with God in heaven.

389. PSYCHOLOGICAL TESTING   *Vocation, discipleship*

Someone suggested that if Jesus had sent his twelve apostles for psychological testing he would have received the following reply: "Thank you for submitting the resumes of the twelve men you have picked for managerial positions in your new organization. After having completed personal interviews for each of them with our psychologist and vocational aptitude consultant, it is the opinion of our staff that most of your nominees are lacking the background, education, and vocational aptitude. They have no team concept. Simon Peter is emotionally unstable and given to fits of temper. Andrew has no qualities for leadership. The two brothers, James and John, place personal interest above company loyalty. Thomas shows a skeptical attitude that would tend to undermine morale. Matthew has been blacklisted by the Jerusalem Better Business Bureau. James, the son of Alphaeus, and Thaddeus, definitely has radical leanings, and registered a high score on the manic-depressive scale. One of the candidates however, shows real potential. He is a man of ability and resourcefulness, mixes with people well, and has contacts in high places. He is highly motivated, ambitious, and responsible. We recommend Judas Iscariot as your CEO and right-hand man."

REFLECTION

We are grateful that Jesus chose the twelve apostles and did not leave the task to a committee, psychologist, or an aptitude consultant. The apostles were ordinary men, with several fishermen among them, possessing important qualities that made them good stewards of the mysteries of God. The qualities of a good fisherman are likewise qualities that every parish should expect of their priest, that faithful parents should seek to possess, and that all Catholics should aspire to. Among them are the following: patience, perseverance, courage, an eye for the right moment and prudence. Such qualities are often mentioned at different times and in different ways by Saint Paul as highly desirable for the disciple of Jesus Christ (Galatians 5:22–23; 1 Corinthians 13:13; Philippians 1:9–10).

390. DIRECTIONS, PLEASE   *Providence, trust*

Reverend Billy Graham tells of a time early in his ministry when he arrived in a small town to preach a sermon. Wanting to mail a letter, he asked a young boy to direct him to the town post office. After the boy gave the visitor directions, Dr. Graham thanked him and said, "If you come to the Baptist Church this evening, you can hear me telling everyone how to get to heaven." The boy replied, "I don't think I'll be there. You don't even know your way to the post office."

REFLECTION

There are times we can be humbled and left speechless when we least expect it, as Dr. Graham was in the unfamiliar town that day. So it is with ourselves when we assume we have control over the direction of our lives but are suddenly reminded through a variety of circumstances that it is God alone who has ultimate control over our lives, over the world. Hopefully, we pray well, work hard, love deeply, and trust God unconditionally. Hopefully, we live our lives in such a way that if we took our last breath this very night, we would be at peace with the knowledge that we have done our best and have lived faithful to our baptism covenant with God. In the end, though, it is God who takes the initiative and accompanies us on our pilgrimage. How we respond to God's loving call is in our hands. With Saint John we can say, "You are worthy, our Lord and God, to receive glory and honor and power, for you created all things, and by your will they existed and were created" (Revelation 4:11).

391. THE END IS NEAR · *Ministry, discipleship*

A local rabbi and priest were on the side of the road, holding up a sign that read, "The End Is Near! Turn Around Now Before It's Too Late!" and showed it to each passing car. One driver who drove by did not appreciate the sign and shouted at them, "Leave us alone, you religious nuts!" All of a sudden they heard a big splash, looked at each other, and the rabbi said to the priest, "Do you think we should have just put up a sign that said, "Bridge Out"?

REFLECTION

People often jump to conclusions by assuming that the message we share always points to our identity. The story illustrates, however, that words are not always what they may seem, that our words can refer to something or someone other than ourselves. This is especially true when we act in any way as a minister of God's work. Our words must ultimately point not to ourselves, but to God. All that we say and do and think must be testimony to the message of Saint John the Baptist, "He must increase; I must decrease" (John 3:30).

392. ROTTEN FROM THE START · *Judgment*

There were twin brothers by the names of John and Joseph. Joseph was single and had an old dilapidated boat. John was married and on the day that his wife died, Joseph's boat filled with water and sank. A few days later the parish priest met Joseph, and mistaking him for John who had lost his wife, said, "I'm sorry to hear of your loss. I'm sure you must feel terrible." Joseph, thinking he was referring to the loss of his boat, said, "I'm not a bit sorry; she was rotten from the start."

REFLECTION

The misunderstanding in this story is humorous, but some misunderstandings can give way to terrible and unfortunate consequences, leading to rash judgment and gossip. Common sense requires that we ask the right questions. "What do you mean by that?" or "What's going on here?" "Do I understand you correctly?" Only then can we be reasonably confident that our assumptions and findings are justified.

393. AT THE FISHING HOLE   *Love for all*

A priest, a deacon, and an atheist were fishing in a boat. The priest said I think I'll go to the car and get a soda. He got out of the boat, walked across the water, got the soda, and then walked back across the water to the boat. The atheist looked at him in amazement. The deacon then said, "I think I'll also go get a soda and a sandwich. He then did the same thing as the priest, walked across the water to the car, got a soda and sandwich, and then walked back across the water into the boat. The atheist said to himself, "Well, if they can walk on water so can I." He proceeded to get out of the boat, but immediately fell into the water. The priest then said to the deacon, "Do you think we should have told him where the rocks are?"

REFLECTION

There may be some humor in this anecdote but it illustrates well G.K. Chesterton's comment that "people without religion do not end up believing nothing, they believe everything." The priest and deacon in the story would have done well to follow the teaching of Christ in the beatitudes about how to be and how to act. It was their opportunity as disciples who hunger and thirst for holiness to identify this fishing trip as an opportunity to show mercy and kindness (Matthew 5:1–12). Ironically, we are often moved by the heartbreak of a movie, by the misery of an accident, or by the tragedy of a natural disaster. Very often, however, do we fail in showing love to those who are so much more a part of our immediate world?

394. YOUNG AND BEAUTIFUL   *Values*

A middle-aged bookstore customer, obviously annoyed, said to one of the store clerks, "Every time I come in here to buy a bestseller, you are sold out. Why can't you people learn to stock your shelves more efficiently?" The clerk asked, "What is the title of the book you wish to purchase?" "How to Remain Young and Beautiful," the woman answered. "Very well," replied the clerk, "I'll place your order at once and mark it urgent!"

REFLECTION

The sense of urgency is one of the important emotional problems of our time. But on what do we spend our energy? We spend our time and energy with relatively unimportant matters and devote little or none to matters of the utmost importance, such as maintaining a right relationship with God, with others, and with all of creation. What is often lacking is a forthright assessment of our fundamental priorities. What do we really value? As Jesus warns us, "Beware, keep alert; for you do not know when the time will come" (Mark 13:33), and "Where your treasure is, there your heart will be also" (Luke 12:34).

395. FINDING THE HYDRANT   *Prophet, discipleship*

A kindergarten teacher was driving a station wagon full of children home one day when a fire engine zoomed past, with a Dalmatian sitting in the front seat. The children started talking about the dog's duties. "They use him to keep crowds back," said one youngster. "No," said another, "he's just for good luck." A third child brought the disagreement to a close. "They use the dog," she said firmly, "to find the fire hydrant."

REFLECTION

This cute story gives a whole new meaning to "word association." In the Christian life as well, there are many signs and symbols that point to more than one reality. The cross, for example, might be described as an instrument of capital punishment used for execution by the Romans in the first century. Others might associate it with the so-called two thieves crucified with Jesus. For the disciple of Christ, the cross is always associated with the unmistakable sign of God's love for humanity. So, when Jesus tells us to take up our cross (Mark 8:34), he means much more than the cross of having a "bad day," an exasperating relationship, a flat tire, or an unfortunate run of bad luck at a Saturday sports event. What Jesus means is that we must have the courage of a prophet to confront injustice, to insist on the truth, and to call for conversion. It means speaking out against evil and being willing to suffer by taking a stand for the sake of truth and righteousness. We express it at the Eucharist when we pray for forgiveness for what we have done and "what we have failed to do." It means dying to self and offering our lives for others as he did.

396. PUNCTUATE IT CORRECTLY   *Jesus*

An English teacher wrote the words, "Woman without her man is nothing" on the blackboard and directed his students to punctuate it correctly. The men wrote: "Woman, without her man, is nothing." The women wrote: "Woman! Without her, man is nothing."

REFLECTION

The real intent of a sentence is understood only when we take the punctuation into account. Likewise, our understanding of Jesus is properly grasped only when we consider the whole of his life, only when we take the time to examine and understand his entire life and ministry. Some people are tempted to imitate the personality traits or the aspects of Jesus' life that have particular appeal, a kind of mix and match whereby we take what is appealing and leave the rest behind. The fact is, though, that we must attend to the entire person of Jesus, all of his words, all of his deeds, and not just those we agree with or that appeal to us. Jesus told us, "Take my yoke upon you, and learn from me" (Matthew 11:29). Saint Paul advises us well in his letter to the Ephesians: "Be imitators of God, as beloved children, and live in love, as Christ loved us and gave himself up for us, a fragrant offering and sacrifice to God" (5:1–2).

397. WHERE WOULD YOU LIKE TO SIT?

Love, prudence

An elderly woman walked into the local country church. The friendly usher greeted her at the door and helped her up the flight of steps. "Where would you like to sit?" he asked politely. "The front row please," she answered. "You really don't want to do that," the usher urged. "The pastor is really a boring preacher." "Do you happen to know who I am?" the woman inquired. "No," the usher responded. "I'm the pastor's mother," she replied indignantly. "And do you know who I am?" he asked. "No," she said. "Good," he answered, and quickly walked away.

REFLECTION

As we know from experience, the spoken word, once expressed, cannot be recaptured. We also know the harm that can be done by an unguarded comment. Our baptism commissions us to preach and teach the good news, to speak well of others, not to needlessly criticize them. Saint Paul reminds us that love, not frank honesty, is the most important among the virtues (1 Corinthians 13:13), but prudence is a virtue we should practice as well.

398. LENGTHY SERMON　　　　　*Homily, word of God*

There was a woman who was visiting a parish church one Sunday. The sermon seemed to go on forever, and some of the parishioners seemed to be falling asleep. Later, outside on the church steps, the woman walked up to some of the other parishioners, extended her hand in greeting, and introduced herself, "Hello, I'm Gladys Dunn." And one gentleman replied, "You're not the only one ma'am; I'm glad he's done too."

REFLECTION

No matter who we are, if we do breathe a sigh of relief at the conclusion of a homily, it might be prudent to keep our opinion of it to ourselves, and reflect on our reaction. Do we see the homily not as a means to entertain us, though that might help, but as a sacred moment during the liturgy when the word of God is opened for us, when we actively search with the homilist for God speaking to us here and now. There is always something to learn, always some benefit for us, even when the presentation is less appealing than we'd like. The time of the homily is not only a sacred liturgical event, but a sacred moment for each worshiper. "Let anyone with ears listen" (Matthew 11:15). Let it not be said of us, "hearing they do not listen, nor do they understand" (Matthew 13:13).

399. EXTRA DOZEN ROSES　　　　　*Misunderstanding*

A young man was very much in love with a beautiful girl. One day she reminded him that the next day was her birthday. He told her he would send her a bouquet of roses...one for each year of her life. That evening he called the local florist and ordered twenty-one roses with instructions to deliver them the first thing in the morning. As the florist was preparing the order, he decided that since the young man was such a good customer, he would put an extra dozen roses in the bouquet. The poor fellow never did find out what upset the young girl.

REFLECTION

Misunderstanding can cause lost friendships, alienate family members, and embitter associates, even when the intention was well meant. We should always do our best to give another the benefit of the doubt until we have all the facts to properly evaluate the situation. If there has been a misunderstanding, what steps can we take to clari-

fy and amend the situation? As Jesus instructed us, "In everything do to others as you would have them do to you; for this is the law and the prophets" (Matthew 7:12).

400. A DRINK OF WATER   *Perseverance, faith*

A man was crawling through the desert on his hands and knees, desperate for a drink of water. He came upon a person selling neckties. "Would you like to buy a nice necktie?" asked the salesman. "All I want is a drink of water," cried the man. The salesman had no water, so the poor fellow crawled on across the sand. Eventually he came upon a beautiful restaurant. "It must be a mirage," he thought, but as he drew closer he saw it was real. With his last ounce of energy, he struggled up to the entrance and asked the doorman, "Please, sir, may I have a drink of water?" The doorman replied, "Sorry. Gentlemen are not admitted without neckties."

REFLECTION

Life is a marvelous gift, but at times it can seem awfully unfair and very hard. At those times, which can often stretch on and on, we can too easily lose heart and lose our way. During such times we ought to recall the very difficult yet virtuous lives of those in the Sacred Scriptures and in the Sacred Tradition of the church who persisted in faith in spite of the challenges and suffering that invaded their lives. They didn't ask, "Is this fair?" They were willing to persevere in faith, despite the cost. With Saint Paul they believed that "neither death, nor life, nor angels, nor rulers, nor things present, nor things to come, nor powers, nor height, nor depth, nor anything else in all creation, will be able to separate us from the love of God in Christ Jesus our Lord" (Romans 8:38–39).

401. DRINKING BUDDIES   *Prudence*

A scrawny little guy was sitting at a bar staring at his beer. Suddenly, a burly truck driver sat down beside him, grabbed the guy's glass, and gulped down the beer. The little fellow burst into tears. "Oh, come on, pal," said the truck driver. "I was just joking. Here, I'll buy you another." "No, that's not it," the man blubbered. "This has been the worst day of my life. I got fired. My car was stolen. I had to walk home, and when I got there, I found my wife with another man. So

I grabbed my wallet and came here. And just when I'm about to end it all," said the sobbing man, "you show up and drink my beer laced with poison!"

R E F L E C T I O N

There are times in our lives when we speak before we think and the result is disastrous, causing unintended hurt and misunderstanding. There are also times when we act before we think, which can have even more drastic results. Teasing another or playing a practical joke is one thing. Doing so carelessly, disregarding possible results, is quite another. We should never do anything in such haste that it might lead to unnecessary suffering. Instead, we would do well to follow Saint Paul's counsel to: "clothe yourselves with the new self, created according to the likeness of God in true righteousness and holiness. So then, putting away falsehood, let all of us speak the truth to our neighbors, for we are members of one another" (Ephesians 4:24–25).

402. THE BEAR AND TWO TRAVELERS
Trust, divine presence

Two men were hiking together in the woods when a bear suddenly confronted them. One of the men climbed up quickly into a tree and concealed himself in the branches. The other, seeing that he was about to be attacked, fell flat on the ground, and when the bear came up and felt him with his snout, he held his breath, and pretended that he was dead. The bear soon became disinterested and left. The other man descended from the tree, and jokingly inquired of his friend what it was the bear had whispered in his ear. "He gave me this advice," his companion replied. "Never travel with a friend who deserts you at the approach of danger."

R E F L E C T I O N

Jesus, our Immanuel, has promised to be with us always—even when it seems that he is far away—to be our companion as we travel through life to our final union with God. So often in times of crisis and difficulty all we can do is hang on by our fingernails and trust Jesus, trust that our friend and brother will never abandon us. Such trust in Jesus will not undo the trial or the spiritual darkness, but it will light the path for us. The end of Saint Matthew's Gospel (28:20) should be the seed of our courage: "Remember, I am with you always, to the end of the age."

403. HOW LONG ARE YOU IN FOR?

Freedom, grace, spirit

The prison inmate greeted the new arrival with the question, "How long are you in for?" "Twenty-five years," the new prisoner replied. "Then you take the bed nearest the door," said the old timer. "You'll be getting out first."

REFLECTION

Living our day-to-day life may sometimes seem like being in prison. There is always someone or something that seems to hold us back, something that restricts us, even when we want to live as a genuine disciple. This inability to be completely free may lead us to wonder, "When will my restless soul be at peace? When will I be 'getting out' so that I will be completely free?" The answer, of course, is that everyone, even Jesus, has to live with limitations, restraints. The only absolute freedom we have is to choose life (Deuteronomy 30:19), to try to live in imitation of Jesus to the best of our ability and with God's assistance. "Where the Spirit of the Lord is, there is freedom" (2 Corinthians 3:17). Freedom, after all, is the right to live not as we wish, but as we ought.

404. IS THIS CALL NECESSARY? *Laity, ministry, baptism*

Annoyed with her teenage daughter who had been calling her boyfriend too frequently, a mother posted the following sign near the telephone: "Is this call necessary?" The daughter posted another sign that read: "How can I tell until I've made it?"

REFLECTION

Like the mother in this story, some people ask similar questions about the active participation of laity in the church: "Is it necessary? To what extent should the laity be actively involved in the church?" The answer is "Absolutely!" One of the most significant directives of the Second Vatican Council was the call for the laity to be more actively engaged in church matters (Lumen gentium, 31). This summons has been echoed time and again through other church documents and has been the subject of countless homilies, books, and conferences. As well, we see this important call to the laity outlined in the Catechism of the Catholic Church *(897–913) and in the emergence of many ministries for the laity within the church.*

405. DIDN'T MARRY
Matrimony, sacrament

A man asked his friend why he never married? The friend replied, "Well, I guess I just never met the right woman. I guess I've been looking for the perfect girl." "Oh, come on now," said the man, "surely you've met at least one woman you wanted to marry." "Yes, there was one...the one perfect girl I really ever met." "Well, why didn't you marry her?" His friend answered, "She was looking for the perfect man."

REFLECTION

With experience we soon realize that there is no such thing as the perfect human being, unless we are referring to Jesus or his mother, Mary. In seeking a husband or a wife it is always important to first seek God's will. Ultimately, we fall in love with the one we are to be with until death, not because he or she is perfect, but despite the fact that he or she is not. The book of Genesis reminds us that marriage comes from the loving hand of God, who fashioned male and female in the divine image (Genesis 1:27). A man "leaves his father and his mother and clings to his wife, and they become one flesh" (Genesis 2:24). Jesus repeats and reaffirms these teachings in Mark 10:6–8: "But from the beginning of creation, 'God made them male and female.' 'For this reason a man shall leave his father and mother and be joined to his wife, and the two shall become one flesh.'" Christian marriage is a sacrament not just at the time of the wedding ceremony, but throughout the couple's married life. It is a sacramental state of life.

406. WHERE ARE THE ANTIQUES?
Silence, reflection

A married couple touring through the back hills of Arkansas came upon a house with a sign in front, Antiques. They knocked on the door and were welcomed warmly by two elderly women. When the visitors asked, "Where are the antiques?" one of the ladies answered sheepishly, "We're the antiques." Then, over a cup of tea, they confessed to their trick. They were lonely. They had no nearby relatives and had recently lost their brother. They came up with the idea of putting out the sign, knowing that people who like antiques are usually nice people. "Notice," said one of the women, "the sign didn't read Antiques for Sale."

The other added, "We really meet a lot of nice people. And we feel that God doesn't mind our little trick."

REFLECTION

How sad it is that in a country of millions there are still people who enjoy little contact, fellowship, or intimacy with other human beings. Being alone is one thing. It can become an opportunity to grow in greater love and intimacy with God, a time for prayerful reflection, a time for listening to the Spirit. Read about Elijah's experience in 1 Kings 19, hearing the voice of God in the silence. Being lonely is something quite different. It is often the catalyst for less than virtuous activities. As the old saying puts it, "An idle mind is the devil's workshop."

407. STAND UP   *Judging*

A man sobering up from the night before was sitting through the Sunday homily, finding it long and boring. Still feeling hung over and tired, he finally nodded off. The priest had been watching him all along, noticing his apparent hangover and was disgusted. At the end of the homily, the priest decided to make an example of him. He said to the congregation, "All those wishing to have a place in heaven, please stand!" The whole church stood up except for the sleeping man. Then the priest said even more loudly, "And he who would like to find a place in hell, please stand!" The weary man caught only the last part and groggily stood up, only to find that he was the only one in the congregation standing. Confused and embarrassed, he said, "I don't know what we're voting on here, Father, but it sure seems like you and I are the only ones standing for it!"

REFLECTION

If the congregation could see what the preacher sees when preaching, they would be surprised, amused, or perhaps scandalized. There are those who look at their watches, read the bulletin, or adjust their hair; who yawn or bite their fingernails, or gawk around the church or engage in conversation. And there are the rare instances similar to the sleeping man. Regardless of what the homilist or others in the assembly might consider inappropriate, there is never a reason for a member of the assembly to be singled out or judged. As Mother Teresa of Calcutta reminds us, "If you judge people, you have no time to love them," or as Jesus says it, "Do not judge, and you will not be judged; do not condemn, and you will not be condemned. Forgive, and you will be forgiven" (Luke 6:37).

408. LAYING AN EGG?   *Body of Christ, stewardship*

A farmer was bragging to tourists from the city about what a good farmer he was. "I'm the old-fashioned type of farmer," he said. "I can plow, milk cows, prune trees, feed hogs, and anything else that has to be done around the place. I don't guess there is anything that goes on that I can't do." One of the visitors asked, "Can you lay an egg?"

REFLECTION

Even those who can do many things, can't do everything. Nor should they try to. In working to build the kingdom of God, we should, through experience and reflection, discern what our talents are and use them judiciously, as part of the church, the body of Christ. The letter to the Ephesians expresses it this way: "The gifts he gave were that some would be apostles, some prophets, some evangelists, some pastors and teachers, to equip the saints for the work of ministry, for building up the body of Christ....But speaking the truth in love, we must grow up in every way into him who is the head, into Christ, from whom the whole body, joined and knitted together by every ligament with which it is equipped, as each part is working properly, promotes the body's growth in building itself up in love" (Ephesians 4:11–16).

409. DO IT YOURSELF   *Presence of Jesus, Christian living*

With a tooth badly needing attention, a missionary nun went to the dentist's office deep in a mountain village of Bolivia. The dentist's wife informed her that her husband was out but, eager to help the Sister, the wife suggested, "I'll give you the surgical instruments and you can do it yourself!"

REFLECTION

The sister must have been caught off guard when she learned that the dentist's wife was willing to give her the surgical tools and expect her to treat her own dental emergency without the expert attention of the dentist. We too would be surprised if when Jesus had ascended into heaven (Mark 16:19; Luke 24:50–51; Acts 1:9–11), he had not left us "tools" to attend to our spiritual needs without his expert pres-

ence. This is not what Jesus did. Rather, he remained with us in many ways and gave us what we need to grow in love. He gave us the church to guide us, the sacraments to sustain us, his presence in the Eucharist to nourish us, his word to teach us, and his mother and the community of fellow pilgrims to be witnesses of saintly living and to intercede for us.

410. GRACE BEFORE MEALS *Faith, reason*

A man visited his relative, a farmer. Before dinner, the farmer bowed his head and said grace. The visitor jeered, "This is old-fashioned. No one with an education prays at table any more." The farmer admitted that he might be a little old-fashioned and conceded that there were some on his farm who did not pray before their meals. Feeling justified, the relative remarked, "So enlightenment is finally reaching the farm. Who are these wise ones?" The farmer replied, "My pigs."

REFLECTION

We all know of people who have made insulting comments such as, "I've finally outgrown my Catholic faith" or "I used to be Catholic, too, until I knew better." The anecdote about the farmer is appropriate for those who make such comments and for those who equate a life devoid of prayer with education, a life devoid of faith with sophistication, and a life devoid of virtuous living with enlightenment. An authentically human life can never be defined as faith without reason any more than it can be measured by wisdom without faith. Both are needed; both are human acts. Adherents of faith alone become blind, as do those who subscribe to reason alone. Ours must always be a faith seeking understanding. In the words of Saint Augustine, "I believe in order to understand; and I understand, the better to believe."

411. PARISH DONATION *Money*

An anonymous caller telephoned the rectory office and asked to speak to the head hog of the trough. The secretary responded, "How rude! I'll have you know we would never ever refer to our pastor as a hog." "Okay, then just take a message," insisted the caller. "Tell him I've come into a bit of money so I was calling to donate $75,000 to the parish." The secretary replied, "Hold the phone, dear! I think I see that pig coming down the hall right now."

REFLECTION

The old saying remains true: "The love of money is a root of all kinds of evil" (1 Timothy 6:10). Although the donation to the parish was a generous one, it does not justify the secretary compromising herself for financial gain. She may have the interests of the parish at heart, but her loyalty to the pastor is uncertain. Is her insult of the pastor justifiable? Does the end justify the means? What limit do we set to financial gain? We get our cue from Jesus, "For what will it profit them to gain the whole world and forfeit their life?" (Mark 8:36). The rest of the quote from 1 Timothy goes like this: "in their eagerness to be rich some have wandered away from the faith."

412. ECUMENICAL EFFORTS *Thinking like Jesus*

At an ecumenical meeting, representatives from each of the participating communities were discussing the results of their independent efforts to present the faith and gain new members. The Methodist minister said, "The revival worked out well for us! We gained four new families." The Baptist preacher said, "We did better than that! We gained six new families." The Catholic pastor said, "Well, we did even better than that! Our ten biggest troublemakers have left our church!"

REFLECTION

A blessing for some may be a burden for others. This can be said of many things: winning the lottery, a company promotion, an unexpected pregnancy, a surprise visit from a relative or friend. Whether it is money, children, or a reunion, each can be the source of a great opportunity to grow in greater love with others, have greater positive change, and discover valuable and lasting insights into one's spiritual life. On the other hand, the same new experiences can initiate an endless litany of disastrous results involving sin and even death. It becomes a question of whether we see things from our own limited perspective or from Jesus'. Saint Paul reminds us that we who have been baptized into Christ "have the mind of Christ" (1 Corinthians 2:16). May the words of the psalmist console us: "Surely there is a reward for the righteous; surely there is a God who judges on earth" (Psalm 58:11).

413. ABLE TO DANCE? *Prayer*

A famous athlete with a good sense of humor suffered a severely twisted knee. When the doctor examined him he found a torn cartilage. The athlete asked the doctor, "When my knee heals, will I be able to dance?" "Of course you will," the doctor reassured him. "Then you're a miracle healer," exclaimed the sportsman. "I never could before."

REFLECTION

Cures are not those that enable people to do something they were unable to do previously. A man with a broken leg should pray for it to function properly, not for the ability to win a marathon if he had never run one. A woman who has lost her hearing should pray for the ability to hear normally again, not to hear in a superhuman way. Beyond this, we may also pray for cures that are spiritual in nature. One who may generally be susceptible to depression may pray that the burden be lifted, not that he or she not ever experience anything negative in life. Our prayer, in other words, may be insistent, frequent, urgent in tone, but always reasonable. See Luke 11:5–13; 18:1–8, 9–14.

414. DINNER AGAIN *Eucharist, Holy Communion*

While attending a private dinner party one evening, British director Alfred Hitchcock, whose famously portly profile betrayed a fondness for food, was dismayed to find that very small portions were being served. At the end of the evening, the host bid Hitchcock farewell. "I do hope you will dine with us again soon," she added. "By all means," Hitchcock dryly replied, "How about now?"

REFLECTION

Hitchcock's disappointment could never be ours when it comes to being nourished by the Bread of Life and the Cup of Eternal Salvation. Like those in the gospel passage of the feeding of the five thousand (Matthew 14:16–21), when we receive Jesus in the Eucharist, we receive our fill because every portion given in Holy Communion is the total Christ. In terms of quality, we could not receive any more or any less.

415. FINAL MEAL   *Eucharist, real presence*

Three men, an Italian, a Frenchman, and a Spaniard, were condemned to be executed. Their captors told them that they would be given one final meal before the execution. They asked the Frenchman what he wanted. "Give me some good French wine, some brie, and French bread," he said. So they gave it to him, he ate it, and then they executed him. Next it was the Italian's turn. "Give me a big plate of pasta," said the Italian. So they brought it to him, he ate it, and then they executed him. Finally, they asked the Spaniard what he wanted. "I want a big bowl of strawberries," said the Spaniard. "Strawberries! They aren't even in season yet!" To this the Spaniard retorted, "So, I'll wait."

REFLECTION

Unlike the request for out-of-season strawberries for the Spaniard's last meal, Jesus' last meal before his execution included bread and wine which, transformed into himself, remains in season for all people all of the time. Every time we "eat this bread and drink this blood" we do so in memory of the One who is really and substantially present under the appearances of bread and wine. This is the constant faith of the church. "As often as you eat this bread and drink the cup, you proclaim the Lord's death until he comes" (1 Corinthians 11:26).

416. NEXT SPEAKER   *Preaching, speech*

At dinner banquets there are often a number of speakers to offer words of wisdom. At one such event there were several speakers and each speech seemed to be longer than the previous. As each speaker finished, more and more people took the opportunity to leave the banquet. Finally there was only one person left listening to the speech. Reminiscing about the event some time later, he recalled, "And I listened. And I listened. And I listened. I felt like going up and helping him turn the pages because he wasn't turning them very fast. Finally, he finished his speech. The speaker then pointed to me and said: 'I'm glad that you appreciate my beautiful thoughts. I'm so happy you stayed till the end.' And I looked at him and replied, 'But I'm the next speaker.'"

REFLECTION

As important as our message might be, even the most patient of listeners have their limits. Jesus, the greatest communicator, didn't preach the entire gospel message in one sitting. As well, he used different methods of verbal technique in speaking to individuals or crowds. If we push the limits in orating, in conversations, in preaching, in teaching, not only might the only ones left listening be ourselves and God, but the passage from Sacred Scripture that says "In all toil there is profit, but mere talk leads only to poverty" (Proverbs 14:23) might be fulfilled.

417. MUCH NEEDED SLEEP   *Homily, Scripture*

A Methodist minister once observed that several members of his congregation had fallen asleep, so he shouted, "Fire! Fire!" Several in the congregation awoke and shouted back, "Where? Where?" "In the place of punishment," added the preacher, "for those who sleep under the ministry of the holy gospel."

REFLECTION

Selective hearing is always a problem when it comes to Liturgy of the Word. We can become fixated on one or two points in the proclamation of the Scripture and in the homily and assume that the bulk of what is said is meant for the others and not for me. In an effort to enter into the mystery of the unraveling of Scripture at Mass, we would do well before it begins to follow the advice that Eli gave to Samuel, "if he calls you, you shall say, 'Speak, Lord, for your servant is listening'" (1 Samuel 3:9). At every Mass God speaks to us.

418. HOLD YOUR MONKEY   *Love, equality*

A woman got on a bus holding a baby. The bus driver said, "That's the ugliest baby I've ever seen." In a huff, the woman slammed her fare into the fare box and took an aisle seat near the rear of the bus. The man seated next to her sensed that she was agitated and asked her what was wrong. "The bus driver insulted me," she fumed. The man sympathized and said, "Why, he's a public servant and shouldn't say things to insult passengers." "You're right," she said. "I think I'll go back up there and give him a piece of my mind." "That's a good idea," the man said. "Here, let me hold your monkey."

REFLECTION

We must never see another human as anything less than human. No matter how homely or unattractive another person appears, no matter how misformed, there

is never a reason to be uncharitable in word or action to someone who, like our-
selves, is made "in the image of God" (Genesis 9:6). Regardless who a person is or
what a person might look like, it is crucial to be mindful that all human beings are
brothers or sisters of Christ and have been redeemed in his blood. They too are des-
tined for eternal life (Ephesians 1:7). It is important, therefore, when meeting
someone with a facial disfigurement, an unusual skin condition, an unusual
height or weight variation—in short, people who look different—that we not stare
at him or her, not look away or look through them as if they are invisible. We who
are disciples of Jesus Christ must refrain from contributing to stigmatizing people
who appear different.

419. PETS AND HEAVEN   *Animals, heaven*

A cat and a mouse died on the same day and went to heaven. There they met
God, who asked them, "How do you like it so far?" The mouse replied, "It's
great, but I always wanted a skateboard. Can I have a skateboard?" God said,
"Sure," and gave him a skateboard. The next day God saw the cat and asked him,
"How do you like it here so far?" The cat replied, "Great. In fact, I'm especially
pleased that you have meals-on-wheels here!"

REFLECTION

We live in an age in which pets seem to enjoy exaggerated, and sometimes even
greater, rights than some humans. Even Saint Francis of Assisi would have found
this unusual. No wonder people ask whether pets go to heaven. The classic way to
answer this is to distinguish between the immortal soul of a human and a tempo-
ral soul of an animal. Human beings have immortal souls and are destined to live
forever. Animals have temporal souls that gives them animation enabling them to
live and move and breathe, but the purpose for their existence ends at death.
Human beings are made in the image of God. Animals are created by God for peo-
ple's use and enjoyment (Genesis 1:28). Humans are in need of a Savior because of
Adam's sin (Romans 5:12–23). Animals are incapable of sin, incapable of being
able to know and love their creator. They do not need a savior because they cannot
make a decision for or against God. Having answered the question whether pets go
to heaven, and assuming the answer is not satisfactory for some pet lovers, the fol-
lowing can be said, particularly for a child. In heaven it is God's desire that we be

completely happy. If our happiness is dependent on having our pets with us in heaven, then God will provide.

420. EXPIRE TOGETHER — *Heaven, judgment*

The woman in charge of a parish magazine drive stood to make her appeal to the assembled parishioners. "Please, my fellow parishioners," she said, "start your subscriptions this month, so that we can all expire together."

REFLECTION

With some effort, we may be able to orchestrate our magazine subscriptions to expire together but even as a community of faith we cannot take our last breath simultaneously. As Saint Paul reminds us in 2 Corinthians 5:10, we will stand before God to be judged not as a group or as a community, but as individuals at a time of God's choosing. The apostle had previously described the reward awaiting those who were judged righteous by Christ: "What no eye has seen, nor ear heard, nor the human heart conceived, what God has prepared for those who love him" (1 Corinthians 2:9).

421. WORDS AT A FUNERAL — *Afterlife*

There were three men sitting on a bench. The first man asked the other two: "What do you want your family and friends to say at your funeral?" One man said, "I guess I'd want them to say I was a nice guy and I took care of my family." The other said, "I'd want them to say that I was faithful right to the end." The first man said, "That's all nice, but me…I want them to say: Look! He's moving!"

REFLECTION

Wouldn't most of us want our death delayed? Short of being another miracle story like Lazarus (John 11:44) or the daughter of Jairus (Luke 8:55), we would even settle for being the recipient of a simple mistake or medical error, having been pronounced dead prematurely. Indeed, we intuitively seek life, even in death. With the Holy Spirit we seek to move always in the direction of life. And no wonder! For all who have been conceived are guaranteed one thing: They will have eternal life. The question is, "Where? Forever in God's loving embrace, or not?"

422. DEATH OF GOD   *Faith*

Some years ago *The Tonight Show* was being taped in Burbank, California. Suddenly, everything shook and everyone realized that they were experiencing an earthquake. Johnny Carson spoke up and said, "I want to announce that the death of God meeting scheduled for tonight has been canceled."

REFLECTION

Immediate belief in God comes fast for those who are suddenly caught in life and death situations. Such a spontaneous sense of faith is apparent in times of crisis, such as earthquakes and other natural disasters. We saw this on the occasion of September 11, 2001, when our churches were suddenly filled throughout the country following the terrorist attacks. We need not only our physical eyes but also eyes of faith that take us into the realm of God where we are given the opportunity to believe, to pray, and to see with an unusual clarity the very reason for our existence. Without faith, we are blind to the reality of truth. No wonder the letter to the Hebrews declared, "Faith is the assurance of things hoped for, the conviction of things not seen" (11:1).

423. LAST RESPECTS   *Church*

The new pastor in a small Midwestern town spent the first four days making personal visits to each of the parishioners homes, inviting them to come to his first Masses. The following Sunday the church was all but empty. Accordingly, the new pastor placed a notice in the local newspaper stating that, because the parish was dead, it was everyone's duty to give it a decent funeral. The funeral would be held the following Sunday afternoon, the notice said. Morbidly curious, a large crowd turned out for the "funeral." In front of the pulpit, they saw a closed coffin, covered with flowers. After the pastor delivered a eulogy, he opened the coffin and invited the assembly to come forward and pay their final respects to their dead parish. Filled with curiosity as to what would represent the corpse of a "dead parish," all the people eagerly lined up to look in the coffin. Each "mourner" peeped and then quickly turned away with a guilty, sheepish look. In the coffin, tilted at the correct angle, was a large mirror.

REFLECTION

Although individual parishes throughout the world may come and go, the church as the people of God, as the bride of Christ and the sacrament of Christ, stands as a prophet in our midst and will exist until the end of time (Matthew 28:19–20; John 14:18). As prophet, one of its greatest and most difficult functions is to call us to task for our actions or for our inactions, to remind us of our baptism calling, to prod us to peer inside and see where we are and where we are going. But no one, not even Christ or his church, can force us to change our ways, a decision and responsibility that rests with us alone. We must be humble enough not to let our pride and "independence" get in the way. We must be courageous and loving enough to pray that we might accomplish God's will "on earth as it is in heaven" (Matthew 6:10).

424. THE EGG MAN   *Humility*

John Dewey, the American philosopher and educator whose writings and teachings had profound influence on education in the United States, focused on learning-by-doing rather than rote learning and dogmatic instruction. He spent his retirement selling eggs and vegetables to his neighbors on Long Island. One day he delivered eggs to a wealthy customer by entering through the front door only to be rebuked that deliveries were made at the back. Sometime later he gave a lecture to a woman's club and was amused to overhear his wealthy customer whisper to her friend, "Why, he looks just like our egg man!"

REFLECTION

John Dewey practiced his philosophy of education in a unique and humble way. What he teaches us is that whatever our accomplishments, there is always something we can learn, even in the most mundane activities. For John Dewey it was selling eggs. Everything we do, he taught us, whether great or ordinary, can be an opportunity to learn not only the task at hand but a number of virtues as well. Among the most difficult of the virtues is that of humility. Insofar as John Dewey sought to learn and live the virtue of humility, he was imitating, perhaps without knowing it, three great figures from the Scriptures: Moses, Mary, and Jesus. Of Moses, the Bible says, "Moses was very humble, more so than anyone else on the face of the earth" (Numbers 12:3). Saint Luke speaks of Mary as the humble ser-

vant of the Lord, and because of her humility, the Almighty did great things for her and all generations forever would call her blessed (Luke 1:48–49). Of Jesus, Saint Paul tells us "he humbled himself and became obedient to the point of death—even death on a cross. Therefore God also highly exalted him and gave him the name that is above every name, so that at the name of Jesus every knee should bend, in heaven and on earth and under the earth, and every tongue should confess that Jesus Christ is Lord, to the glory of God the Father" (Philippians 2:8–11).

SCRIPTURAL PASSAGES CITED

Old Testament

New Testament

TOPIC INDEX